ACTIVITY BOOK

DISCOVERING FRENCH BLEU

LISTENING ACTIVITIES

WRITING ACTIVITIES

READING AND CULTURE ACTIVITIES

POUR *COMMUNIQUER*

Communicative Expressions and Thematic Vocabulary

Jean-Paul Valette
Rebecca M. Valette

D.C. Heath and Company,
a Division of Houghton Mifflin Company

Overview

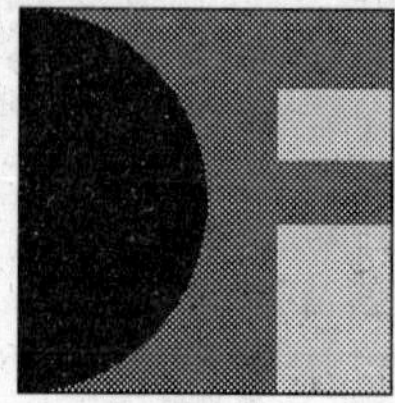

The **DISCOVERING FRENCH–*BLEU*** Activity Book is an integrated workbook that provides additional practice to allow students to build their control of French and develop French proficiency.

The activities provide guided communicative practice in meaningful contexts and frequent opportunity for self-expression.

Activity Book PE Copyright (ii)

D.C. Heath and Company, a Division of Houghton Mifflin Company

Printed in the United States of America

International Standard Book Number: 0-669-43478-7

8 9 10 -MZ- 01 00

Contents

Contents, *continued*

To the Student

Your Activity Book is divided into nine units. Each unit has four sections:

Listening Activities

The Listening Activities (called Cassette Worksheets) have the pictures you will need to complete the recorded activities. The 36 lessons correspond to the 36 lessons in the student text. When you work with the Cassette Program, you will need your textbook as well as your Activity Book with you, so that you can follow along for the vocabulary sections and the **À votre tour** sections.

Writing Activities

The Writing Activities will give you the chance to develop your writing skills and put into practice what you have learned in class. The 36 lessons correspond to the 36 lessons in the student text. Starting in Unit 4, the exercises are coded to correspond to a particular *part* of the lesson. For example, **A** at the beginning of an exercise or group of exercises means that the material is related to the structures or vocabulary presented in Section A of that lesson. The last activity is called **Communication** and encourages you to express yourself in various additional communicative situations.

Reading and Culture Activities

The Reading and Culture Activities contain realia (illustrations and objects from real life) from French-speaking countries and various kinds of cultural activities. There is one set of activities for each unit in the student text.

Communicative Expressions and Thematic Vocabulary

The **Pour Communiquer** section summarizes all of the vocabulary introduced in the lessons of each unit. The words and expressions are grouped into categories that will make it easier for you to review the material.

UNITÉ 1
Bonjour!

LISTENING ACTIVITIES
Leçons 1–4

WRITING ACTIVITIES
Leçons 1–4

READING AND CULTURE ACTIVITIES
Unité 1

Communicative Expressions and Thematic Vocabulary

Nom ______________________________

Classe ____________________ Date ______________

CASSETTE WORKSHEET Leçon 1 La rentrée

Section 1 La rentrée *(Back to school)*

A. *Compréhension orale.* Listening comprehension.

This is the first day of school. Students are greeting their friends and meeting new classmates.

PHILIPPE: Bonjour! Je m'appelle Philippe.
STÉPHANIE: Et moi, je m'appelle Stéphanie.

MARC: Je m'appelle Marc. Et toi?
ISABELLE: Moi, je m'appelle Isabelle.

JEAN-PAUL: Comment t'appelles-tu?
NATHALIE: Je m'appelle Nathalie.
JEAN-PAUL: Bonjour.
NATHALIE: Bonjour.

B. *Écoutez et répétez.* Listen and repeat.

Section 2 Qui est-ce? *(Who is it?)*

C. *Compréhension orale.* Listening comprehension.

▶ (a.) François
b. Frank

1. a. Nathalie
b. Nicole

2. a. Sylvie
b. Cécile

3. a. Jean-Claude
b. Jean-Paul

4. a. Lucie
b. Juliette

Nom ______________________________

CASSETTE WORKSHEET Leçon 1 (cont.)

D. ***Compréhension orale.*** Listening comprehension.

a. ___ Monsieur Fazère
b. ___ Olivier LeGrand
c. _1_ Florence Clément
d. ___ Madame Bertin
e. ___ Mademoiselle Lacour
f. ___ Charles Dumont
g. ___ Monsieur Martin
h. ___ Monsieur Ronchon
i. ___ Jeanne Dupont

E. ***Compréhension orale.*** Listening comprehension.

1. a. ___ Michèle b. ___ Hélène
2. a. ___ Fatou b. ___ Nicolas
3. a. ___ Paul b. ___ Loriza

Section 3 L'alphabet et les signes orthographiques
(The alphabet and spelling marks)

F. ***Écoutez et répétez.*** Listen and repeat.

A B C D E F G H I J K L M
N O P Q R S T U V W X Y Z

G. ***Écoutez et répétez.*** Listen and repeat.

´ accent aigu **Cécile**
` accent grave **Michèle**
^ accent circonflexe **Jérôme**
¨ tréma **Noël**
¸ cédille **François**

Nom ____

CASSETTE WORKSHEET Leçon 1 (cont.)

H. ***Écoutez et écrivez.*** Listen and write.

1. ___ ___ ___ ___

2. ___ ___ ___ ___ ___ ___

3. ___ ___ ___ ___ ___ ___

4. ___ ___ ___ ___ ___ ___

5. ___ ___ ___ ___ ___ ___ ___ ___ ___

Section 4 Les nombres de 0 à 10 *(Numbers from 0 to 10)*

I. ***Écoutez et répétez.*** Listen and repeat.

0 (zéro)	**1** (un)	**2** (deux)	**3** (trois)	**4** (quatre)	**5** (cinq)
	6 (six)	**7** (sept)	**8** (huit)	**9** (neuf)	**10** (dix)

J. ***Écoutez et écrivez.*** Listen and write.

Éric: ___ ___ ___ - ___ ___ ___ ___

Marie: ___ ___ ___ - ___ ___ ___ ___

Jean-Jacques: ___ ___ ___ - ___ ___ ___ ___

Nom ______________________________

Classe ____________________ Date ____________

CASSETTE WORKSHEET Leçon 2 Tu es français?

Section 1 Tu es français? *(You're French?)*

A. *Compréhension orale*

It is the opening day of school and several of the students meet in the cafeteria at lunchtime. Marc discovers that not everyone is French.

MARC: Tu es français?
JEAN-PAUL: Oui, je suis français.
MARC: Et toi, Patrick, tu es français aussi?
PATRICK: Non! Je suis américain. Je suis de Boston.
MARC: Et toi, Stéphanie, tu es française ou américaine?
STÉPHANIE: Je suis française.
MARC: Tu es de Paris?
STÉPHANIE: Non, je suis de Fort-de-France.
MARC: Tu as de la chance!

B. *Écoutez et répétez.* Listen and repeat.

Section 2 Quelle nationalité? *(What nationality?)*

C. *Compréhension orale*

		▶	1	2	3	4	5	6	7	8
A	**français**	✓								
B	**française**									

Nom ____

CASSETTE WORKSHEET Leçon 2 (cont.)

D. *Compréhension orale*

	(British flag)		(American flag)		(Canadian flag)	
	A	B	C	D	E	F
	anglais	anglaise	américain	américaine	canadien	canadienne
▶					✓	
1						
2						
3						
4						
5						
6						
7						

E. *Compréhension orale*

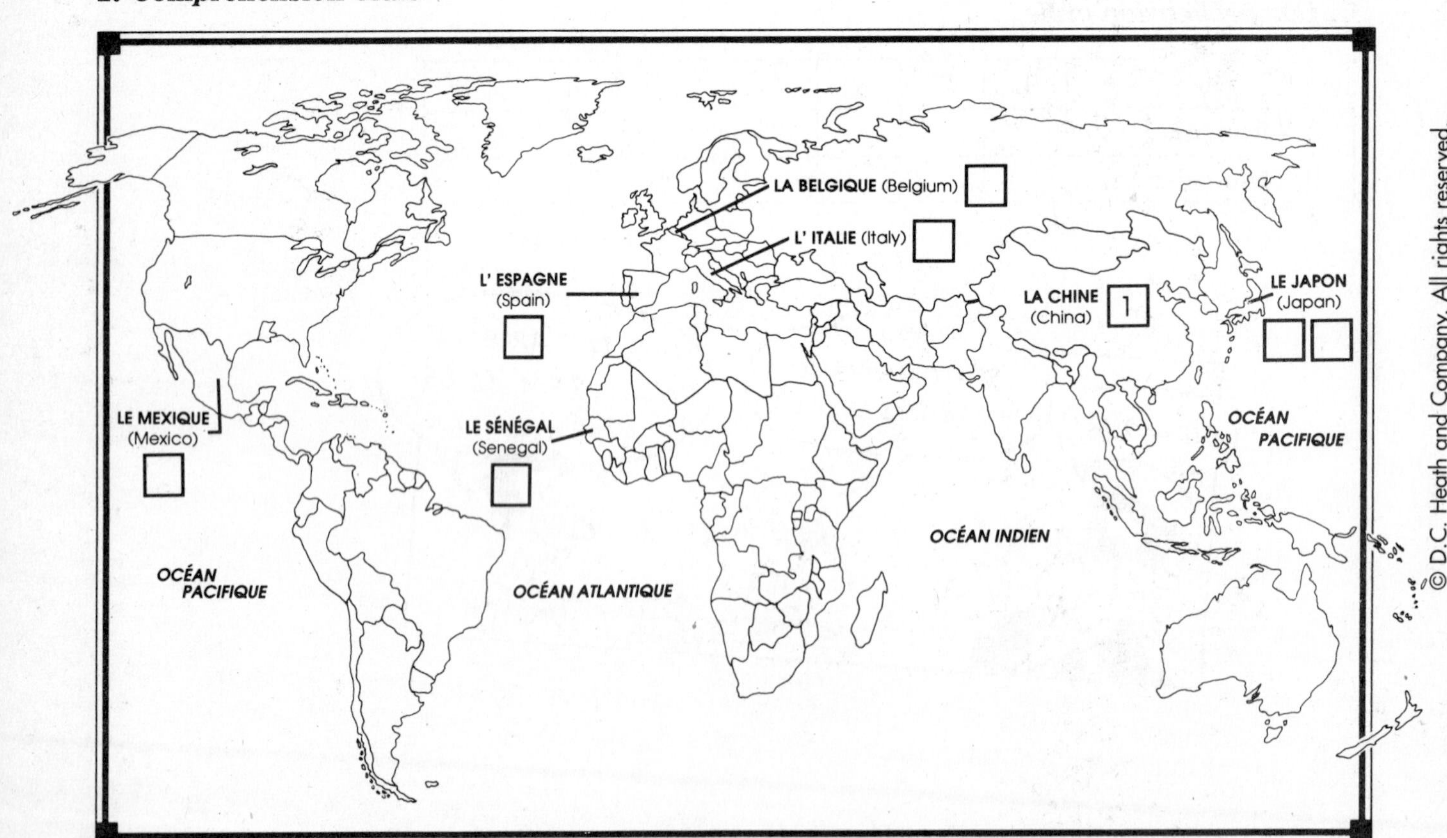

CASSETTE WORKSHEET Leçon 2 (cont.)

Section 3 **Les nombres de 10 à 20**

F. ***Écoutez et répétez.*** Listen and repeat.

10 (dix) **11** (onze) **12** (douze) **13** (treize) **14** (quatorze) **15** (quinze)

16 (seize) **17** (dix-sept) **18** (dix-huit) **19** (dix-neuf) **20** (vingt)

G. ***Écoutez et écrivez.*** Listen and write.

▶ Philippe

Paul

François

Marc

Jérôme

Jean-Michel

Frédéric

Patrick

Robert

Thomas

CASSETTE WORKSHEET Leçon 2 (cont.)

Section 4 Prononciation

H. ***Les lettres muettes*** (Silent letters)

Écoutez: **Pari~~s~~**

In French, the last letter of a word is often not pronounced.

- Final "e" is always silent.

  Répétez: **Sophi~~e~~ Philipp~~e~~ Stéphani~~e~~ anglais~~e~~ français~~e~~**
  onz~~e~~ douz~~e~~ treiz~~e~~ quatorz~~e~~ quinz~~e~~ seiz~~e~~

- Final "**s**" is almost always silent.

  Répétez: **Pari~~s~~ Nicola~~s~~ Jacque~~s~~ anglai~~s~~ françai~~s~~ troi~~s~~**

- The letter "**h**" is always silent.

  Répétez: **~~H~~élène ~~H~~enri T~~h~~omas Nat~~h~~alie Cat~~h~~erine**

Nom ______________________________

Classe ______________________ Date ____________

CASSETTE WORKSHEET Leçon 3 Salut! Ça va?

Section 1 Salut! Ça va?

A. ***Compréhension orale***

On the way to school, François meets his friends.

FRANÇOIS: Salut, Isabelle!
ISABELLE: Salut! Ça va?
FRANÇOIS: Ça va! Merci!

FRANÇOIS: Salut, Nathalie! Ça va?
NATHALIE: Ça va bien! Et toi?
FRANÇOIS: Moi aussi.

ISABELLE: Ça va, Philippe?
PHILIPPE: Ah non! Zut! Ça va mal!

François also meets his teachers.

FRANÇOIS: Bonjour, monsieur.
M. MASSON: Bonjour, François.

FRANÇOIS: Bonjour, madame.
MME CHOLLET: Bonjour, François.

FRANÇOIS: Bonjour, mademoiselle.
MLLE LACOUR: Bonjour, François.

After class, François says good-bye to his teacher and his friends.

FRANÇOIS: Au revoir, mademoiselle.
MLLE LACOUR: Au revoir, François.

NATHALIE: Au revoir, François.
FRANÇOIS: Au revoir, Nathalie.

B. ***Écoutez et répétez.*** Listen and repeat.

Section 2 Ça va?

C. ***Compréhension orale***

Ça va bien!

a. ____

Ça va très bien!

b. ____

Ça va comme ci, comme ça.

c. ____

Ça va mal.

d. ____

Ça va très mal.

e. ____

CASSETTE WORKSHEET Leçon 3 (cont.)

D. ***Questions et réponses***

▶ —Ça va?

—**Ça va comme ci, comme ça.**

CASSETTE WORKSHEET Leçon 3 (cont.)

Section 3 Les nombres de 20 à 60

E. ***Écoutez et répétez.*** Listen and repeat.

20	**21**	**22**	**23**	**24**	**25**	**26**
27	**28**	**29**	**30**	**31**	**32**	**33 . . .**
40	**41 . . .**		**44**	**45**	**46 . . .**	
50	**51 . . .**		**57**	**58**	**59**	**60**

F. ***Écoutez et écrivez.*** Listen and write.

Louis Bertrand ___ ___ . ___ ___ . ___ ___ . ___ ___

Marie-Claire Dulac ___ ___ . ___ ___ . ___ ___ . ___ ___

Charles Leclerc ___ ___ . ___ ___ . ___ ___ . ___ ___

Stéphanie Ladoux ___ ___ . ___ ___ . ___ ___ . ___ ___

ALLÔ
CHIENS!
30.41.96.63
Le chien d'abord !

Nom ______________________________________

UNITÉ 1

CASSETTE WORKSHEET Leçon 3 (cont.)

Section 4 Prononciation

G. ***Les consonnes finales*** (Final consonants)

Écoutez: **un deux trois**

In French, the last consonant of a word is often not pronounced.

- Remember: Final "**s**" is usually silent.

  Répétez: **trois français anglais**

- Most other final consonants are usually silent.

  Répétez: **Richard Albert Robert salut**
  américain canadien bien deux

EXCEPTION: The following final consonants are usually pronounced: "**c**," "**f**," "**l**," and sometimes "**r**."

Répétez: **Éric Daniel Lebeuf Pascal Victor**

However, the ending **-er** is usually pronounced /e/.

Répetez: **Roger Olivier**

Nom ______________________________

Classe ____________________ Date ____________

CASSETTE WORKSHEET Leçon 4 Le français pratique: L'heure

Section 1 Dialogue A: Un rendez-vous

A. ***Compréhension orale***

Jean-Paul and Stéphanie are sitting in a café. Stéphanie seems to be in a hurry to leave.

STÉPHANIE: Quelle heure est-il?
JEAN-PAUL: Il est trois heures.
STÉPHANIE: Trois heures?
JEAN-PAUL: Oui, trois heures.
STÉPHANIE: Oh là là. J'ai un rendez-vous avec David dans vingt minutes.
Au revoir, Jean-Paul.
JEAN-PAUL: Au revoir, Stéphanie. À bientôt!

B. ***Écoutez et répétez.***

Section 2 Quelle heure est-il? (Part 1)

C. ***Compréhension orale***

▶

1.

2.

3.

4.

5.

D. ***Questions et réponses***

▶

1.

2.

3.

4.

▶

Quelle heure est-il?
Il est huit heures.

5.

6.

7.

CASSETTE WORKSHEET Leçon 4 (cont.)

Section 3 Dialogue B: À quelle heure est le film?

E. ***Compréhension orale***

Stéphanie and David have decided to go to a movie.

STÉPHANIE: Quelle heure est-il?
DAVID: Il est trois heures et demie.
STÉPHANIE: Et à quelle heure est le film?
DAVID: À quatre heures et quart.
STÉPHANIE: Ça va. Nous avons le temps.

F. ***Écoutez et répétez.***

Section 4 Quelle heure est-il? (Part 2)

G. ***Compréhension orale***

▶ 1:15

1. __:__ **2.** __:__

3. __:__ **4.** __:__

H. ***Questions et réponses***

▶

1.

2.

3.

4.

5.

6.

CASSETTE WORKSHEET Leçon 4 (cont.)

Section 5 À quelle heure?

I. *Compréhension orale*

▶ le film 4 h 15

1. la classe de français ________
2. le dîner ________
3. le film ________
4. le train de Toulouse ________

Section 6 L'heure officielle

J. *Compréhension orale*

▶ 17 h 00

– 12

5:00 P.M.

1. [ ] – 12 [ ]

2. [ ] – 12 [ ]

3. [ ] – 12 [ ]

À quelle heure est le train de Nice?
Le train de Nice est à six heures dix.
INFORMATIONS

CASSETTE WORKSHEET Leçon 4 (cont.)

À votre tour!

Section 1. Nathalie et Marc

 Allez à la page 30. *Turn to page 30 in your Student Text.*

Section 2. Et toi?

 Allez à la page 30.

Section 3. Conversation dirigée

 Allez à la page 30.

Section 4. Minidialogues

 Allez à la page 31.

Nom ____________________

Classe ____________ Date ________

WRITING ACTIVITIES **Leçon 1** La rentrée

1. Au Club International

You have met the following young people at the Club International. Six of them have names of French origin. Circle these names. Then write them in the box below, separating the boys and the girls.
(Note: Don't forget the accent marks!)

Carlos Suárez	Mustapha Ibrahim
Birgit Eriksen	Jérôme Dupuis
Hélène Rémy	Janet Woodford
Jean-François Petit	Raúl González
Michiko Sato	Marie-Noëlle Laîné
Frédéric Lemaître	Svetlana Poliakoff
Heinz Mueller	Stéphanie Mercier

FLASH culturel

French is spoken not only in France. Today about thirty countries use French as their official language (or one of their official languages). Which continent has the largest number of French-speaking countries?

☐ Europe ☐ Africa ☐ Asia ☐ South America

→ page 20

WRITING ACTIVITIES Leçon 1 (cont.)

2. Allô!

First write down your phone number and the numbers of two friends or relatives. Then write out the numbers as you would say them in French.

1. Moi

☐ ☐ ☐-☐ ☐ ☐ ☐

_____ / _____ / _____ / – / _____ / _____ / _____ / _____

2. Nom *(name)*: ____________________

☐ ☐ ☐-☐ ☐ ☐ ☐

_____ / _____ / _____ / – / _____ / _____ / _____ / _____

3. Nom *(name)*: ____________________

☐ ☐ ☐-☐ ☐ ☐ ☐

_____ / _____ / _____ / – / _____ / _____ / _____ / _____

3. Communication: En français!

On the bus you meet a new French student. Write out what you would say — in French!

1. *Say hello.*

____

2. *Give your name.*

____

3. *Ask the French student his/her name.*

____

FLASH culturel

French is the official language in 25 African countries. The largest of these countries is Zaïre in central Africa. Other countries where French is spoken by many of the citizens are: Algeria, Tunisia, and Morocco in North Africa; Senegal and the Ivory Coast in West Africa; and the island of Madagascar off the coast of East Africa.

La Tunisie.

Le Maroc.

ALGÉRIE

Nom ______________________________

Classe ______________________ Date ______________

WRITING ACTIVITIES Leçon 2 Tu es français?

1. Présentations *(Introductions)*

The following people are introducing themselves, giving their names and their nationalities. Complete what each one says.

Je m'appelle Cédric.

Je suis ________________.

Je m'appelle Liz.

Je suis ________________.

Je m'appelle Tina.

Je suis ________________.

Je m'appelle Pierre.

Je suis ________________.

Je m'appelle Bob.

Je suis ________________.

Je m'appelle Véronique.

Je suis ________________.

FLASH culturel

Martinique and Guadeloupe are two French-speaking islands in the Caribbean. In which other Caribbean country is French spoken?

☐ Cuba ☐ Puerto Rico ☐ Haiti ☐ The Dominican Republic

→ page 22

WRITING ACTIVITIES Leçon 2 (cont.)

2. Maths

Write out the answers to the following arithmetic problems.

▶ 4 + 7 = onze

1. 9 + 3 = __________
2. 8 + 6 = __________
3. 10 + 7 = __________
4. 17 + 2 = __________
5. 5 x 3 = __________
6. 2 x 10 = __________

3. Communication: En français!

You are at a party and have just met two French-speaking students: Philippe and Marie-Laure.

1. *Say hello to them.*

____

2. *Give your name.*

____

3. *Say that you are American.*

____

4. *Ask Philippe if he is French.*

____

5. *Ask Marie-Laure if she is Canadian.*

____

• BOSTON •
HAÏTI
COURRIER

FLASH culturel

Haiti is a former French colony. Toward the end of the eighteenth century, the black slaves who worked in the sugar cane plantations revolted against their French masters. In 1804, Haiti became an independent country. It is the first republic established by people of African origin.

Today French, which is the official language of Haiti, is spoken by many Haitians, along with Creole. Many people of Haitian origin live in the United States, especially in Florida, New York, and Boston. If you meet young Haitians, you might want to speak French with them.

Nom ______________________________

Classe ____________________ Date ____________

WRITING ACTIVITIES Leçon 3 Salut! Ça va?

1. Loto *(Bingo)*

You are playing Loto in Quebec. The numbers below have all been called. If you have these numbers on your card, circle them.

seize trente et un vingt-deux cinquante quarante-neuf quinze quarante trente-quatre vingt-neuf soixante quarante-huit douze cinquante-deux onze dix-sept vingt et un vingt trente-cinq trente-sept cinquante-six sept cinquante-quatre cinquante-neuf trois

5	14	26	37	49
7	15	29	40	52
9	18	X	41	54
11	21	33	46	59
12	22	35	48	60

How many numbers did you circle? ____________

How many rows of five did you score? ____________

FLASH culturel

France is not the only European country where French is spoken. In which of the following countries do one fifth of the people speak French?

☐ Germany ☐ Italy ☐ Spain ☐ Switzerland

→ page 24

WRITING ACTIVITIES Leçon 3 (cont.)

2. Bonjour!

The following people meet in the street. How do you think they will greet each other? Fill in the bubbles with the appropriate expressions.

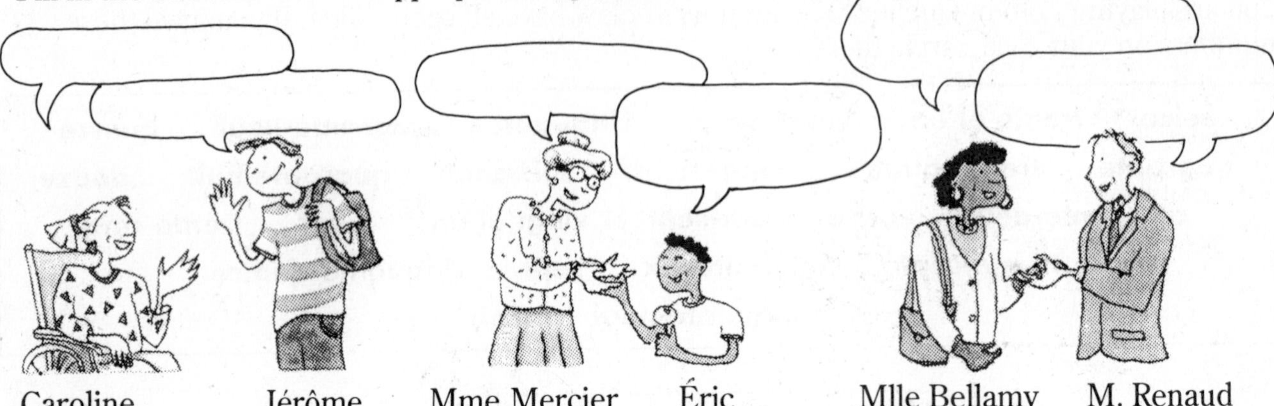

3. Ça va?

How do you think the following people would answer the question **Ça va?**

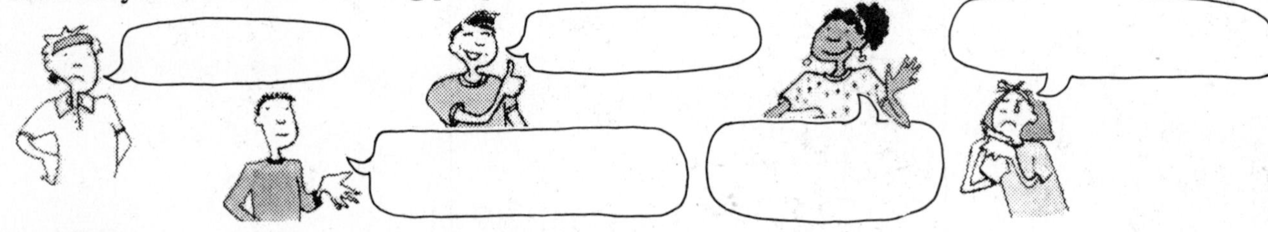

4. Communication: En français!

You have just enrolled in a French school as an exchange student.

1. On the way to school, you meet your friend Catherine.

   Say hello to her. ______________________________

   Ask her how things are going. ______________________________

2. Now you meet Mademoiselle Lebrun, your new music teacher.

   Say hello to her. ______________________________

   Ask her how she is. ______________________________

FLASH culturel

Although all of these countries border on France, only Switzerland has a sizeable French-speaking population. The main French-speaking city of Switzerland is Geneva **(Genève),** which is the headquarters of the International Red Cross and the seat of several other international organizations.

Nom ______________________________

Classe ____________________ Date ______________

WRITING ACTIVITIES Leçon 4 Le français pratique: L'heure

1. Oui ou non?

Watches do not always work well. Read the times below and compare them with the times indicated on the watches. If the two times match, check **oui.** If they do not match, check **non.**

	oui	non
▶ Il est une heure dix.	☐	☐
▶ Il est une heure vingt-cinq.	☐	☐
1. Il est deux heures et demie.	☐	☐
2. Il est trois heures et quart.	☐	☐
3. Il est cinq heures moins vingt.	☐	☐
4. Il est sept heures moins le quart.	☐	☐
5. Il est huit heures cinq.	☐	☐
6. Il est onze heures cinquante-cinq.	☐	☐

FLASH culturel

In many French-speaking countries, official time is given using a 24-hour clock. For example, on this Canadian TV schedule, the movie *Driving Miss Daisy* begins at 22 h 40 (**vingt-deux heures quarante).** What would be the corresponding time on our 12-hour clock?

☐ 2:40 P.M. ☐ 8:40 P.M. ☐ 9:40 P.M. ☐ 10:40 P.M.

Super Écran

VENDREDI 22 MARS

14h50	LAWRENCE D'ARABIE
18h20	ONCLE BUCK
20h05	LES SIMPSON
21h00	TREMORS
22h40	MISS DAISY ET SON CHAUFFEUR

→ **page 26**

WRITING ACTIVITIES Leçon 4 (cont.)

2. Quelle heure est-il?

Stéphanie's watch is not working. Tell her what time it is. Write out your responses.

1:00	1. ______________________ .	7:30	4. ______________________ .
12:00	2. ______________________ .	8:45	5. ______________________ .
3:15	3. ______________________ .	10:50	6. ______________________ .

3. Communication: En français!

A. Conversation avec Caroline You are in a café with your friend Caroline. You plan to see a movie together. Complete the dialogue.

CAROLINE: Quelle heure est-il?

YOU: ______________________________
(Look at your watch and tell her the time.)

CAROLINE: À quelle heure est le film?

YOU: ______________________________
(Name a time about half an hour from now.)

B. Conversation avec Julien You are in a hurry to keep an appointment with Mme Pascal, your math teacher. You meet your friend Julien. Complete the dialogue.

YOU: ______________________________
(Ask Julien what time it is.)

JULIEN: Il est onze heures dix. Pourquoi *(why)*?

YOU: ______________________ avec Madame Pascal.
(Say you have an appointment with Madame Pascal.)

JULIEN: À quelle heure?

YOU: ______________________________
(Tell him at quarter past eleven, and say good-bye.)

FLASH culturel

With the 24-hour clock, times are expressed as follows:

- A.M. hours go from 0 h 01 (one minute after midnight) to 12 h 00 (noon).
- P.M. hours go from 12 h 01 to 24 h 00.

To calculate the P.M. equivalent of 24-hour clock times, simply subtract 12.

22 h 40 =
22:40–12 =
10:40 P.M.

Nom ____________________

Classe ____________________ Date ____________

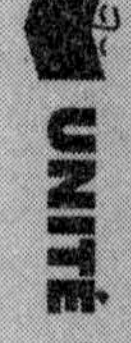

READING AND CULTURE ACTIVITIES Unité 1

A. En voyage *(On a trip)*

1. Why would you go to Le Napoli?

- ☐ To shop for food.
- ☐ To have dinner.
- ☐ To see a movie.
- ☐ To plan a trip to Italy.

Le Napoli
Restaurant - Pizzéria
Spécialités - Grillades
7, Av. des Poilus - Place Cavet
83110 Sanary-sur-mer
☎ 94 74 03 34

2. In which country is the Bonaparte located?

- ☐ In France.
- ☐ In Canada.
- ☐ In Switzerland.
- ☐ In Belgium.

RESTAURANT

BONAPARTE
CUISINE DE FRANCE
443, rue St-François-Xavier
Vieux-Montréal
Reservations: **844-4368**

3. Why would you call the number shown in this ad?

- ☐ To buy a train ticket.
- ☐ To rent a video.
- ☐ To have your phone repaired.
- ☐ To reserve a room.

HOTEL LES CLEMATITES**
18 chambres
Télévision - Téléphone
Plein centre Ville
19, rue Vaugelas 74000 ANNECY
Tél. 50.52.84.33 - Fax 50.45.49.06

4. Why did someone buy this ticket?

- ☐ To visit a historical site.
- ☐ To see a historical movie.
- ☐ To listen to classical music.
- ☐ To tour a battleship.

La COUVERTOIRADE
AVEYRON
e Nant
Nº
MONUMENT HISTORIQUE
ADULTE
Conservez votre ticket. **Nº 80810**

READING AND CULTURE ACTIVITIES Unité 1 (cont.)

5. If you were in France, where would you see this sign?

- ☐ In a train.
- ☐ In an elevator.
- ☐ On a highway.
- ☐ In a stadium.

6. If you were driving on this highway, you would exit to the right . . .

- ☐ if you needed gas
- ☐ if you wanted to take pictures
- ☐ if you were looking for a campground
- ☐ if you were meeting a flight

Nom ____

READING AND CULTURE ACTIVITIES Unité 1 (cont.)

B. Carte de visite

Marie-Françoise Bellanger

photographe

47, rue du Four
Paris 6^e

Tél. 42.21.30.15

A friend of yours has given you the calling card of her cousin in France. Fill in the blanks below with the information that you can find out about this cousin by reading the card.

- Last name ____
- First name ____
- City of residence ____
- Profession ____

READING AND CULTURE ACTIVITIES Unité 1 (cont.)

C. Agenda

Look at the following page from Stéphanie's pocket calendar.

8 ...... 14 ......
9 ...... 15 ......
10 ...... 16 ......
11 ...... 17 ......
12 ...... 18 ......
13 ...... 19 ......

SAMEDI **21**

(10) Octobre

42e Semaine

OCT

classe de piano 10 h 00

rendez-vous avec Jean-Paul 4 h 00

téléphoner à Christine 7 h 30

8 ...... 14 ......
9 ...... 15 ......
10 ...... 16 ......
11 ...... 17 ......
12 ...... 18 ......
13 ...... 19 ......

- What does Stéphanie have scheduled for Saturday morning at 10 A.M.?

  ____

- When is Stéphanie going to meet Jean-Paul?

  ____

- What is Stéphanie planning to do at 7:30?

  ____

UNITÉ 1

COMMUNICATIVE EXPRESSIONS AND THEMATIC VOCABULARY

Unité 1 Bonjour!

CULTURAL CONTEXT: Meeting people

COMMUNICATIVE EXPRESSIONS

Greeting people

Bonjour! **Au revoir!**
Salut!

Asking people how they are

(informally)	**Ça va?**	**Ça va . . .**	**bien.**
	Comment vas-tu?		**mal**
			comme ci, comme ça
(formally)	**Comment allez-vous?**		**très bien**
			très mal

Asking a classmate's name

Comment t'appelles-tu?
Je m'appelle . . .

Asking a friend which city he/she is from

Tu es de [Boston]?
Je suis de [San Francisco].

Asking a friend about his/her nationality

Tu es . . . ?	**français**	**française**
Je suis . . .	**anglais**	**anglaise**
	américain	**américaine**
	canadien	**canadienne**

Asking the time

Quelle heure est-il?

Il est . . .	**une heure**	**midi**
	deux heures	**minuit**
	trois heures et quart	**neuf heures du matin**
	six heures et demie	**cinq heures de l'après-midi**
	sept heures moins le quart	**dix heures du soir**
	huit heures dix	
	onze heures moins vingt	

Asking at what time something begins

À quelle heure est . . . ?
— À quelle heure est le concert?
— Le concert est à huit heures.

Saying at what time you have an appointment or date

J'ai un rendez-vous à [quatre heures].

COMMUNICATIVE EXPRESSIONS AND THEMATIC VOCABULARY

VOCABULARY

Numbers: 0–60

zéro	**dix**	**vingt**	**trente**
un	**onze**	**vingt et un**	
deux	**douze**	**vingt-deux**	**quarante**
trois	**treize**	**vingt-trois**	
quatre	**quatorze**	**vingt-quatre**	**cinquante**
cinq	**quinze**	**vingt-cinq**	
six	**seize**	**vingt-six**	**soixante**
sept	**dix-sept**	**vingt-sept**	
huit	**dix-huit**	**vingt-huit**	
neuf	**dix-neuf**	**vingt-neuf**	

Other expressions

oui	**et**	**moi**	**Monsieur**
non	**ou**	**et toi?**	**Madame**
merci	**aussi**		**Mademoiselle**
zut!			

UNITÉ 2
Les copains et la famille

LISTENING ACTIVITIES
Leçons 5–8

WRITING ACTIVITIES
Leçons 5–8

READING AND CULTURE ACTIVITIES
Unité 2

Communicative Expressions and Thematic Vocabulary

Nom ______________________________

Classe ______________________ Date ______________

CASSETTE WORKSHEET Leçon 5 Copain ou copine?

Section 1 Copain ou copine?

A. *Compréhension orale*

Today, Jean-Paul is visiting his friend Philippe. Philippe seems to be expecting someone.

PHILIPPE: Tiens! Voilà Dominique!
JEAN-PAUL: Dominique? Qui est-ce? Un copain ou une copine?
PHILIPPE: C'est une copine.

PHILIPPE: Salut, Dominique! Ça va?
DOMINIQUE: Oui, ça va! Et toi?
JEAN-PAUL: C'est vrai! C'est une copine!

B. *Écoutez et répétez.*

Section 2 Qui est-ce?

C. *Compréhension orale*

	A	B	C	D	E	F
	un ami	une amie	un copain	une copine	un prof	une prof
▶				✓		
1						
2						
3						
4						
5						

D. *Questions et réponses*

▶ — Tiens, voilà Isabelle!
— Qui est-ce?
— **C'est une copine.**

1. un copain? une copine?
2. un copain? une copine?
3. un ami? une amie?
4. un ami? une amie?
4. un ami? une amie?
6. un prof? une prof?

CASSETTE WORKSHEET Leçon 5 (cont.)

Section 3 Les nombres de 60 à 79

E. ***Écoutez et répétez.***

60	61	62	63	64	65	66	67	68	69
70	71	72	73	74	75	76	77	78	79

F. ***Écoutez et écrivez.***

Jean-Michel Descroix ___ ___ . ___ ___ . ___ ___ . ___ ___

Christine Albert ___ ___ . ___ ___ . ___ ___ . ___ ___

Roger Boulanger ___ ___ . ___ ___ . ___ ___ . ___ ___

Mireille Chardin ___ ___ . ___ ___ . ___ ___ . ___ ___

Section 4 Prononciation

G. ***La liaison***

Écoutez: **un ami**
Répétez: **un ami** **un Américain** **un Anglais** **un artiste**

In general, the "**n**" of **un** is silent. However, in the above words, the "**n**" of **un** is pronounced as if it were the first letter of the next word. The two words are linked together in LIAISON.

Liaison occurs between two words when the second one begins with a VOWEL SOUND, that is, with "**a**", "**e**", "**i**", "**o**", "**u**", and sometimes "**h**" and "**y**".

Contrastez et répétez:

LIAISON: **un ami** **un Américain** **un Italien** **un artiste**
NO LIAISON: **un copain** **un Français** **un Canadien** **un prof**

Nom ______________________________

Classe ____________________ Date ____________

CASSETTE WORKSHEET Leçon 6 Une coïncidence

Section 1 Une coïncidence

A. ***Compréhension orale***

Isabelle is at a party with her new Canadian friend Mark. She wants him to meet some of the other guests.

ISABELLE: Tu connais la fille là-bas?
MARC: Non. Qui est-ce?
ISABELLE: C'est une copine. Elle s'appelle Juliette Savard.
MARC: Elle est française?
ISABELLE: Non, elle est canadienne. Elle est de Montréal.
MARC: Moi aussi!
ISABELLE: Quelle coïncidence!

B. ***Écoutez et répétez.***

Section 2 Qui est-ce?

C. ***Compréhension orale***

1. a. une amie b. une copine
c. Denise d. Danielle
e. américaine f. canadienne
g. de Québec h. de Montréal

2. a. un ami b. un copain
c. américain d. canadien
e. de Boston f. de Baltimore
g. Patrick h. Paul

D. ***Questions et réponses***

▶ — Elle est française?
— Oui, elle est française.

— Comment s'appelle-t-elle?
— Elle s'appelle Isabelle.

▶ Isabelle

1. Marc

2. Philippe

3. Nathalie

4. Patrick

CASSETTE WORKSHEET Leçon 6 (cont.)

Section 3 Les nombres de 80 à 100

E. ***Écoutez et répétez.***

80	**81**	**82**	**83**	**84**	**85**	**86**	**87**	**88**	**89**	
90	**91**	**92**	**93**	**94**	**95**	**96**	**97**	**98**	**99**	**100**

F. ***Écoutez et écrivez.***

Florence	Juliette	Philippe	Laure

Delphine	Julien	Olivier	Caroline

Section 4 Prononciation

G. ***La voyelle nasale*** /ɛ̃/

In French, there are three nasal vowel sounds.

Écoutez: **cinq** **onze** **trente**

Practice the sound /ɛ̃/ in the following words. Note that this vowel sound can have several different spellings.

➡ Be sure not to pronounce an "**n**" or "**m**" after the nasal vowel.

Répétez: **"in"** **cinq quinze vingt vingt-cinq quatre-vingt-quinze**
"ain" **americain Alain copain**
"(i)en" **bien canadien tiens!**
"un" **un**
Tiens! **Voilà Alain. Il est américain. Et Julien? Il est canadien.**

Nom ____

Classe ______________________________ Date ______________

CASSETTE WORKSHEET Leçon 7 Les photos d'Isabelle

Section 1 Les photos d'Isabelle

A. *Compréhension orale*

Isabelle is showing her family photo album to her friend Jean-Paul.

ISABELLE: Voici ma mère.
JEAN-PAUL: Et le monsieur, c'est ton père?
ISABELLE: Non, c'est mon oncle Thomas.
JEAN-PAUL: Et la fille, c'est ta cousine?
ISABELLE: Oui, c'est ma cousine Béatrice. Elle a seize ans.
JEAN-PAUL: Et le garçon, c'est ton cousin?
ISABELLE: Non, c'est un copain.
JEAN-PAUL: Un copain ou ton copain?
ISABELLE: Dis donc, Jean-Paul, tu es vraiment trop curieux!

B. *Écoutez et répétez.*

Nom ____

CASSETTE WORKSHEET Leçon 7 (cont.)

Section 2 **La famille d'Isabelle**

UNITÉ 2

C. *Compréhension orale*

a. ____ Papa
(mon père)

b. __1__ Maman
(ma mère)

c. ____ Papi
(mon grand-père)

d. ____ Mamie
(ma grand-mère)

e. ____ Nicolas
(mon frère)

f. ____ Valérie
(ma soeur)

g. ____ Médor
(mon chien)

h. ____ Félix
(mon chat)

i. ____ Oncle Thomas
(mon oncle)

j. ____ Tante Christine
(ma tante)

k. ____ Cédric
(mon cousin)

l. ____ Béatrice
(ma cousine)

Nom ____________________

CASSETTE WORKSHEET Leçon 7 (cont.)

Section 3 **Quel âge as-tu?**

D. ***Compréhension orale***

▶ Marc a 13 ans.

1. Karen a ___ ans.
2. Pierre a ___ ans.
3. Jean-François a ___ ans.
4. Sylvie a ___ ans.
5. Annie a ___ ans.
6. Bernard a ___ ans.

E. ***Compréhension orale***

1. Madame Galand a ___ ans.
2. Mademoiselle Rivière a ___ ans.
3. Monsieur Giraud a ___ ans.
4. Monsieur Pascal a ___ ans.
5. Madame Mercier a ___ ans.

CASSETTE WORKSHEET Leçon 7 (cont.)

F. *Questions et réponses*

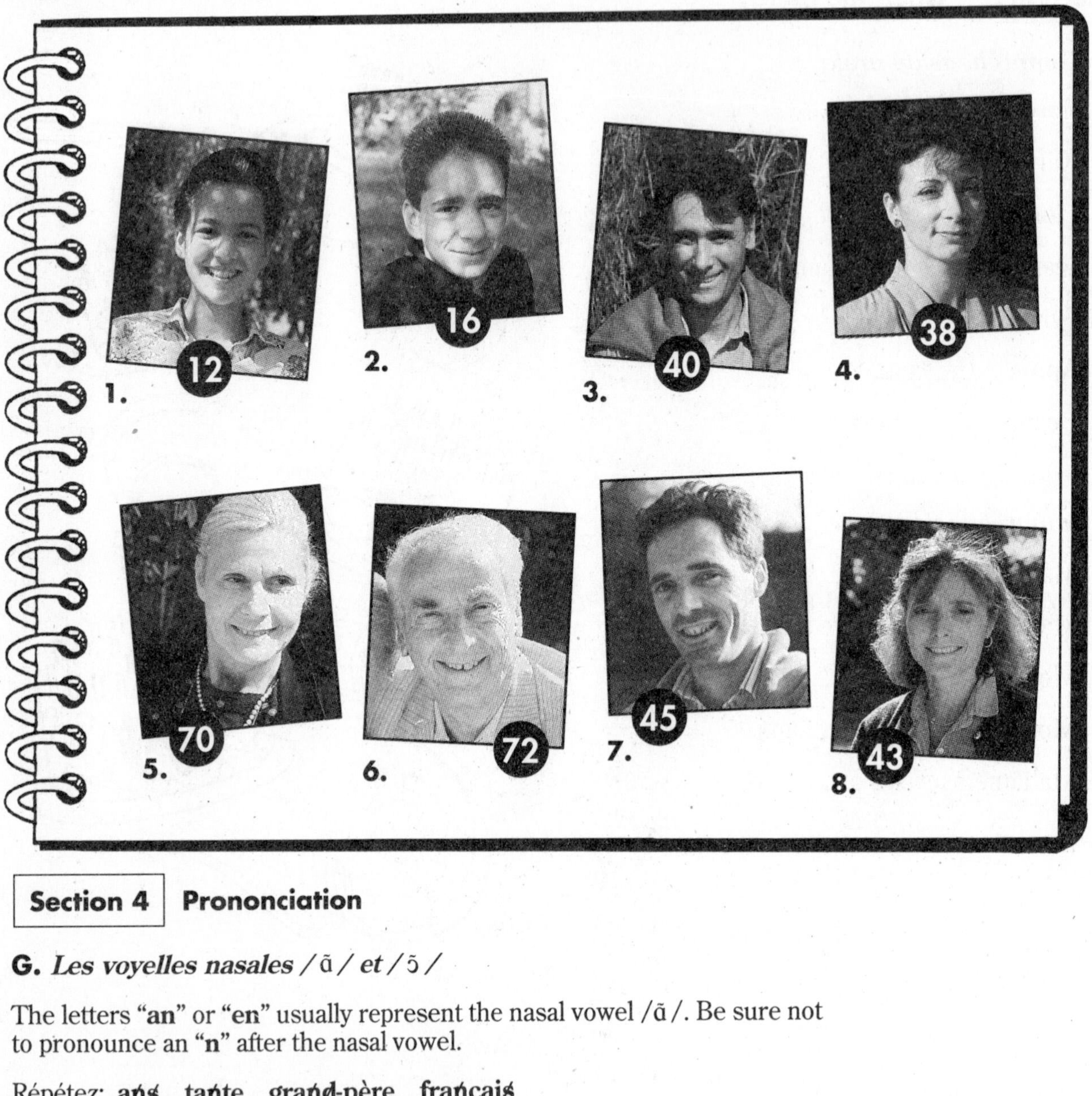

1. 12
2. 16
3. 40
4. 38
5. 70
6. 72
7. 45
8. 43

Section 4 **Prononciation**

G. *Les voyelles nasales* / ɑ̃ / *et* / ɔ̃ /

The letters "**an**" or "**en**" usually represent the nasal vowel / ɑ̃ /. Be sure not to pronounce an "**n**" after the nasal vowel.

Répétez: **ans tante grand-père français**
anglais quarante cinquante
trente comment Henri Laurent

The letters "**on**" represent the nasal vowel / ɔ̃ /. Be sure not to pronounce an "**n**" after the nasal vowel.

Répétez: **non mon ton bonjour oncle**
garçon onze

Contrastez: **an—on tante—ton onze—ans**
Mon oncle François a trente ans.

Nom ____ **DISCOVERING FRENCH - BLEU**

Classe _____________________________ Date ___________

CASSETTE WORKSHEET Leçon 8 Le français pratique: Le jour et la date

Section 1 Quel jour est-ce?

A. *Compréhension orale*

For many people, the days of the week are not all alike.

Dialogue 1. Vendredi

PHILIPPE: Quel jour est-ce?
STÉPHANIE: C'est vendredi!
PHILIPPE: Super! Demain, c'est samedi!

Dialogue 2. Mercredi

NATHALIE: Ça va?
MARC: Pas très bien.
NATHALIE: Pourquoi?
MARC: Aujourd'hui, c'est mercredi.
NATHALIE: Et alors?
MARC: Demain, c'est jeudi! Le jour de l'examen.
NATHALIE: Zut! C'est vrai! Au revoir, Marc.
MARC: Au revoir, Nathalie. À demain!

B. *Écoutez et répétez.*

Section 2 Les jours de la semaine

C. *Écoutez et écrivez.*

▶ Christine arrive mardi.

▶ Christine

1. Pauline
2. Bertrand
3. Céline
4. Didier
5. Agnès
6. Guillaume
7. Véronique

a. lundi
b. mardi
c. mercredi
d. jeudi
e. vendredi
f. samedi
g. dimanche

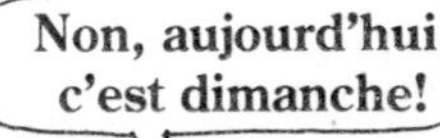

Non, aujourd'hui, c'est dimanche!
Aujourd'hui, c'est samedi?

UNITÉ 2

Nom ______________________________

CASSETTE WORKSHEET Leçon 8 (cont.)

UNITÉ 2

Section 3 Anniversaire

D. ***Compréhension orale***

François wants to know when Isabelle's birthday is.

FRANÇOIS: C'est quand, ton anniversaire?
ISABELLE: C'est le 18 mars!
FRANÇOIS: Le 18 mars? Pas possible!
ISABELLE: Si! Pourquoi?
FRANÇOIS: C'est aussi mon anniversaire.
ISABELLE: Quelle coïncidence!

E. ***Écoutez et répétez.***

Section 4 Quel jour est-ce?

F. ***Compréhension orale***

▶ C'est le __2__ février.

1. C'est le ____ mars.
2. C'est le ____ juin.
3. C'est le ____ juillet.
4. C'est le ____ août.
5. C'est le ____ septembre.
6. C'est le ____ novembre.

CASSETTE WORKSHEET Leçon 8 (cont.)

G. *Questions et réponses*

▶ — Quel jour est-ce?
— **C'est le 5 décembre.**

▶ 

1. 

2. 

3. 

4. 

5. 

6. 

7. 

Section 5 **C'est quand, votre anniversaire?**

H. *Compréhension orale*

▶ Alice: le 18/7

1. Béatrice: le ________
2. Françoise: le ________
3. Julie: le ________
4. Delphine: le ________
5. Denis: le ________
6. Paul: le ________

CASSETTE WORKSHEET Leçon 8 (cont.)

À votre tour!

Section 1. Nathalie et Philippe

 Allez à la page 52.

Section 2. Et toi?

 Allez à la page 52.

Section 3. Conversation dirigée

 Allez à la page 52.

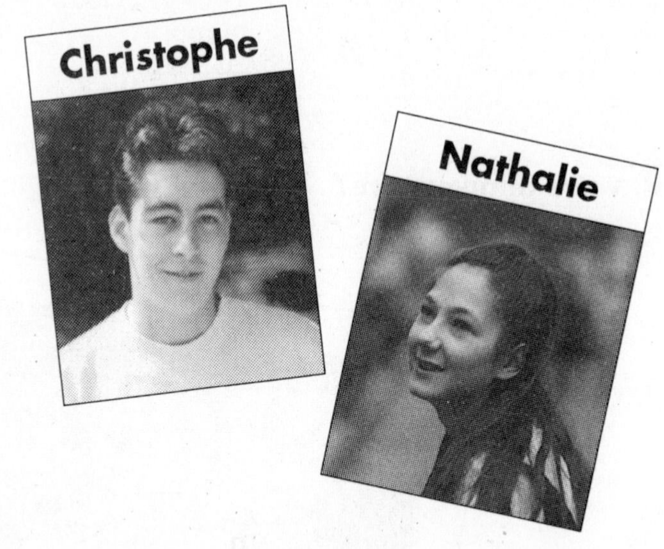

Nom ______________________________

Classe ____________________ Date __________

WRITING ACTIVITIES Leçon 5 Copain ou copine?

1. Pour détectives

You have found a notebook in which several people are mentioned only by their initials. Read the descriptions and determine who is male and who is female. Circle the corresponding letter.

▶ J.G. est un journaliste français.	(M)	F
▶ C.C. est une actrice italienne.	M	(F)
1. B.H. est un musicien anglais.	M	F
2. V.C. est un pianiste.	M	F
3. S.F. est une photographe américaine.	M	F
4. E.M. est une artiste française.	M	F
5. P.N. est un excellent acteur.	M	F
6. T.B. est un artiste américain.	M	F
7. P.V. est un cousin de San Francisco.	M	F
8. V.U. est une cousine de Montréal.	M	F

2. Descriptions

Describe the following people. For each one, write two sentences using two different nouns from the box. Be sure to use **un** or **une** as appropriate.

garçon	**ami**	**copain**	**monsieur**	**prof**
fille	**amie**	**copine**	**dame**	**prof**

▶ *C'est une fille.*

Christine ______________________

Jean-François ______________________ ______________________

M. Martinot ______________________ ______________________

Mme Pichon ______________________ ______________________

FLASH culturel

The **Tour de France** is an international bicycle race that is held in France every summer. How long does it last?

☐ 10 hours ☐ 24 hours ☐ 10 days ☐ 3 weeks

→ page 48

WRITING ACTIVITIES Leçon 5 (cont.)

UNITÉ 2

3. Les nombres

Fill in the six missing numbers in the grid. Then write out these numbers in French.

60		62	63	64
65	66	67		69
		72	73	74
75		77		79

- ____________________
- ____________________
- ____________________
- ____________________
- ____________________
- ____________________

4. Communication: En français!

1. You are walking in town with your French friend Catherine. Catherine waves hello to a girl on a bicycle.
Ask Catherine who it is.

____

2. You see Jean-Louis who is sitting in a café.
Point him out and tell Catherine that he is a friend.

____

3. You see your friend Juliette coming in your direction.
Express your surprise and explain to Catherine who is approaching.

____

FLASH culturel

The **Tour de France** is the longest and most strenuous bicycle race in the world. It is divided into about 20 stages (or **étapes**) and lasts approximately three weeks. During the race, the participants cover about 3,000 kilometers, riding along the valleys and climbing the high mountains of France. The American cyclist Greg Lemond is a three-time winner of the **Tour de France**.

Nom ______________________________

Classe ____________________ Date ____________

WRITING ACTIVITIES Leçon 6 Une coïncidence

1. *Le, la* ou *l'*?

Write **le, la,** or **l'** in front of the following nouns, as appropriate.

▶ la copine

1. ____ garçon
2. ____ monsieur
3. ____ fille
4. ____ ami
5. ____ copain
6. ____ amie
7. ____ prof: M. Lenoir
8. ____ prof: Mme Dupin

2. Photos de vacances

Last summer you went on an international camping trip and took pictures of some of your friends. Give each person's name and nationality.

▶ Il s'appelle Jim.

Il est anglais.

____

____

____

____

____

____

FLASH culturel

In the United States, there are many places that have names of French origin. Which of the following states is named after a French king?

☐ Georgia ☐ North Carolina ☐ Louisiana ☐ Virginia

→ page 50

Nom ______________________________

WRITING ACTIVITIES Leçon 6 (cont.)

3. Loto

Imagine that you are playing **Loto** in France. The following numbers have been called. Read them carefully and put an "X" on the numbers that appear on your **Loto** card.

soixante-treize **soixante-quatre** **quatorze** **cinquante-trois** **huit**
quatre-vingt-douze **vingt-trois** **quatre-vingt-neuf** **soixante-quinze**
cinquante-huit **trente-sept** **quarante-cinq** **soixante-quatorze** **seize**
vingt et un **quatre-vingt-six** **soixante-dix-huit** **quatre-vingt-un**

Which row did you complete to win **Loto:** the top, the middle, or the bottom?

____

Now write in digits the numbers that were not on your card.

____

		21		45			73	81	92
	17				53		74	86	95
8			39			64	78		99

4. À votre tour *(Your turn)*

Now it's your turn to call out the **Loto** numbers. Write out in French what you would say.

1. (95) ______________ 3. (27) ______________ 5. (79) ______________
2. (83) ______________ 4. (62) ______________ 6. (90) ______________

5. Communication: Dialogues

Complete the following mini-dialogues by filling in the missing words.

1. —Philippe ______________ français?
   —Non, ______________ est canadien.
2. —Tu ______________ le garçon là-bas?
   —Oui, c'est ______________ copain.
3. —______________ s'appelle ______________ prof?
   —______________ s'appelle Madame Vallée.

FLASH culturel

Louisiana was named in honor of the French king Louis XIV (1638–1715). Louisiana was once a French colony and extended up the entire Mississippi basin. The U.S. purchased it from France in 1803. Today, French is still spoken in the state of Louisiana by some people in the "Cajun" areas.

Nom ______________________________

Classe ____________________ Date ______________

DISCOVERING FRENCH - *BLEU*

WRITING ACTIVITIES Leçon 7 Les photos d'Isabelle

1. La famille de Catherine

Catherine has taken a picture of her family. Identify each of the people on the photograph.

▶ Suzanne est ___la soeur___ de Catherine.

1. M. Arnaud est ______________ de Catherine.
2. Jean-Michel est ______________ de Catherine.
3. Mme Laurent est ______________ de Catherine.
4. Mme Arnaud est ______________ de Catherine.
5. M. Laurent est ______________ de Catherine.
6. Hugo, c'est ______________.
7. Mimi, c'est ______________.

FLASH culturel

At what age can a French teenager drive a car?

☐ 15 ☐ 16 ☐ 17 ☐ 18

→ page 52

UNITÉ 2

Nom ______________________________

UNITÉ 2

WRITING ACTIVITIES Leçon 7 (cont.)

2. *Mon ou ma?*

Philippe is talking about his friends and relatives, as well as other people he knows. Complete his statements with **mon** or **ma,** as appropriate.

1. __________ cousine s'appelle Christine.
2. __________ frère est à Paris.
3. __________ copine Susan est anglaise.
4. __________ amie Cécile a seize ans.
5. __________ ami Jean-Pierre a quinze ans.
6. __________ prof d'anglais est américaine.
7. __________ prof d'histoire est canadien.
8. __________ mère est journaliste.

3. Quel âge?

Look at the years in which the following people were born. Then complete the sentences below by giving each person's age.

1. (1980) Corinne ______________________________.
2. (1985) Jean-Philippe ______________________________.
3. (1971) Mademoiselle Richaume ______________________________.
4. (1958) Monsieur Lambert ______________________________.

4. Communication: En français!

1. *Tell how old you are.*

____

2. *Ask a friend how old he/she is.*

____

3. *Ask a friend how old his/her brother is.*

____

FLASH culturel

In principle, you have to be 18 to get your driver's license in France. However, if you take driving lessons in an authorized school **(une auto-école),** you can drive at the age of 16 when accompanied by a licensed adult.

Nom ______________________________

Classe ______________________ Date ____________

WRITING ACTIVITIES Leçon 8 Le français pratique: Le jour et la date

1. La semaine

Can you fit the seven days of the week into the following French puzzle?

1. S _ _ _ _ _
2. _ E _ _ _
3. M _ _ _ _ _ _ _
4. _ A _ _ _
5. _ I _ _ _ _ _ _
6. _ _ N _ _
7. _ E _ _ _ _ _ _

2. Les mois

Complete the grid with the names of the missing months.

janvier		**mars**
avril	**mai**	
		septembre
octobre	**novembre**	

FLASH culturel

In France, **le quatorze juillet** is a very important date. What do the French do on that day?

- ☐ They vote.
- ☐ They pay their taxes.
- ☐ They celebrate their national holiday.
- ☐ They honor their war veterans.

→ page 54

UNITÉ 2

Nom ______________________________

UNITÉ 2

WRITING ACTIVITIES Leçon 8 (cont.)

3. Joyeux anniversaire! *(Happy birthday!)*

Ask five friends when their birthdays are. Write out the information in French on the chart below.

	NOM	ANNIVERSAIRE
▶	*David*	*le trois juillet*
1.		
2.		
3.		
4.		
5.		

4. Communication: En français!

Answer the following questions in complete sentences.

1. Quel jour est-ce aujourd'hui?

   ____

2. Et demain?

   ____

3. Quelle est la date aujourd'hui?

   ____

4. C'est quand ton anniversaire?

   ____

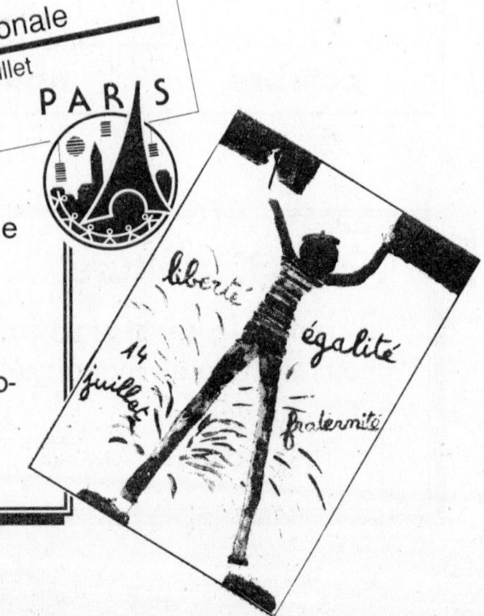

FLASH culturel

On July 14, or "Bastille Day" as it is known in the United States, the French celebrate their national holiday. On July 14, 1789, a Parisian mob stormed **la Bastille,** a state prison which had come to symbolize the king's tyranny. This important historical event marked the beginning of the French Revolution and led to the establishment of a republican form of government for the first time in French history.

Nom ______________________________________

Classe ____________________________ Date ______________

READING AND CULTURE ACTIVITIES Unité 2

A. En voyage

1. CEEL is a language school in Geneva. They teach four languages including German **(allemand)**, which is one of the official languages of Switzerland. Which of the following languages do they NOT teach?

- ☐ English.
- ☐ French.
- ☐ Spanish.
- ☐ Italian.

2. This brochure advertises a film festival in Montreal. When is the festival being held?

- ☐ Early spring.
- ☐ Early summer.
- ☐ Late summer.
- ☐ Late fall.

FESTIVAL DES FILMS DU MONDE

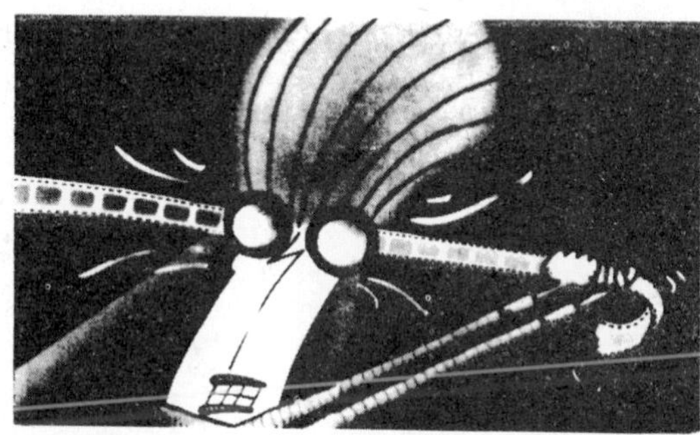

MONTREAL

21 AOÛT - 1er SEPT.

TRANSPORTEUR OFFICIEL

AIR CANADA

READING AND CULTURE ACTIVITIES Unité 2 (cont.)

3. This is a card of phone numbers that was distributed in Strasbourg, France.

NUMÉROS D'URGENCE

SAMU (Service d'Aide Médicale d'Urgence	15
POLICE	17
POMPIERS	18
PHARMACIE	88.41.12.45
TAXIS	88.61.54.13

- You would dial 15 if you had . . .
  - ☐ a medical emergency
  - ☐ a problem with your telephone
  - ☐ a fire to report
  - ☐ a burglary to report

- To get a prescription filled, you would call . . .
  - ☐ 15
  - ☐ 18
  - ☐ 88.41.12.45
  - ☐ 88.61.54.13

- If you needed transportation to get to the airport, you would call . . .
  - ☐ 15
  - ☐ 18
  - ☐ 88.41.12.45
  - ☐ 88.61.54.13

4. The following flyer was distributed in Paris.

MAIRIE DE PARIS
NOUVEAU THEATRE MOUFFETARD
73, rue Mouffetard Paris 5e
Métro Monge
Tél. 43.31.11.99
50 représentations exceptionnelles
du 8 Novembre au 1er Janvier
EMMANUEL DECHARTRE
CLAUDINE COSTER
ROBERT PARTY
LE PRINCE DE HOMBOURG
Tragédie romantique en 5 actes
de HEINRICH VON KLEIST
Mise en scène : Jacques MAUCLAIR
Version française de J. CURTIS
Musique originale de Greco CASADESUS

- What does this flyer advertise?
  - ☐ A play.
  - ☐ A concert.
  - ☐ A piano recital.
  - ☐ A ballet.

- How many performances will there be?
  - ☐ 5
  - ☐ 8
  - ☐ 15
  - ☐ 50

- When is the last performance?
  - ☐ January 1.
  - ☐ June 1.
  - ☐ July 14.
  - ☐ November 8.

READING AND CULTURE ACTIVITIES Unité 2 (cont.)

B. Les boutiques du Palais des Congrès

In this ad, the shops at the Paris Convention Center **(le Palais des Congrès)** are announcing a large sale. Look at the ad carefully.

- What is the French word for *sale?*

  ____

- On what day does the sale begin?

  ____

- On what day does the sale end?

  ____

- Is there parking available? ____________

  For how many cars? ______________

C. «Un bon patriote»

Look at this Paris ticket for "Un bon patriote."

- Where is the performance being held?

  ____

- How much does the ticket cost?

  ____

- What is the date on the ticket?

  ____

- What day of the week is the performance?

  ____

- What time does the performance begin?

  ____

READING AND CULTURE ACTIVITIES Unité 2 (cont.)

D. Une carte

Jean-Claude bought this card and has just signed it.

- To whom is he planning to send it?

____

- What is the special occasion?

____

Heureux Anniversaire
Bonheur
Chance
Prospérité
Santé
À ma grand-mère
à l'occasion de
son 58 ème
anniversaire
Jean-Claude

COMMUNICATIVE EXPRESSIONS AND THEMATIC VOCABULARY

Unité 2 Les copains et la famille

▶ CULTURAL CONTEXT: Talking about people

COMMUNICATIVE EXPRESSIONS

Introducing or pointing someone out

Voici . . . **Voilà . . .**

Inquiring about people and mentioning their nationality

Tu connais . . . ?

Il est [français].
Elle est [française].

Qui est-ce?
C'est . . .

Asking about someone's name and age

Comment s'appelle . . . ?
Il/Elle s'appelle . . .

Quel âge as-tu?
J'ai [14] ans.

Quel âge a . . . ?
Il/Elle a [15] ans.

Talking about days, dates, and birthdays

Quel jour est-ce?
C'est [mardi].

Quelle est la date?
C'est le [10 novembre].
C'est le premier [mai].

C'est quand, ton anniversaire?
C'est le [2 juillet].

VOCABULARY

People, family members, pets

un garçon	**une fille**	**un frère**	**une soeur**	**un chat**
un ami	**une amie**	**un cousin**	**une cousine**	**un chien**
un copain	**une copine**			
		un père	**une mère**	
un monsieur	**une dame**	**un oncle**	**une tante**	
un prof	**une prof**	**un grand-père**	**une grand-mère**	

UNITÉ 2

COMMUNICATIVE EXPRESSIONS AND THEMATIC VOCABULARY

VOCABULARY *(continued)*

Days and months

	un jour	un mois	
aujourd'hui	**lundi**	**janvier**	**juillet**
demain	**mardi**	**février**	**août**
	mercredi	**mars**	**septembre**
	jeudi	**avril**	**octobre**
	vendredi	**mai**	**novembre**
	samedi	**juin**	**décembre**
	dimanche		

Numbers: 60–100

soixante	**soixante-dix**	**quatre-vingts**	**quatre-vingt-dix**	**cent**
soixante et un	**soixante et onze**	**quatre-vingt-un**	**quatre-vingt-onze**	
soixante-deux	**soixante-douze**	**quatre-vingt-deux**	**quatre-vingt-douze**	
soixante-trois	**soixante-treize**	**quatre-vingt-trois**	**quatre-vingt-treize**	
soixante-quatre	**soixante-quatorze**	**quatre-vingt-quatre**	**quatre-vingt-quatorze**	
soixante-cinq	**soixante-quinze**	**quatre-vingt-cinq**	**quatre-vingt-quinze**	
soixante-six	**soixante-seize**	**quatre-vingt-six**	**quatre-vingt-seize**	
soixante-sept	**soixante-dix-sept**	**quatre-vingt-sept**	**quatre-vingt-dix-sept**	
soixante-huit	**soixante-dix-huit**	**quatre-vingt-huit**	**quatre-vingt-dix-huit**	
soixante-neuf	**soixante-dix-neuf**	**quatre-vingt-neuf**	**quatre-vingt-dix-neuf**	

Other expressions

un, une	**tiens!**
le, la, l'	**à demain!**
mon, ma	**à samedi!**
ton, ta	

UNITÉ 2

UNITÉ 3
Bon appétit!

LISTENING ACTIVITIES
Leçons 9–12

WRITING ACTIVITIES
Leçons 9–12

READING AND CULTURE ACTIVITIES
Unité 3

Communicative Expressions and Thematic Vocabulary

Nom ______________________________

Classe ______________________ Date ____________

CASSETTE WORKSHEET Leçon 9 Tu as faim?

Section 1 Tu as faim?

A. *Compréhension orale*

Pierre, Philippe, and Nathalie are on their way home from school. They stop to get something to eat. Today it is Pierre's turn to treat his friends.

Scène 1. Pierre et Nathalie

PIERRE: Tu as faim?
NATHALIE: Oui, j'ai faim.
PIERRE: Qu'est-ce que tu veux, un sandwich ou une pizza?
NATHALIE: Donne-moi une pizza, s'il te plaît.
PIERRE: Voilà.
NATHALIE: Merci.

Scène 2. Pierre et Philippe

PIERRE: Et toi, Philippe, tu as faim?
PHILIPPE: Oh là, là, oui, j'ai faim.
PIERRE: Qu'est-ce que tu veux, un sandwich ou une pizza?
PHILIPPE: Je voudrais un sandwich . . . euh . . . et donne-moi aussi une pizza.
PIERRE: C'est vrai! Tu as vraiment faim!

B. *Écoutez et répétez.*

UNITÉ 3

Section 2 Je voudrais . . .

C. *Compréhension orale*

a. _____ trois croissants

b. _____ une glace à la vanille

c. _____ un hot dog

d. __1__ un sandwich

e. _____ un sandwich au jambon et un sandwich au pâté

f. _____ un steak-frites et une salade

D. *Compréhension orale*

a. _____ *l'Express*

b. _____ 20 francs

c. _____ un album d'Astérix

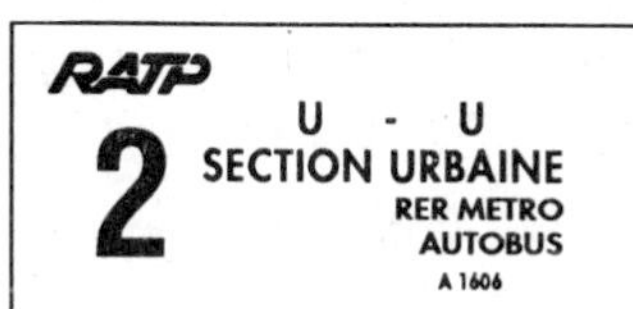

d. _____ un ticket de métro

Nom ______________________________

CASSETTE WORKSHEET Leçon 9 (cont.)

Section 3 Au café

E. ***Questions et réponses***

▶ — Tu veux un sandwich ou une pizza?
— **Je voudrais un sandwich.**

▶

1.

2.

3.

4.

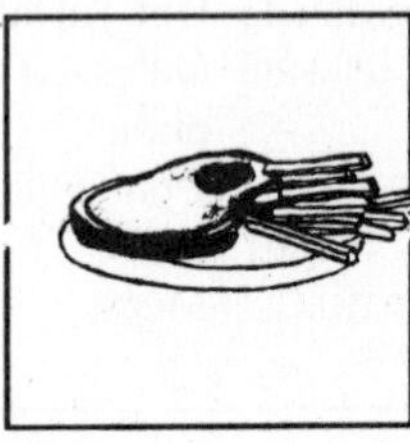

5.

UNITÉ 3

Section 4 Prononciation

F. ***L'intonation***

Écoutez: **Voici un steak . . . et une salade.**

When you speak, your voice rises and falls. This is called INTONATION. In French, as in English, your voice goes down at the end of a statement. However, in French, your voice rises after each group of words in the middle of a sentence. (This is the opposite of English, where your voice drops a little when you pause in the middle of a sentence.)

Répétez: **Je voudrais une pizza.**

Je voudrais une pizza et un sandwich.

Je voudrais une pizza, un sandwich et un hamburger.

Voici un steak.

Voici un steak et une salade.

Nom ______________________________

Classe ____________________ Date ______________

CASSETTE WORKSHEET Leçon 10 Au café

Section 1 Au café

A. *Compréhension orale*

Jean-Paul and Isabelle are tired and thirsty after an afternoon of shopping. Jean-Paul invites Isabelle to a café.

Scène 1

JEAN-PAUL: Tu as soif?
ISABELLE: Oui, j'ai soif.
JEAN-PAUL: On va dans un café? Je t'invite.
ISABELLE: D'accord!

Scène 2

LE GARÇON: Vous désirez, mademoiselle?
ISABELLE: Un jus d'orange, s'il vous plaît.
LE GARÇON: Et vous, monsieur?
JEAN-PAUL: Hmmm . . . Donnez-moi une limonade, s'il vous plaît.

Scène 3

LE GARÇON: La limonade, c'est pour vous, mademoiselle?
JEAN-PAUL: Non, c'est pour moi.
LE GARÇON: Ah, excusez-moi. Voici le jus d'orange, mademoiselle.
ISABELLE: Merci.

B. *Écoutez et répétez.*

CASSETTE WORKSHEET Leçon 10 (cont.)

Section 2 *S'il vous plaît ou s'il te plaît?*

C. ***Compréhension orale***

How to say *please:*

Formal form: **s'il vous plaît**

ISABELLE: Un jus d'orange, s'il vous plaît.
JEAN-PAUL: Donnez-moi une limonade, s'il vous plaît.

Informal form: **s'il te plaît**

JEAN-PAUL: Donne-moi un soda, s'il te plaît.

D. ***Écoutez et écrivez.***

1

a. ____ s'il vous plaît
b. ____ s'il te plaît

2

a. ____ s'il vous plaît
b. ____ s'il te plaît

3

a. ____ s'il vous plaît
b. ____ s'il te plaît

4

a. ____ s'il vous plaît
b. ____ s'il te plaît

5

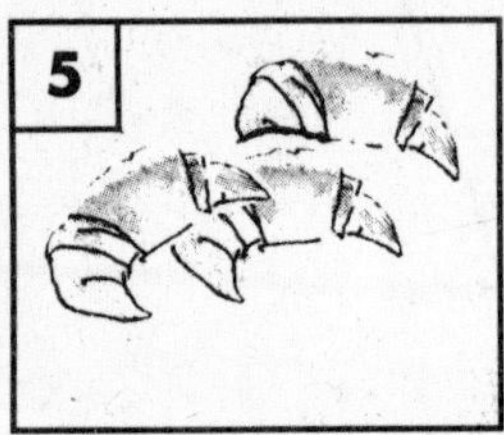

a. ____ s'il vous plaît
b. ____ s'il te plaît

6

a. ____ s'il vous plaît
b. ____ s'il te plaît

7

a. ____ s'il vous plaît
b. ____ s'il te plaît

8

a. ____ s'il vous plaît
b. ____ s'il te plaît

9

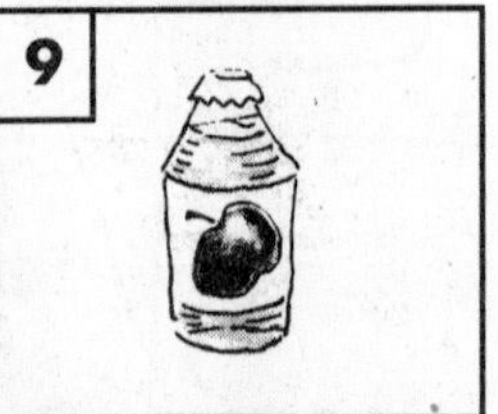

a. ____ s'il vous plaît
b. ____ s'il te plaît

10

a. ____ s'il vous plaît
b. ____ s'il te plaît

CASSETTE WORKSHEET Leçon 10 (cont.)

Section 3 S'il te plaît, donne-moi . . .

E. *Questions et réponses*

▶ — Tu veux un café ou un thé?
— S'il te plaît, donne-moi un café.

▶ 

1 

2 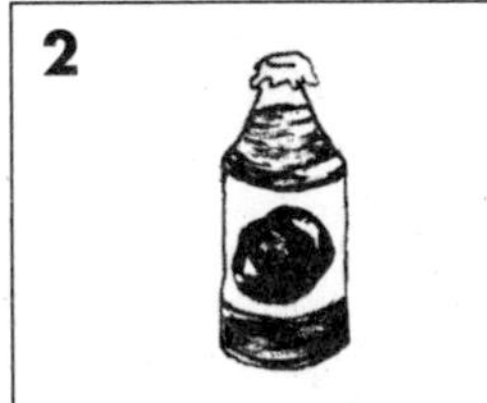

3 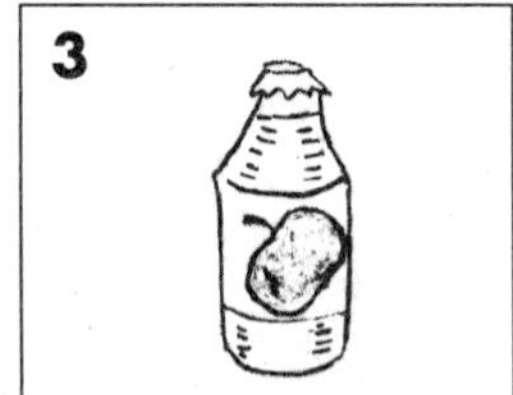

4 

Section 4 Vous désirez?

F. *Questions et réponses*

▶ — Vous désirez?
— Je voudrais un thé, s'il vous plaît.

▶ 

1 

2 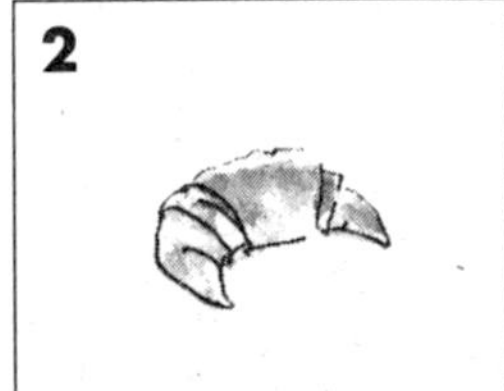

3 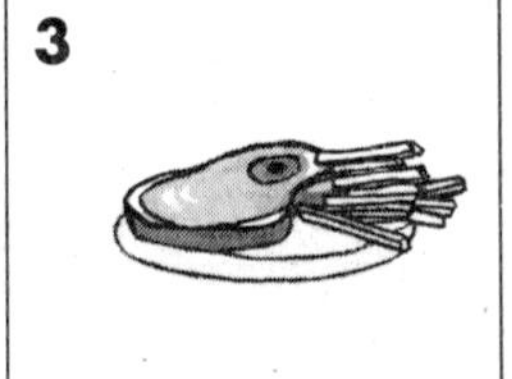

4 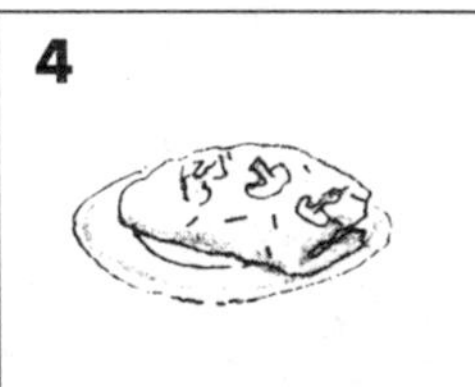

Nom ____

CASSETTE WORKSHEET Leçon 10 (cont.)

Section 5 **Prononciation**

G. ***L'accent final***

Écoutez: **un chocolat**

In French, the rhythm is very even and the accent always falls on the *last* syllable of a word or group of words.

Répétez: **Philippe Thomas Alice Sophie Dominique**
un café **Je voudrais un café.**
une salade **Donnez-moi une salade.**
un chocolat **Donne-moi un chocolat.**

UNITÉ 3

Nom ______________________________

Classe ____________________ Date __________

DISCOVERING FRENCH – *BLEU*

CASSETTE WORKSHEET Leçon 11 Ça fait combien?

Section 1 Ça fait combien?

A. ***Compréhension orale***

At the café, Jean-Paul and Isabelle are ready to leave. Jean-Paul calls the waiter so he can pay the check.

JEAN-PAUL: S'il vous plaît?
LE GARÇON: Oui, monsieur.
JEAN-PAUL: Ça fait combien?
LE GARÇON: Voyons, un jus d'orange, 12 francs, et une limonade, 10 francs. Ça fait 22 francs.
JEAN-PAUL: 22 francs . . . Très bien . . . Zut! Où est mon porte-monnaie . . .? Dis, Isabelle, prête-moi 30 francs, s'il te plaît.

B. ***Écoutez et répétez.***

Section 2 C'est combien?

C. ***Compréhension orale***

▶ 60 francs

1. ____ francs

2. ____ francs

3. ____ francs

4. ____ francs

5. ____ francs

CASSETTE WORKSHEET Leçon 11 (cont.)

Section 3 Au café

D. *Questions et réponses*

1. 
2. 
3. 
4. 

Section 4 Prononciation

E. *La consonne "r"*

Écoutez: **Marie**

The French consonant "**r**" is not at all like the English "**r**". It is pronounced at the back of the throat. In fact, it is similar to the Spanish "jota" sound of José.

Répétez: **Marie Paris orange Henri**
franc très croissant fromage
bonjour pour Pierre quart
Robert Richard Renée Raoul
Marie, prête-moi trente francs.

Nom ____

Classe ____________________________ Date ____________

CASSETTE WORKSHEET Leçon 12 Le français pratique: Le temps

Section 1 Le temps

A. *Compréhension orale*

It is nine o'clock Sunday morning. Cécile and her brother Philippe have planned a picnic for the whole family. Cécile is asking about the weather.

CÉCILE: Quel temps fait-il?
PHILIPPE: Il fait mauvais!
CÉCILE: Il fait mauvais?
PHILIPPE: Oui, il fait mauvais! Regarde! Il pleut!
CÉCILE: Oh, zut, zut et zut!
PHILIPPE: !!!???
CÉCILE: Et le pique-nique?
PHILIPPE: Le pique-nique? Ah, oui, le pique-nique! . . . Écoute, ça n'a pas d'importance.
CÉCILE: Pourquoi?
PHILIPPE: Pourquoi? Parce que Papa va nous inviter au restaurant.
CÉCILE: Super!

B. *Écoutez et répétez.*

Section 2 Quel temps fait-il?

C. *Compréhension orale*

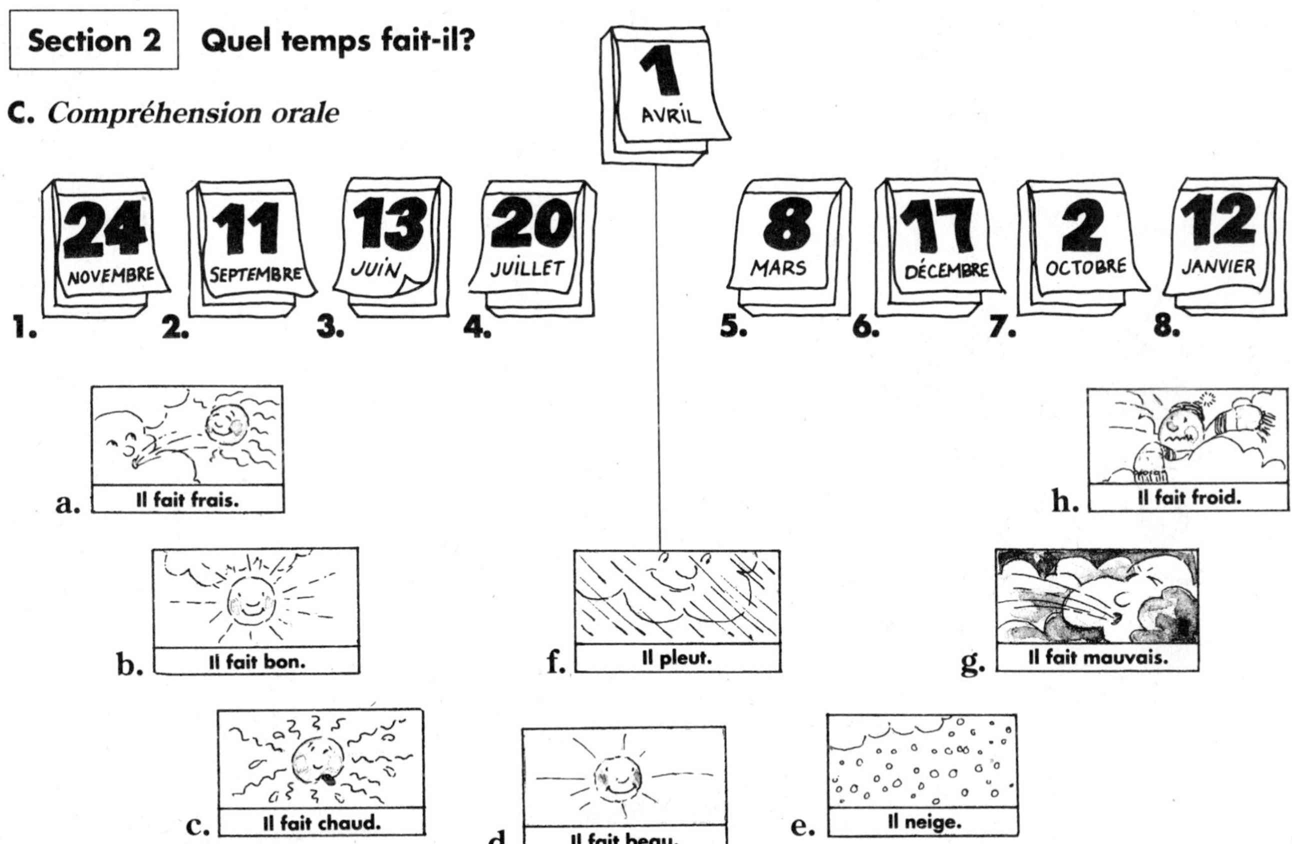

CASSETTE WORKSHEET Leçon 12 (cont.)

D. ***Questions et réponses***

1 

2 

3 

4 

5 

6 

À votre tour!

Section 1. Isabelle et Jean-Paul

 Allez à la page 72.

Section 2. Et toi?

 Allez à la page 72.

Section 3. Conversation dirigée

 Allez à la page 72.

Nom ______________________________

Classe ____________________ Date ____________

WRITING ACTIVITIES Leçon 9 Tu as faim?

1. *Un ou une?*

Complete the names of the following foods with **un** or **une,** as appropriate.

1. ________ sandwich

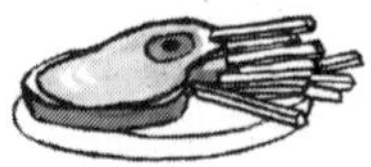
5. ________ steak-frites

2. ________ pizza

6. ________ salade

3. ________ steak

7. ________ croissant

4. ________ crêpe

8. ________ omelette

UNITÉ 3

2. Conversations

Complete the conversations with expressions from the box.

1. —Tu as faim?
   —Oui, ____________ faim.
2. —Qu'est-ce que ________________ ?
   —Je ________________ une glace.
3. —S'il te plaît, ____________ un sandwich.
   —Voilà un sandwich.
   —____________ !

merci
tu veux
j'ai
je voudrais
donne-moi

FLASH culturel

Camembert, brie, and roquefort are all products of French origin. What are they?

☐ pastries ☐ cheeses ☐ perfumes ☐ crackers

→ page 74

WRITING ACTIVITIES Leçon 9 (cont.)

3. Communication: En français!

A. You have invited your French friend Philippe to your home.

1. *Ask Philippe if he is hungry.*

____

2. *Ask him if he wants a sandwich.*

____

3. *Ask him if he wants an ice cream cone.*

____

B. You are in a French restaurant with a friend.

1. *Tell your friend that you are hungry.*

____

2. *Tell her what type of food you would like to have.*

____

FLASH culturel

France produces over 400 varieties of cheese, among which **camembert, brie,** and **roquefort** are the best known. In a traditional French meal, cheese is served as a separate course, after the salad and before the dessert. It is eaten with bread, and occasionally with butter.

Nom ______________________________

Classe ______________________ Date ____________

WRITING ACTIVITIES Leçon 10 Au café

1. Les boissons

Find the French names of eight beverages in the following grid. The names can be read horizontally, vertically, or diagonally. Then list these beverages, using **un** or **une,** as appropriate.

J	O	J	B	M	N	C	I	X	Y	A	Z
M	U	U	R	E	W	H	L	Q	B	C	F
J	U	S	D	E	T	O	M	A	T	E	R
K	V	D	D	L	G	C	C	U	K	N	Z
X	D	E	A	E	L	O	H	T	L	Z	C
Y	B	P	A	F	R	L	C	H	X	T	P
Z	S	O	D	A	C	A	F	É	J	M	B
O	N	M	C	K	B	T	I	N	K	A	Y
L	I	M	O	N	A	D	E	S	D	O	C
S	Q	E	T	F	I	P	D	V	I	G	L
H	T	W	M	R	O	S	Y	I	U	N	J

- ______________________
- ______________________
- ______________________
- ______________________
- ______________________
- ______________________
- ______________________
- ______________________

2. Mes préférences

In the chart below, list which three of the above beverages you like the best and which three you like the least.

1. ______________________ 4. ______________________
2. ______________________ 5. ______________________
3. ______________________ 6. ______________________

FLASH culturel

Which of the following beverages is most likely to be served with a French meal?

☐ milk ☐ coffee ☐ iced tea ☐ mineral water

→ page 76

WRITING ACTIVITIES Leçon 10 (cont.)

3. Communication: En français!

A. Your French friend Marc has dropped by your house.

1. *Ask him if he is thirsty.*

____

2. *Ask him if he wants a soda or a glass of orange juice.*

____

B. You are in a French café with a friend.

1. *Tell your friend that you are thirsty.*

____

2. *Tell the waiter (or waitress) to bring you a beverage of your choice.*

____

C'est original, c'est Perrier.
perrier

FLASH culturel

The French drink a lot of mineral water. In fact, they have the highest consumption of mineral water in the world: about 60 liters per person per year. These mineral waters, some plain and some carbonated, come from natural springs in various parts of the country and are widely exported. The best known are Évian, Vittel, Perrier, and Vichy.

Nom ______________________________

Classe ____________________ Date ____________

WRITING ACTIVITIES Leçon 11 Ça fait combien?

1. C'est combien?

Identify the items pictured and give their prices.

▶ 

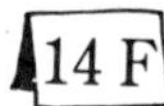

Voici un sandwich.

Il coûte quatorze francs.

1.  7 F ______________________________

____

2. 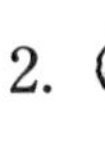 24 F ______________________________

____

3. 28 F 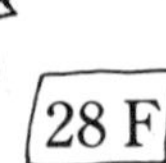 ______________________________

____

4.  45 F ______________________________

____

5.  13 F ______________________________

____

6.  30 F ______________________________

____

UNITÉ 3

FLASH culturel

On their paper money, the French honor people who have made significant contributions to the world of science and art. The largest French banknote is the 500-franc bill which is worth about $80. It bears the portrait of Blaise Pascal. Who is Pascal?

☐ a mathematician ☐ a philosopher ☐ a musician ☐ a painter

→ page 78

Nom ______________________________

WRITING ACTIVITIES Leçon 11 (cont.)

2. Communication: En français!

Imagine that you are at Le Rallye with two French friends, Olivier and Valérie.

Use the menu to write out the following conversation (in French, of course!).

Le Rallye

Boissons		**Sandwichs**	
Café	10 F	Sandwich au jambon	20 F
Thé	10 F	Sandwich au fromage	20 F
Chocolat	15 F	**Et aussi:**	
Soda	15 F	Croissant	10 F
Limonade	12 F	Pizza	18 F
Jus d'orange	15 F	Salade	15 F
Eau minérale	8 F	Omelette	20 F
Glaces		Hamburger	26 F
Glace au café	12 F	Steak	34 F
Glace à la vanille	12 F	Steak-frites	40 F

LE GARÇON: ______________________________
May I help you?

TOI: ______________________________
I would like [a food and a beverage].

VALÉRIE: ______________________________
Please give me [a food and a beverage].

OLIVIER: ______________________________
I would like [a food and a beverage], please.

TOI: ______________________________
How much does that come to?

LE GARÇON: ______________________________
That comes to [the price of what was ordered].

TOI: ______________________________
Hey, Olivier, loan me fifty francs, please.

UNITÉ 3

FLASH culturel

Blaise Pascal (1623–1662) was both a philosopher and a mathematician. By age 12, he could read Greek and Latin and was well versed in higher mathematics. At 19, he invented a calculating machine which is considered by many to be the forerunner of today's computers. As you may know, a modern computer language has been named in his honor.

Nom ______________________________

Classe ______________________ Date ______________

WRITING ACTIVITIES Leçon 12 Le français pratique: Le temps

1. Les quatre saisons

Write the names of the seasons associated with the following pictures.

______________ ______________ ______________ ______________

2. La météo *(Weather report)*

Look at the map of France and describe the weather in the cities indicated below.

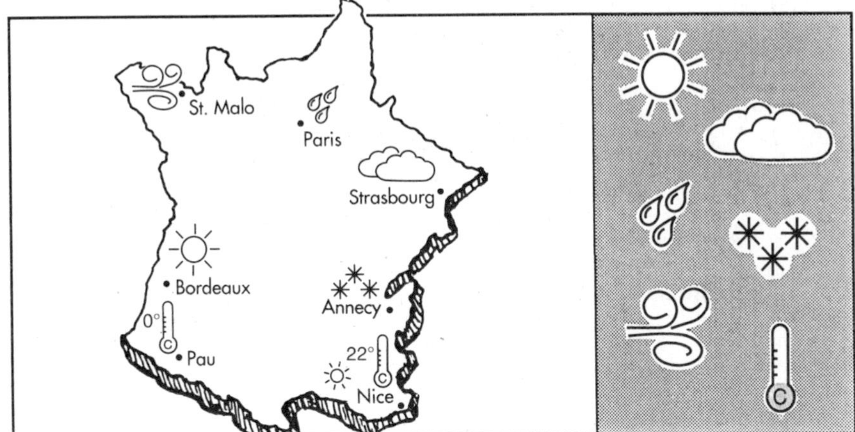

1. À Pau, ______________________.
2. À Nice, ______________________.
3. À Bordeaux, ______________________.
4. À Strasbourg, ______________________.
5. À Annecy, ______________________.
6. À Saint Malo, ______________________.
7. À Paris, ______________________.

FLASH culturel

If you went to France for Christmas vacation, what kind of weather should you expect?

☐ rain ☐ snow ☐ cold weather ☐ mild weather

→ page 80

WRITING ACTIVITIES Leçon 12 (cont.)

3. Communication: Quel temps fait-il?

Describe the weather in the city where you live.

1. Aujourd'hui, ______________________________.
2. En été, ______________________________.
3. En automne, ______________________________.
4. En hiver, ______________________________.
5. Au printemps, ______________________________.

4. Communication: As-tu faim? As-tu soif?

When we go to a café, what we order often depends on the weather. Read each of the weather descriptions and then indicate what you would like to eat and/or drink.

Le Temps	Au Café S'il vous plaît, . . .	
▶ Il fait froid.	donnez-moi	un croissant et un chocolat.
1. Il fait chaud.	donnez-moi	______________________________.
2. Il pleut.	donnez-moi	______________________________.
3. Il neige.	donnez-moi	______________________________.
4. Il fait frais.	donnez-moi	______________________________.

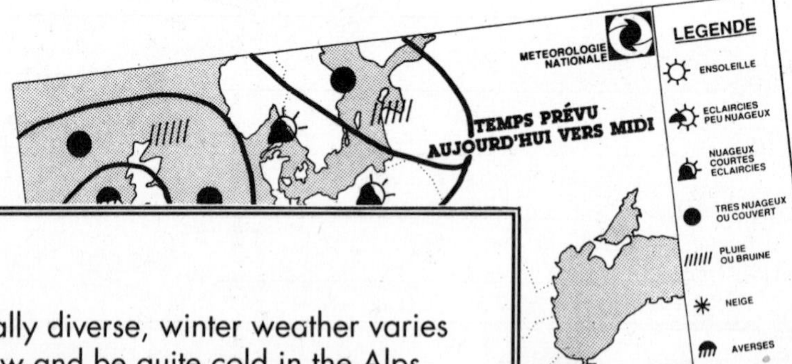

FLASH culturel

Since France is very geographically diverse, winter weather varies from region to region. It may snow and be quite cold in the Alps, the Pyrenees, and the mountains of central France. The weather may be rather mild along the Mediterranean and in southern France. In the rest of the country it may be cool and sometimes rainy.

Nom ______________________________

Classe ____________________ Date ____________

READING AND CULTURE ACTIVITIES Unité 3

A. Le petit déjeuner

Read the breakfast request that Monsieur Chardon hung on the doorknob of his hotel room.

1. When does M. Chardon want his breakfast served?
- ☐ Before 7 A.M.
- ☐ Around 7:15 A.M.
- ☐ Around 7:45 A.M.
- ☐ He does not say.

2. What kind of juice is he ordering?
- ☐ Orange juice.
- ☐ Grapefruit juice.
- ☐ Apple juice.
- ☐ Tomato juice.

3. What does he want to eat?
- ☐ Toast.
- ☐ A muffin.
- ☐ A croissant.
- ☐ A Danish pastry.

4. What hot beverage is he ordering?
- ☐ Coffee.
- ☐ Hot chocolate.
- ☐ Tea with lemon.
- ☐ Tea with milk.

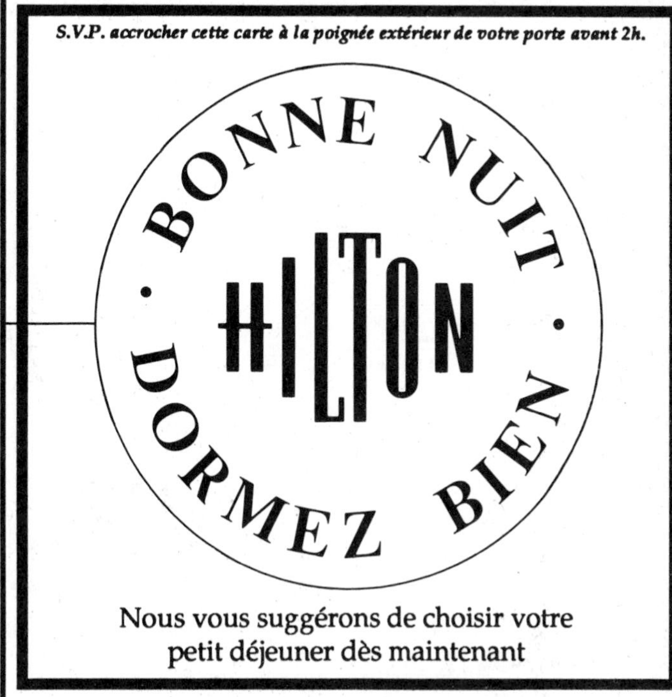

S.V.P. accrocher cette carte à la poignée extérieur de votre porte avant 2h.
BONNE NUIT
HILTON
DORMEZ BIEN
Nous vous suggérons de choisir votre petit déjeuner dès maintenant

Nom (en lettres moulées): CHARDON

No de chambre: 89 Nbre de personnes: 1

Servir entre

☐ 6:30 — 7:00	☐ 8:00 — 8:30	☐ 9:30 — 10:00
☑ 7:00 — 7:30	☐ 8:30 — 9:00	☐ 10:00 — 10:30
☐ 7:30 — 8:00	☐ 9:00 — 9:30	☐ 10:30 — 11:00

LE CONTINENTAL

Votre choix de

☑ Jus d'orange frais ou ☐ Jus de pamplemousse ou ☐ Jus de pomme
☐ Jus de tomate

☐ Croissant ou ☑ Pâtisserie danoise
☐ Muffin

☑ Café	☐ Thé avec lait	☐ Lait
☐ Décaféiné	☐ Thé avec citron	☐ Chocolat chaud

READING AND CULTURE ACTIVITIES Unité 3 (cont.)

B. La météo

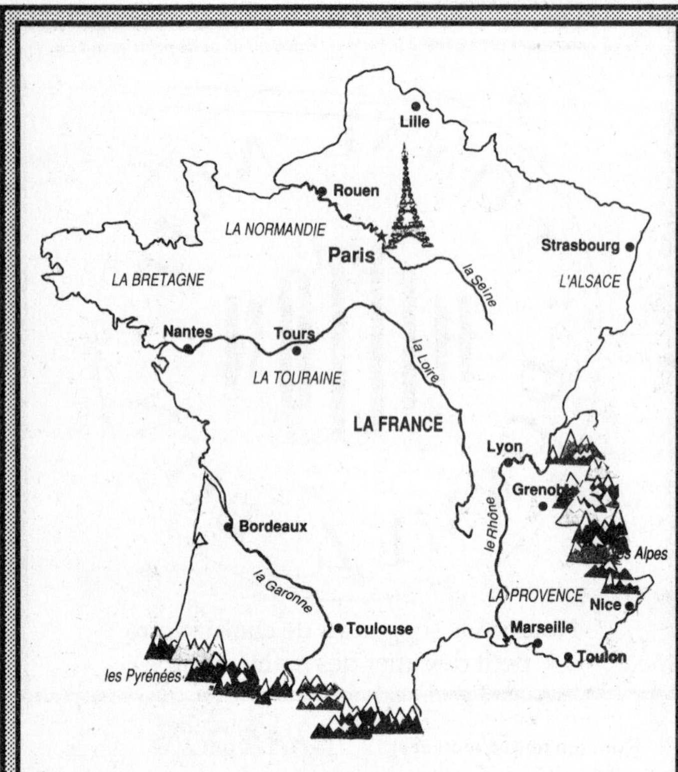

La météo en bref:
23 janvier

Dans le nord de la France il fait assez froid.

Dans la région parisienne, il pleut.

Dans les Alpes, il neige.

Cependant sur la Côte d'Azur, à Nice et à Cannes, il fait beau temps.

1. What is the weather like in Paris?
- ☐ It's sunny.
- ☐ It's windy.
- ☐ It's rainy.
- ☐ It's snowing.

2. What is the weather like in the Alps?
- ☐ It's sunny.
- ☐ It's windy.
- ☐ It's rainy.
- ☐ It's snowing.

3. What is the weather like in Nice?
- ☐ It's sunny.
- ☐ It's windy.
- ☐ It's rainy.
- ☐ It's snowing.

READING AND CULTURE ACTIVITIES Unité 3 (cont.)

C. À la Terrasse Mailloux

The Terrasse Mailloux is a restaurant in Quebec City. This morning you visited the Citadelle with a classmate, and now you have stopped at the Terrasse Mailloux for lunch.

Together with your classmate, read the menu carefully and select three dishes that you will each have.

- Write down the dishes you have selected.
- Then enter the prices for what you have chosen and total up each bill.

MOI		MON COPAIN/MA COPINE	
PLAT	PRIX	PLAT	PRIX
______	______	______	______
______	______	______	______
______	______	______	______
TOTAL	______	TOTAL	______

Terrasse Mailloux

entrées

Frites (French fries)	0.80
Frites avec sauce hot chicken (French fries with hot chicken sauce)	1.00
Frites avec sauce spaghetti (French fries with spaghetti sauce)	1.65
Oignons français (Onion rings)	1.50

salades

Au poulet (Chicken)	3.95
Au homard (en saison) Lobster (in season)	9.50
Salade du chef (Chef's salad)	1.50

pizza 9''

Fromage (Cheese)	3.25
Pepperoni	3.75
Garnie (All dressed)	4.25

sandwichs
(servis avec frites et salade de choux)
(served with French fries and cole slaw)

Salade aux oeufs (Egg salad)	2.00
Jambon (Ham)	2.50
Poulet (Chicken)	2.25
Tomates et bacon (Tomato & bacon)	2.50
Croque Monsieur	3.25

desserts

Salade de fruits (Fruit salad)	1.25
Tartes (Pies)	1.00
Gâteau moka (Mocha cake)	1.50
Gâteau Forêt Noire (Black Forest cake)	1.75

COMMUNICATIVE EXPRESSIONS AND THEMATIC VOCABULARY

Unité 3 Bon appétit!

▶ CULTURAL CONTEXT: Having a snack in France

COMMUNICATIVE EXPRESSIONS

Saying that you are hungry or thirsty

J'ai faim. **J'ai soif.**
Tu as faim? **Tu as soif?**

Offering a friend something

Tu veux . . . ?
Qu'est-ce que tu veux?

Asking a friend for something

Je voudrais . . . **s'il te plaît**
Donne-moi . . .
Prête-moi . . .

Ordering in a café

Vous désirez?
Je voudrais . . . **s'il vous plaît**

Asking how much something costs

C'est combien?
Ça fait combien?
Ça fait [50 francs].

Combien coûte [un sandwich/une pizza]?
Il/Elle coûte . . .

Talking about the weather

Quel temps fait-il?
Il fait | **beau.** **Il neige.**
| **bon** **Il pleut.**
| **chaud**
| **frais**
| **froid**
| **mauvais**

UNITÉ 3

COMMUNICATIVE EXPRESSIONS AND THEMATIC VOCABULARY

VOCABULARY

Foods you can order in a café

un croissant
un hamburger
un hot dog
un sandwich
un steak
un steak-frites

une crêpe
une glace
une omelette
une pizza
une salade

Beverages you can order in a café

un café
un chocolat
un thé

une limonade

un jus d'orange
un jus de pomme
un jus de raisin
un jus de tomate
un soda

The seasons

l'automne
l'été
l'hiver
le printemps

en automne
en été
en hiver
au printemps

UNITÉ 3

UNITÉ 4
Qu'est-ce qu'on fait?

LISTENING ACTIVITIES
Leçons 13–16

WRITING ACTIVITIES
Leçons 13–16

READING AND CULTURE ACTIVITIES
Unité 4

Communicative Expressions and Thematic Vocabulary

Nom ______________________________

Classe ____________________ Date ____________

CASSETTE WORKSHEET Leçon 13 Le français pratique: Mes activités

Section 1 Préférences

A. ***Écoutez et répétez.***

Allez à la page 90.

Section 2 J'aime téléphoner

B. ***Compréhension orale***

a. ____ danser

b. ____ écouter la musique

c. ____ jouer au tennis

d. ____ jouer au volley

e. ____ manger

f. ____ nager

g. ____ parler anglais

h. ____ regarder la télé

i. __1__ téléphoner

j. ____ voyager

Nom ____________________

CASSETTE WORKSHEET Leçon 13 (cont.)

Section 3 Tu aimes écouter la radio?

C. *Questions et réponses*

▶ —Tu aimes écouter la radio?
—Oui, j'aime écouter la radio.
(Non, je n'aime pas écouter la radio.)

UNITÉ 4

CASSETTE WORKSHEET Leçon 13 (cont.)

D. *Questions*

▶ — Quelle est la question?
— **Tu aimes écouter la radio?**

▶ 

1. 

2. 

3. 

4. 

5. 

6. 

7. 

Section 4	Invitations

E. *Compréhension orale*

1. At a party. a. ____ accepts b. ____ declines
2. By the tennis courts. a. ____ accepts b. ____ declines
3. At home. a. ____ accepts b. ____ declines

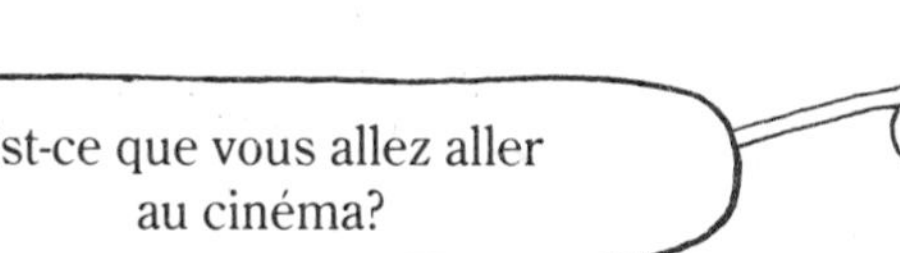

Est-ce que vous allez aller au cinéma?

Nom ______________________________

CASSETTE WORKSHEET Leçon 13 (cont.)

Section 5 Dialogue: Tennis?

F. *Écoutez et écrivez.*

1. Quelle est la question de Nicolas?

   «Est-ce que tu ______________________ avec moi?»

2. Quelle est la réponse de Jean-Claude?

   «Je __________, mais je ______________________.»

3. Quelle est la réponse de Nathalie?

   «Je __________, mais je ______________________.»

4. Quelle est la réponse de Marie?

   «______________________________________.»

5. À quelle heure est le match de tennis?

   «À ____________________________________.»

UNITÉ 4

À votre tour!

Section 6. Créa-dialogue

▶ Est-ce que tu veux jouer au tennis avec moi?

1. Est-ce que tu veux jouer au basket avec moi?
2. Est-ce que tu veux manger une pizza?
3. Est-ce que tu veux regarder la télé?
4. Est-ce que tu veux jouer au ping-pong?
5. Est-ce que tu veux dîner au restaurant?

EXCUSES:

a. Je dois étudier.
b. Je dois travailler.
c. Je dois téléphoner à une copine.
d. Je dois dîner avec ma cousine.
e. Je dois parler avec ma mère.
f. Je dois chanter avec la chorale.

Section 7. Conversation dirigée

Allez à la page 95.

Nom ______________________________

Classe ____________________ Date ____________

CASSETTE WORKSHEET Leçon 14 Qui est là?

Section 1 Qui est là?

A. ***Compréhension orale***

It is Wednesday afternoon. Pierre is looking for his friends but cannot find anyone. Finally he sees Hélène at the Café Bellevue and asks her where everyone is.

PIERRE: Où est Jacqueline?
HÉLÈNE: Elle est à la maison.
PIERRE: Et Jean-Claude? Il est là?
HÉLÈNE: Non, il n'est pas là.
PIERRE: Où est-il?
HÉLÈNE: Il est en ville avec une copine.
PIERRE: Et Nicole et Sandrine? Est-ce qu'elles sont ici?
HÉLÈNE: Non, elles sont au restaurant.
PIERRE: Alors, qui est là?
HÉLÈNE: Moi, je suis ici.
PIERRE: C'est vrai, tu es ici! Eh bien, puisque tu es là, je t'invite au cinéma. D'accord?
HÉLÈNE: Super! Pierre, tu es un vrai copain!

B. ***Écoutez et répétez.***

Section 2 Où es-tu?

C. ***Compréhension orale***

Je suis . . .

	A	B	C	D
	au café	**au cinéma**	**en classe**	**à la maison**
▶		✓		
1				
2				
3				
4				
5				

CASSETTE WORKSHEET Leçon 14 (cont.)

Section 3 Où êtes-vous?

D. ***Compréhension orale***

Nous sommes . . .

	A	B	C	D	E
	en classe	**à Paris**	**en ville**	**en vacances**	**en France**
▶				✓	
1					
2					
3					
4					
5					

Section 4 Où sont-ils?

E. ***Questions et réponses***

▶ —Est-ce qu'il est à la maison ou au restaurant?
—Il est au restaurant.

UNITÉ 4

CASSETTE WORKSHEET Leçon 14 (cont.)

Section 5 Dialogue: Où est Jean-Claude?

F. ***Compréhension orale***

Frédéric sees his friend Nathalie on the way home from school.

FRÉDÉRIC: Salut!
NATHALIE: Salut, Frédéric!

FRÉDÉRIC: Jean-Claude ______________ avec toi?
NATHALIE: Non, il est avec Sandrine.

FRÉDÉRIC: ______________ ?

NATHALIE: Ils sont ______________ de l'Univers.

FRÉDÉRIC: ______________ Nathalie, salut!
NATHALIE: Salut!

FRÉDÉRIC: Salut, Sandrine!
SANDRINE: Salut, ça va?

FRÉDÉRIC: Oui, ça va. Jean-Claude n'est pas ______________ ?
SANDRINE: Bien, non.

FRÉDÉRIC: Où ______________ ?
SANDRINE: Il est avec sa soeur Catherine.
FRÉDÉRIC: Où?
SANDRINE: Au McDonald.
FRÉDÉRIC: Ah bon! Merci Sandrine. Salut!

CATHERINE: Tiens, Frédéric, ça va?
FRÉDÉRIC: Oui, ça va . . . ton frère n'est pas avec toi?

CATHERINE: Non, il est ______________ .
FRÉDÉRIC: Ah bon! Salut!

CATHERINE: ______________ !

FRÉDÉRIC: Bonjour, madame.
LA MÈRE: Bonjour, Frédéric.

FRÉDÉRIC: ______________ parler à Jean-Claude?

LA MÈRE: ______________ . Il est en haut *(upstairs)*.

FRÉDÉRIC: Jean-Claude? ______________ ?

JEAN-CLAUDE: Eh, ben, oui. ______________ là.

UNITÉ 4

CASSETTE WORKSHEET Leçon 14 (cont.)

Section 6 Prononciation

G. *La voyelle /a/*

Écoutez: **chat**

The letter "**a**" alone always represents the sound /a/ as in the English word *ah*. It never has the sound of *"a"* as in English words like *class, date,* or *cinema.*

Répétez: **chat ça va à la là-bas avec ami voilà**
classe café salade dame date Madame Canada
Anne est au Canada avec Madame Laval.

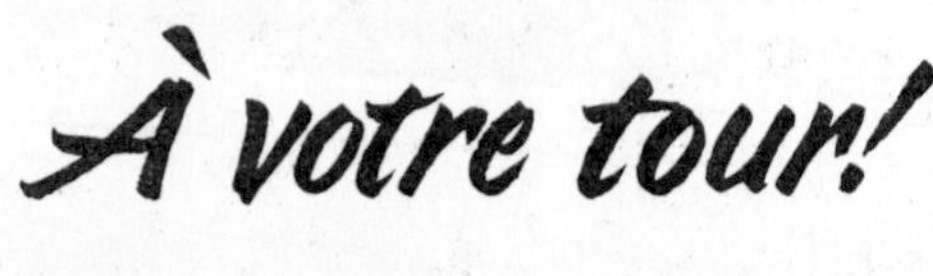

Section 7. Allô!

 Allez à la page 104.

Section 8. Créa-dialogue

 Allez à la page 104.

UNITÉ 4

Nom ______________________

Classe ______________________ Date ______________

CASSETTE WORKSHEET Leçon 15 Une boum

Section 1 Une boum

A. *Compréhension orale*

Jean-Marc has been invited to a party. He is trying to decide whether to invite Béatrice or Valérie. First he talks to Béatrice.

JEAN-MARC: Dis, Béatrice, tu aimes danser?
BÉATRICE: Bien sûr, j'aime danser!
JEAN-MARC: Est-ce que tu danses bien?
BÉATRICE: Oui, je danse très, très bien.
JEAN-MARC: Et ta cousine Valérie? Est-ce qu'elle danse bien?
BÉATRICE: Non, elle ne danse pas très bien.
JEAN-MARC: Alors, c'est Valérie que j'invite à la boum.
BÉATRICE: Mais pourquoi elle? Pourquoi pas moi?
JEAN-MARC: Écoute, Béatrice, je ne sais pas danser! Alors, je préfère inviter une fille qui ne danse pas très bien. C'est normal, non?

B. *Écoutez et répétez.*

Section 2 J'étudie

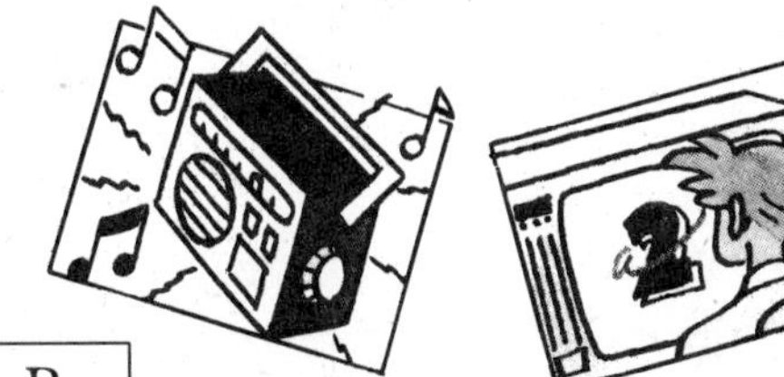

C. *Compréhension orale*

	A		B	
▶	✓	J'étudie.		Je n'étudie pas.
1		J'étudie.		Je n'étudie pas.
2		Je travaille.		Je ne travaille pas.
3		Je travaille.		Je ne travaille pas.
4		Je regarde la télé.		Je ne regarde pas la télé.
5		Je joue au Monopoly.		Je joue au Nintendo.
6		Elle joue très mal.		Elle joue très bien.
7		Je mange.		Je ne mange pas.
8		Je mange un sandwich.		Je mange une omelette.
9		Je mange une crêpe.		Je mange une pizza.
10		J'écoute la radio.		J'écoute mon walkman.
11		Je téléphone.		Je ne téléphone pas.
12		Je téléphone à un copain.		Je téléphone à une copine.

UNITÉ 4

CASSETTE WORKSHEET Leçon 15

Section 3 Tu téléphones?

D. *Compréhension orale*

1. Tu téléphones?

a. ____ oui b. ____ non

2. Tu regardes la télé?

a. ____ oui b. ____ non

3. Est-ce que tu étudies?

a. ____ oui b. ____ non

4. Tu dînes à la maison ce soir?

a. ____ oui b. ____ non

Section 4 Est-ce qu'il travaille?

E. *Questions et réponses*

▶ — Est-ce qu'il travaille?
— Non, il ne travaille pas.

CASSETTE WORKSHEET Leçon 15 (cont.)

Section 5 Jean-Paul à la boum

F. ***Compréhension orale***

First Jean-Paul goes up to Dominique.

JEAN-PAUL: ______________________ danser?

DOMINIQUE: Oui, j'aime ______________________.

JEAN-PAUL: Est-ce que tu danses ______________________?

DOMINIQUE: Oui, je danse très, très bien. Et toi?

JEAN-PAUL: Euh non, ______________________.

Then Jean-Paul goes over to Nathalie.

JEAN-PAUL: Tu aimes danser?

NATHALIE: Oui, j'aime danser . . . mais ______________________ très bien.

JEAN-PAUL: ______________________ danser avec moi?

NATHALIE: Je te dis (*I'm telling you*), je ne danse pas très bien.

JEAN-PAUL: Moi non plus (*me neither*), je ne danse pas ______________.

NATHALIE: Bon, ______________.

CASSETTE WORKSHEET Leçon 15 (cont.)

Section 6 Pronunciation

G. ***Les voyelles /i/ et /u/***

Écoutez: /u/ **où** /i/ **ici**

The vowel sounds **/i/** and **/u/** are easy to say. Remember to pronounce the French "**i**" as in **Mimi** and not as in the English *him*.

Répétez: /i/ **ici Philippe il**
Mimi Sylvie visite
Philippe visite Paris avec Sylvie.

/u/ **où nous vous**
écoute joue toujours
Vous jouez au foot avec nous?

Section 7. Allô!

 Allez à la page 116.

Section 8. Créa-dialogue

 Allez à la page 116.

UNITÉ 4

Nom ______________________________

Classe ____________________ Date ____________

CASSETTE WORKSHEET Leçon 16 Une interview

Section 1 Une interview

A. *Compréhension orale*

Nicolas is at a café with his new friend Fatou. He's interviewing her for an article in his school newspaper.

NICOLAS: Bonjour, Fatou. Ça va?
FATOU: Oui, ça va.
NICOLAS: Tu es sénégalaise, n'est-ce pas?
FATOU: Oui, je suis sénégalaise.
NICOLAS: Où est-ce que tu habites?
FATOU: Je suis de Dakar, mais maintenant j'habite à Paris avec ma famille.
NICOLAS: Est-ce que tu aimes Paris?
FATOU: J'adore Paris.
NICOLAS: Qu'est-ce que tu fais le weekend?
FATOU: Ça dépend. En général, je regarde la télé ou je sors avec mes copains. Dis, Nicolas! Est-ce que je peux te poser une question?
NICOLAS: Oui, bien sûr!
FATOU: Qu'est-ce que tu fais samedi?
NICOLAS: Euh . . . je ne sais pas.
FATOU: Est-ce que tu veux aller avec nous à un concert de musique africaine?
NICOLAS: Super! Où? Quand? Et à quelle heure?

B. *Écoutez et répétez.*

CASSETTE WORKSHEET Leçon 16 (cont.)

Section 2 Où est-ce qu'il va?

C. *Compréhension orale*

	A	B	C	D	E	F
	où?	quand?	à quelle heure?	comment?	à qui?	avec qui?
▶	✓					
1						
2						
3						
4						
5						
6						
7						
8						

Section 3 Qu'est-ce que tu fais?

D. *Compréhension orale*

a. ____

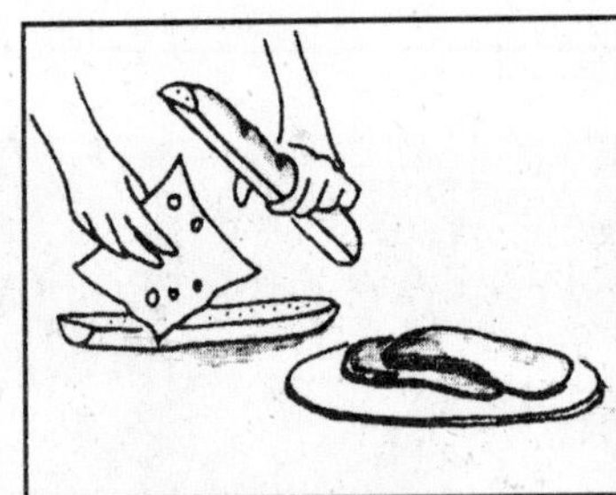

b. __1__

c. ____

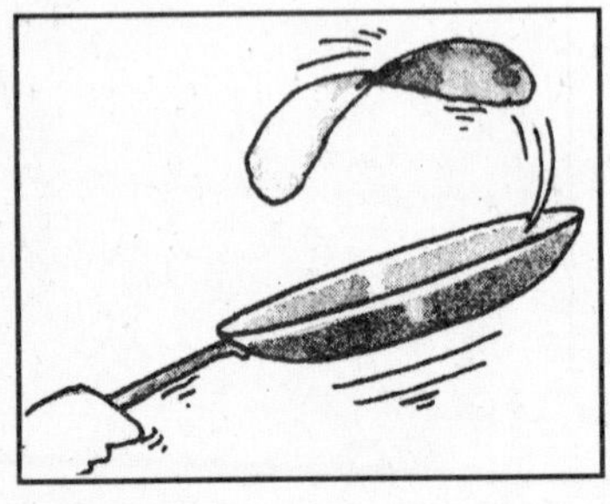

d. ____

e. ____

f. ____

CASSETTE WORKSHEET Leçon 16 (cont.)

Section 4 Questions

E. ***Questions et réponses***

▶ — Qu'est-ce qu'il mange?
— **Il mange un sandwich.**

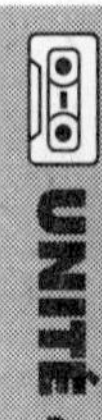

Section 5 Au Sénégal

F. ***Écoutez et écrivez.***

— Bonjour, ______________________ vous vous appelez?

— Je m'appelle Monsieur Li.

— ______________________ français?

— Oui, ______________________ français, et le ouolof aussi.

Nom ______________________

CASSETTE WORKSHEET Leçon 16 (cont.)

Section 6 Prononciation

G. ***La voyelle /y/***

Écoutez: **super!**

The vowel sound /y/, represented by the letter "**u**," does not exist in English. Here is a helpful trick for producing this new sound. First say the French word **si.** Then round your lips as if to whistle and say **si** with rounded lips: /**sy**/. Now say **si-per.** Then round your lips as you say the first syllable: **super!**

Répétez: /y/ **super tu étudie bien sûr**
Lucie Luc
Tu étudies avec Lucie.

Section 7. Allô!

 Allez à la page 126.

Section 8. Créa-dialogue

 Allez à la page 126.

UNITÉ 4

Nom ______________________

Classe ______________________ Date ______________

WRITING ACTIVITIES Leçon 13 Le français pratique: Mes activités

A* **1. Qu'est-ce qu'ils aiment faire?** *(What do they like to do?)*

The following people are saying what they like to do. Complete the bubbles, as in the model.

J'aime téléphoner.

2. Et toi?

Say whether or not you like to do the activities suggested by the pictures.

1. ______________________

2. ______________________

3. ______________________

4. ______________________

5. ______________________

6. ______________________

7. ______________________

8. ______________________

*NOTE: Beginning with this unit, activities are coded to sections in your textbook (Ex: Leçon 13, Section A) for your reference.

WRITING ACTIVITIES Leçon 13 (cont.)

B/C 3. Communication: En français!

1. You are spending your vacation in a French summer camp.

   Ask your friend Patrick . . .

   - *if he likes to swim*

     ____

   - *if he likes to play basketball*

     ____

   - *if he wants to play volleyball with you*

     ____

2. Your friend Cécile is phoning to invite you to go to a restaurant. Unfortunately you have an English exam tomorrow.

   Tell Cécile . . .

   - *that you are sorry*

     ____

   - *that you cannot have dinner at the restaurant with her*

     ____

   - *that you have to study*

     ____

3. At the tennis court, you meet your friend Jean-Claude.

   - *Tell him that you would like to play tennis.*

     ____

   - *Ask him if he wants to play with you.*

     ____

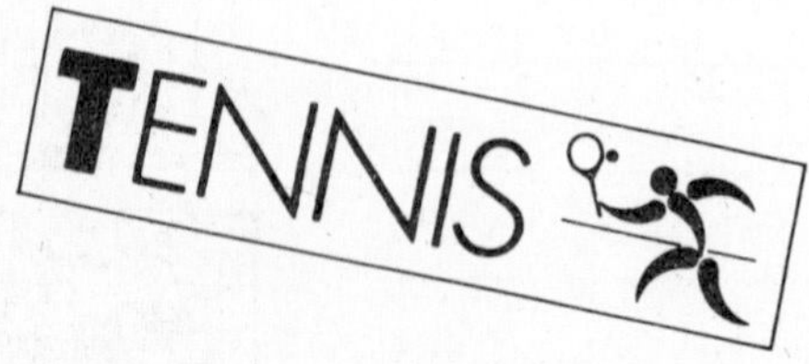

Nom ________________________________

Classe ____________________ Date ______________

WRITING ACTIVITIES Leçon 14 Qui est là?

A 1. Mots croisés *(Crossword puzzle)*

Complete the crossword puzzle with the forms of **être.** Then write the corresponding subject pronoun in front of each form.

▶ nous ______ S O M M E S

1. ______ _ S

2. ______ S _ _ S

3. ______ _ _ _ S

4. ______ S _ _ T

5. ______ _ S _

2. En vacances

The people in parentheses are on vacation. Say where they are, using the appropriate pronouns: **il, elle, ils,** or **elles.**

▶ (Cécile) Elle est ______ à Québec.

1. (Jean-Marc) ______ à Tours.
2. (Catherine et Sophie) ______ à Nice.
3. (Mademoiselle Simon) ______ à Montréal.
4. (Jérôme et Philippe) ______ en Italie.
5. (Isabelle, Thomas et Anne) ______ au Mexique.
6. (Monsieur et Madame Dupin) ______ au Japon.

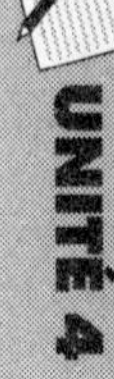

UNITÉ 4

3. Où sont-ils?

Complete the following sentences, saying where the people are.

Nous ______________________.

Vous ______________________.

M. Bernard ______________________.

Éric et Claire ______________________.

WRITING ACTIVITIES Leçon 14 (cont.)

B/C 4. Non!

Answer the following questions in the negative, using pronouns in your answers.

1. Est-ce que tu es français (française)?

____

2. Est-ce que ton copain est canadien?

____

3. Est-ce que ta copine est anglaise?

____

4. Est-ce que tu es au cinéma?

____

5. Est-ce que tes *(your)* parents sont en vacances?

____

5. Communication: En français!

1. The phone rings. It is your French friend Caroline who wants to talk to your brother.

   Tell Caroline that he is not home.

   ____

   Tell her that he is downtown with a friend.

   ____

2. You are phoning your friend Marc. His mother answers.

   Ask her if Marc is there.

   ____

   Ask her if you can please speak with Marc.

   ____

WRITING ACTIVITIES Leçon 15 Une boum

A/B 1. Tourisme

The following people are traveling abroad. Complete the sentences with the appropriate forms of **visiter.**

1. Nous __________ Québec.
2. Tu __________ Fort-de-France.
3. Jean et Thomas __________ Paris.
4. Vous __________ Genève.
5. Hélène __________ San Francisco.
6. Je __________ La Nouvelle Orléans.
7. Marc __________ Tokyo.
8. Monsieur et Madame Dupont __________ Mexico.

2. Qu'est-ce qu'ils font?

Describe what people are doing by completing the sentences with the appropriate verbs. First write the infinitive in the box, and then fill in the correct form in the sentence. Be logical.

manger	**écouter**	*regarder*	**dîner**
jouer	organiser	**parlеr**	

	Infinitive	Sentence
▶	dîner	Nous ___dînons___ au restaurant.
1.		Christine et Claire __________ au tennis.
2.		Vous __________ la télé.
3.		J' __________ la radio.
4.		Tu __________ français avec le professeur.
5.		Jérôme __________ un sandwich.
6.		Nous __________ une boum.

UNITÉ 4

WRITING ACTIVITIES Leçon 15 (cont.)

3. Descriptions

Look carefully at the following scenes and describe what the different people are doing.

▶ Mélanie _____nage_____. Monsieur Boulot ______________________.

Éric et Vincent ______________________. Claire et Philippe ______________________.

Le professeur ______________________. Diane ______________________.

Hélène et Marc ______________________. Jean-Paul et Bernard ______________________.

Nom ______________________________

WRITING ACTIVITIES Leçon 15 (cont.)

C 4. Et toi?

Your French friend Caroline wants to know more about you. Answer her questions, affirmatively or negatively.

1. Tu parles anglais?
   ____
2. Tu parles souvent français?
   ____
3. Tu habites à New York?
   ____
4. Tu étudies l'espagnol?
   ____
5. Tu joues au foot?
   ____
6. Tu dînes souvent au restaurant?
   ____

5. Dimanche

For many people, Sunday is a day of rest. Say that the following people are not doing the activities in parentheses.

▶ (étudier) Tu n'étudies pas.
1. (étudier) Nous ______________________________.
2. (travailler) Vous ______________________________.
3. (parler) Mon copain ______________________ français.
4. (téléphoner) La secrétaire ______________________________.
5. (jouer) Paul et Thomas ______________________ au foot.
6. (voyager) Tu ______________________________.

WRITING ACTIVITIES Leçon 15 (cont.)

6. Communication

You have a new French pen pal named Isabelle. Write her a short letter introducing yourself.

Date your letter.

- *Tell Isabelle your name.*
- *Tell her in which city you live.*
- *Tell her at what school you study.*
- *Tell her whether or not you often speak French.*
- *Tell her what sports you play.*
- *Tell her two things you like to do.*
- *Tell her one thing you do not like to do.*

Sign your letter.

____

Chère Isabelle,

- _______________
- _______________
- _______________
- _______________
- _______________
- _______________

____

- _______________

Amitiés,

____

UNITÉ 4

Nom ______________________________

Classe ____________________ Date ____________

WRITING ACTIVITIES Leçon 16 Une interview

A 1. Dialogue

Complete the following dialogues with the appropriate interrogative expressions.

1. —______________ est-ce que tu habites?
   —J'habite à Dakar.
2. —______________ est-ce que tu dînes?
   —En général, je dîne à huit heures.
3. —______________ est-ce que tu chantes?
   —Je chante assez bien.
4. —______________ est-ce que tu étudies
   —Parce que je veux visiter l'Italie.
5. —______________ est-ce que tu voyages?
   —Je voyage en juillet.
6. —______________ est-ce que ta mère travaille?
   —Elle travaille dans *(in)* un hôpital.

B 2. Répétitions

Philippe did not quite hear what Annie told him and he asks her to repeat what she said. Complete his questions.

ANNIE:	PHILIPPE:
▶ Je joue au tennis avec Vincent.	Avec qui est-ce que tu joues au tennis?
1. Je téléphone souvent à Olivier.	À ______________?
2. Je parle rarement à Valérie.	À ______________?
3. J'étudie avec Jean-Claude.	Avec ______________?
4. Je travaille pour M. Bertrand.	Pour ______________?
5. Je parle anglais avec Vanessa.	Avec ______________?
6. Je parle de Pierre.	De ______________?

WRITING ACTIVITIES Leçon 16 (cont.)

A/B/C **3. Curiosité**

You want to know more about what the following people are doing. Write your questions using subject pronouns and the expressions in parentheses.

▶ Jérôme dîne. (avec qui?)

Avec qui est-ce qu'il dîne?

1. Madame Martin travaille. (où?)

____

2. Nathalie téléphone. (à qui?)

____

3. Antoine organise une boum. (quand?)

____

4. Thomas et Patrick étudient beaucoup. (pourquoi?)

____

5. Hélène et Sylvie jouent au tennis. (à quelle heure?)

____

6. Béatrice étudie. (qu'est-ce que?)

____

D **4. Conversations**

Complete the following mini-dialogues with the appropriate forms of **faire.**

1. —Qu'est-ce que tu ________ à deux heures?
   —Je ________ un match de tennis.
2. —Qu'est-ce que vous ________ maintenant?
   —Nous ________ une salade de fruits.
3. —Où est ta cousine?
   —Elle ________ un voyage au Sénégal.
4. —Où sont Paul et Marc?
   —Ils sont en ville. Ils ________ une promenade.

SÉNÉGAL

Nom ______________________________

WRITING ACTIVITIES Leçon 16 (cont.)

5. Communication

1. You want to invite your friend Nathalie to your home for dinner.

   Ask her . . .

   - *at what time she has dinner* ______________________________
   - *what she likes to eat* ______________________________

2. You are interviewing Madame Ricard, a French businesswoman, for your school newspaper. (Do not forget to address her as **vous!**)

   Ask her . . .

   - *where she lives* ______________________________
   - *where she works* ______________________________
   - *when she travels* ______________________________

3. You meet your friend Marc in the street.

   Ask him . . .

   - *what he is doing now* ______________________________
   - *what he is doing tomorrow* ______________________________

Nom ______________________________

Classe ______________________ Date ______________

DISCOVERING FRENCH – *BLEU*

READING AND CULTURE ACTIVITIES Unité 4

A. En France et en Louisiane

LES CHOEURS
Maurice de Sully
CATHEDRALE NOTRE-DAME DE PARIS

Nous avons besoin de nouvelles voix pour renforcer notre groupe.

CHANTEZ AVEC NOUS...

... J.S. BACH, VIVALDI, MOZART, CHANTS GREGORIENS, REPERTOIRE CONTEMPORAIN.

—INSCRIPTIONS: Père A. Batselaere—

8, rue Massillon Paris 4e – Téléphone: **354 71 53** ou **633 01 01**

1. You would pay attention to this ad if you were interested in . . .
- ☐ singing
- ☐ traveling
- ☐ going to a concert
- ☐ visiting a church

ICI, ON PARLE FRANÇAIS

(FAITES VOTRE DEMANDE EN FRANÇAIS).

CONSEIL POUR LE DÉVELOPPEMENT DU FRANÇAIS EN LOUISIANE — CODOFIL — JAMES DOMENGEAUX Chairman

NOUS SOMMES FIERS DE PARLER FRANÇAIS.

2. If you were traveling in Louisiana, you might see this sign in certain shops. What does it mean?
- ☐ We are French.
- ☐ French is spoken here.
- ☐ We sell French products.
- ☐ We like French people.

3. Here is another sign you might see in Louisiana. What does it mean?
- ☐ We do not speak French.
- ☐ We are proud to speak French.
- ☐ We sell French products.
- ☐ We love people who speak French.

READING AND CULTURE ACTIVITIES Unité 4 (cont.)

B. La Maison des Jeunes et de la Culture

Sandrine Moreau has dropped by Les Marquisats to get more information about their activities. She was asked to fill out the following form.

Je souhaite recevoir régulièrement des informations sur les activités culturelles de la Maison des Jeunes et de la Culture "Les Marquisats" d'Annecy.

Je suis plus particulièrement intéressé par :

☐ CINÉMA ☑ DANSES SPÉCIALES ☐ CONFÉRENCES

☑ STAGES DANSE ☐ JAZZ ☐ ROCK ☐ CHANSON

NOM MOREAU, Sandrine

INSTITUTION / PROFESSION Étudiante

ADRESSE 136, rue Descartes

Annecy

TÉL. ______________ (facultatif).

LES MARQUISATS

M.J.C. 52, RUE DES MARQUISATS
74000 ANNECY TEL. 50.45.08.80

1. Sandrine is especially interested in . . .
- ☐ movies
- ☐ music
- ☐ dance
- ☐ lectures

2. Who is Sandrine?
- ☐ A student.
- ☐ A homemaker.
- ☐ A guitarist.
- ☐ A retired person.

UNITÉ 4

Nom ______________________________

READING AND CULTURE ACTIVITIES Unité 4 (cont.)

C. Conversation

Carefully read the following phone conversation between Carole and her friend Julien.

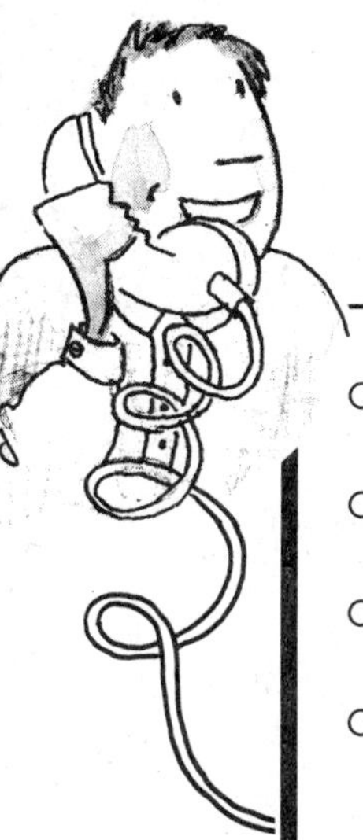

CAROLE: Allô, Julien?
JULIEN: Ah, c'est toi, Carole. Mais où es-tu?
CAROLE: Je suis à Tours.
JULIEN: À Tours? Mais pourquoi es-tu là-bas?
CAROLE: Je fais un voyage avec ma cousine.
JULIEN: Ah bon! Qu'est-ce que vous faites?
CAROLE: Oh là là, nous faisons beaucoup de choses. Nous visitons les châteaux. Nous dînons dans les restaurants. Nous . . .
JULIEN: Quand est-ce que vous rentrez à Paris?
CAROLE: Le quinze août.
JULIEN: Alors, bonnes vacances et bon retour!

- Where is Carole when she calls Julien? ______________________

  Where is Julien? ______________________
- With whom is Carole traveling? ______________________
- What have the two of them been doing?

  ____

  ____
- When is Carole returning home? ______________________

Nom ______________________________

READING AND CULTURE ACTIVITIES Unité 4 (cont.)

D. Invitations

1. You recently received two invitations. (Note: **venir** means *to come.*)

Invitation

Est-ce que tu veux venir dîner avec moi samedi à 7h30? Réponds-moi avant jeudi.

Christophe

- What is Daniel's invitation for? ______________________

  What day and what time? ______________________

- What is Christophe's invitation for? ______________________

  What day and what time? ______________________

- Which invitation are you going to accept, and why?

  ____

  ____

2. Write a note to the person whose invitation you have to turn down.
- Express your regret.
- Explain that you have other plans.
- Sign your note.

Cher ____________,

____

____

____

____

____

UNITÉ 4

COMMUNICATIVE EXPRESSIONS AND THEMATIC VOCABULARY

Unité 4 Qu'est-ce qu'on fait?

▶ CULTURAL CONTEXT: **Daily activities at home, at school, on weekends**

COMMUNICATIVE EXPRESSIONS

Talking about what you like and don't like to do

Qu'est-ce que tu aimes faire?
Est-ce que tu aimes . . . ?
J'aime . . . — **Je n'aime pas . . .**
Je préfère . . .

Talking about what you want and do not want to do

Qu'est-ce que tu veux faire?
Je veux . . . — **Je ne veux pas . . .**
Je voudrais . . .

Inviting a friend

Est-ce que tu veux . . . ? — **. . . avec moi/toi**
Est-ce que tu peux . . . ?

Accepting and turning down an invitation

Oui, bien sûr, . . .	**Je regrette mais je ne peux pas.**
Oui, merci, . . .	**Je dois . . .**
Oui, d'accord, . . .	
je veux bien.	
je veux bien . . .	

Asking and answering yes/no questions

Est-ce que [tu étudies]?	**oui**	**non**
[Tu étudies], n'est-ce pas?	**mais oui**	**mais non**
	bien sûr	
	peut-être . . .	

Asking for specific information

où?	**Où est-ce que tu habites?**
quand?	**Quand est-ce que tu regardes la télé?**
à quelle heure?	**À quelle heure est-ce que tu dînes?**
comment?	**Comment est-ce que tu joues au volley?**
pourquoi?	**Pourquoi est-ce que tu étudies le français?**
parce que . . .	**Parce que je veux visiter Paris.**
qu'est-ce que . . . ?	**Qu'est-ce que tu fais?**
qui?	**Qui travaille?**
	Qui est-ce que tu invites?
à qui?	**À qui est-ce que tu téléphones?**
de qui?	**De qui est-ce que tu parles?**
avec qui?	**Avec qui est-ce que tu joues au tennis?**
pour qui?	**Pour qui est-ce que tu travailles?**

UNITÉ 4

COMMUNICATIVE EXPRESSIONS AND THEMATIC VOCABULARY

VOCABULARY

Things people do

aimer
chanter
danser
dîner au restaurant
écouter la radio
étudier
habiter à [Québec]
inviter
jouer au basket
jouer au foot
jouer au tennis
jouer au volley

manger
nager
organiser une boum
parler anglais
parler espagnol
parler français
regarder la télé
téléphoner
travailler
visiter [Paris]
voyager

faire
faire un match
faire une promenade
faire un voyage
faire attention

être
être d'accord

Places where one can be

où
ici
là
là-bas

à [Paris]
à la maison
au café
au cinéma
au restaurant

en France
en classe
en vacances
en ville

How well? how much? how often? when?

bien
très bien
mal

beaucoup
un peu

rarement
souvent
toujours

maintenant

Other words and expressions

à
de
et
ou

avec
mais
pour

super!
dommage!

ah bon?

UNITÉ 4

UNITÉ 5
Le monde personnel et familier

LISTENING ACTIVITIES
Leçons 17–20

WRITING ACTIVITIES
Leçons 17–20

READING AND CULTURE ACTIVITIES
Unité 5

Communicative Expressions and Thematic Vocabulary

Nom ______________________________

Classe ____________________ Date ____________

CASSETTE WORKSHEET Leçon 17 Le français pratique: Les personnes et les objets

Section 1 La description des personnes

A. *Écoutez et répétez.*

Allez à la page 139.

Section 2 J'ai un walkman

B. *Compréhension orale*

a.  ____ b.  ____ c.  ____ d. ____

e. 1  f.  ____ g.  ____ h. ____

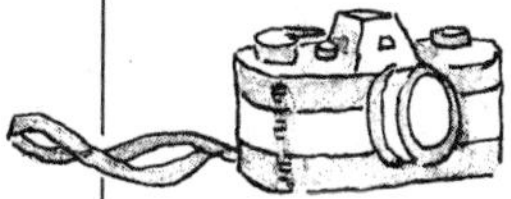

i.  ____ j.  ____ k.  ____ l. ____

CASSETTE WORKSHEET Leçon 17 (cont.)

Section 3 Qu'est-ce que c'est?

C. *Questions et réponses*

▶ — Qu'est-ce que c'est?
— **C'est un appareil-photo.** ▶

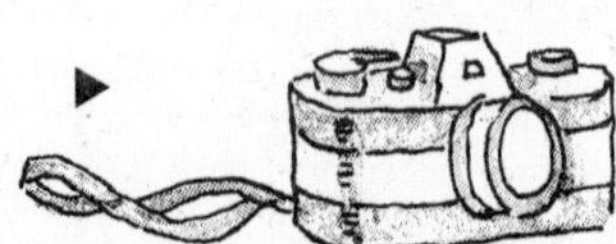

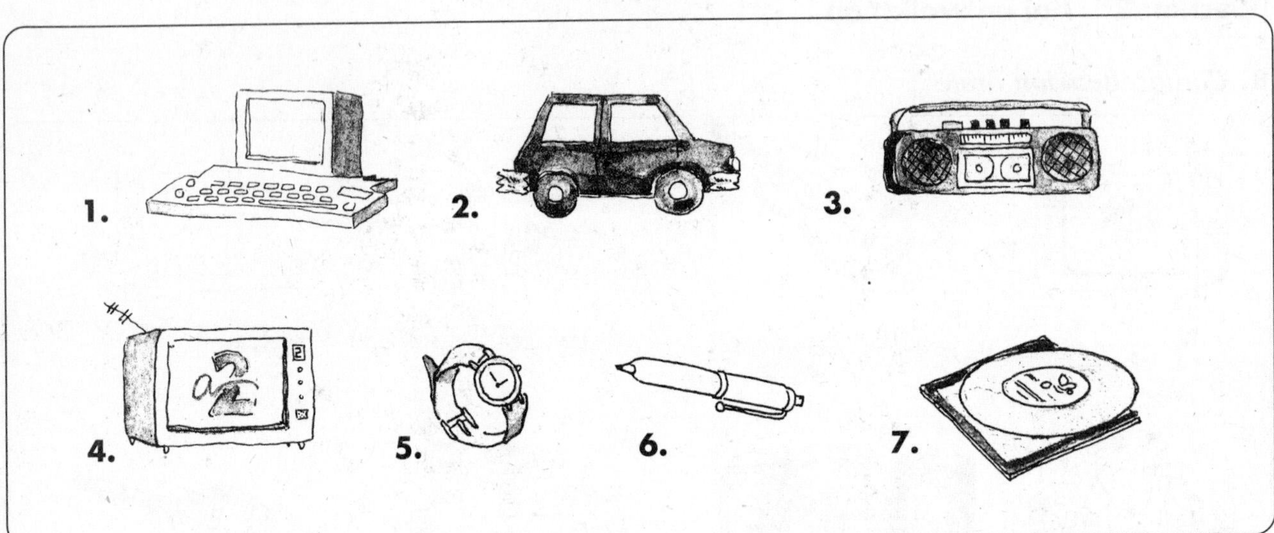

UNITÉ 5

Section 4 Dialogue: Tu as un walkman?

D. *Compréhension orale*

1. Nathalie a un walkman.	vrai	faux
2. Le walkman est dans son sac.	vrai	faux
3. Le sac est sur la table.	vrai	faux
4. Le sac est dans sa chambre.	vrai	faux
5. Le sac est sous son bureau.	vrai	faux
6. Le sac est derrière la porte.	vrai	faux

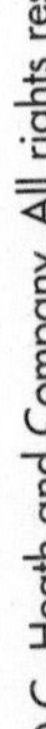

Nom ___________________________________

CASSETTE WORKSHEET Leçon 17 (cont.)

Section 5 Où est-il?

E. *Questions et réponses*

▶ — Est-ce que l'appareil-photo est sur la table ou sous la table?
— **Il est sur la table.**

UNITÉ 5

CASSETTE WORKSHEET Leçon 17 (cont.)

Section 6 Monologue: La chambre de Catherine

F. ***Compréhension orale***

a. ☐ un bureau
b. ☐ une chaise
c. ☐ une table
d. ☐ un lit
e. ☐ des disques
f. ☐ des affiches
g. ☐ des livres
h. ☐ un livre de français
i. ☐ un livre d'anglais
j. ☐ un sac de classe
k. ☐ des crayons
l. ☐ un stylo
m. ☐ une calculatrice
n. ☐ un cahier
o. ☐ un ordinateur
p. ☐ une raquette
q. ☐ une radiocassette
r. ☐ des compact-discs
s. ☐ un appareil-photo

Section 7. Créa-dialogue

 Allez à la page 147.

Section 8. Conversation dirigée

 Allez à la page 147.

Nom ______________________________

Classe ______________________ Date ____________

CASSETTE WORKSHEET Leçon 18 Vive la différence!

Section 1 Vive la différence!

A. ***Compréhension orale***

Listen to Caroline, a French girl from Montpellier, describe herself and her friend Jean-Pierre.

Je m'appelle Caroline.	Il s'appelle Jean-Pierre.
J'habite à Montpellier.	Il habite à Strasbourg.
J'ai des frères.	Il n'a pas de frère, mais il a des soeurs.
J'ai un chien.	Il n'a pas de chien, mais il a deux horribles chats.
J'ai un scooter.	Il a une moto.
J'aime le cinéma.	Il préfère le théâtre.
J'aime les films de science-fiction.	Il préfère les westerns.
J'aime les sports.	Il préfère la musique.
J'étudie l'anglais.	Il étudie l'espagnol.

B. ***Écoutez et répétez.***

Section 2 Tu as un vélo?

C. ***Compréhension orale***

▶ un vélo	(oui)	non
1. a. un vélo	oui	non
b. une mobylette	oui	non
2. une voiture	oui	non
3. une voiture	oui	non
4. une montre	oui	non

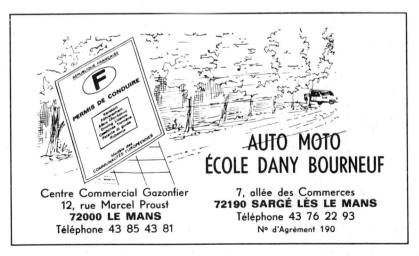

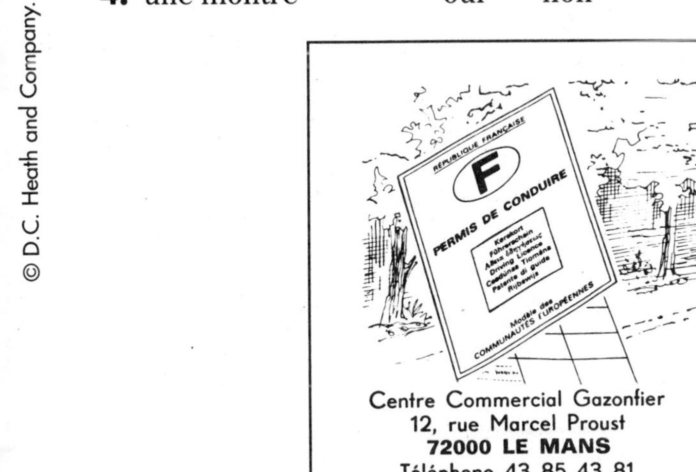

Nom ______________________________

CASSETTE WORKSHEET Leçon 18 (cont.)

Section 3 Qu'est-ce que tu as?

D. *Compréhension orale*

1.	a. un stylo	oui	non
	b. des crayons	oui	non
	c. un cahier	oui	non
	d. une calculatrice	oui	non
	e. des livres	oui	non
	f. un sandwich	oui	non
2.	a. un crayon	oui	non
	b. un stylo	oui	non
3.	a. un walkman	oui	non
	b. des cassettes	oui	non
4.	a. une calculatrice	oui	non
	b. un ordinateur	oui	non
5.	une raquette	oui	non

UNITÉ 5

CASSETTE WORKSHEET Leçon 18 (cont.)

Section 4 Est-ce que tu as un vélo?

E. *Questions et réponses*

▶ —Est-ce que tu as un vélo?
—Oui, j'ai un vélo.
(Non, je n'ai pas de vélo.) ▶

1. 2. 3. 4.
5. 6. 7.

Section 5 Dialogue: J'organise une boum

F. *Compréhension orale*

1.	une chaîne stéréo	oui	non
2.	une radiocassette	oui	non
3.	des cassettes	oui	non
4.	des compact-discs	oui	non
5.	un vélo	oui	non
6.	une mobylette	oui	non

Nom ______________________________

CASSETTE WORKSHEET Leçon 18 (cont.)

Section 6 Prononciation

G. ***Les articles*** **le** ***et*** **les**

Écoutez: **le sac** **les sacs**

Be sure to distinguish between the pronunciation of **le** and **les.** In spoken French, that is often the only way to tell the difference between a singular and a plural noun.

Répétez:						
/lə/	**le**	**le sac**	**le vélo**	**le disque**	**le copain**	**le voisin**
/le/	**les**	**les sacs**	**les vélos**	**les disques**	**les copains**	**les voisins**

Section 7. Allô!

 Allez à la page 158.

Section 8. Créa-dialogue

 Allez à la page 158.

UNITÉ 5

Nom ______________________________

Classe ______________________ Date ______________

DISCOVERING FRENCH – *BLEU*

CASSETTE WORKSHEET Leçon 19 Le copain de Mireille

Section 1 Le copain de Mireille

A. ***Compréhension orale***

Nicolas and Jean-Claude are having lunch at the school cafeteria. Nicolas is looking at the students seated at the other end of the table.

NICOLAS: Regarde la fille là-bas.
JEAN-CLAUDE: La fille blonde?
NICOLAS: Oui! Qui est-ce?
JEAN-CLAUDE: C'est Mireille Labé.
NICOLAS: Elle est mignonne!
JEAN-CLAUDE: Oui, elle est aussi amusante, intelligente et très sympathique.
NICOLAS: Est-ce qu'elle a un copain?
JEAN-CLAUDE: Oui, elle a un copain.
NICOLAS: Il est sympathique?
JEAN-CLAUDE: Très sympathique!
NICOLAS: Et intelligent?
JEAN-CLAUDE: Aussi!
NICOLAS: Dommage! . . . Qui est-ce?
JEAN-CLAUDE: C'est moi!
NICOLAS: Oh . . . Excuse-moi et félicitations!

B. ***Écoutez et répétez.***

Section 2 Je suis américain

C. ***Compréhension orale***

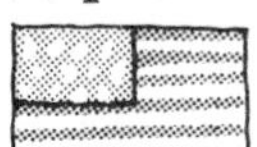

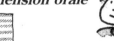

(a.) américain b. américaine

1. a. anglais b. anglaise

2. a. canadien b. canadienne

3. a. chinois b. chinoise

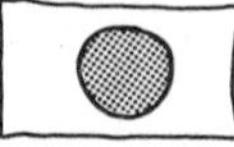

4. a. japonais b. japonaise

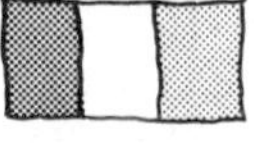

5. a. italien b. italienne

6. a. mexicain b. mexicaine

UNITÉ 5

Nom ______________________________

CASSETTE WORKSHEET Leçon 19 (cont.)

Section 3 La description

D. *Écoutez et répétez.*

Allez à la page 163.

Section 4 Qui est-ce?

E. *Compréhension orale*

▶ (a.) mignon b. mignonne
(c.) sympathique d. sympathiques

1. a. américains b. américaines
c. sympathique d. sympathiques

2. a. espagnol b. espagnole
c. mexicaine d. mexicaines
e. sportif f. sportive
g. intelligente h. intelligentes

3. a. anglais b. anglaise
c. américain d. américaines
e. intéressant f. intéressante
g. strict h. strictes

UNITÉ 5

CASSETTE WORKSHEET Leçon 19 (cont.)

Section 5 **Comment sont-ils?**

F. ***Questions et réponses***

▶ — Est-ce qu'elle est grande ou petite?
— Elle est grande.

CASSETTE WORKSHEET Leçon 19 (cont.)

Section 6 Prononciation

G. ***Les consonnes finales***

Écoutez: **blond** **blonde**

As you know, when the last letter of a word is a consonant, that consonant is often silent. But when a word ends in "**e**," the consonant before it is pronounced. As you practice the following adjectives, be sure to distinguish between the masculine and the feminine forms.

	MASCULINE ADJECTIVE (no final consonant sound)		FEMININE ADJECTIVE (final consonant sound)
Répétez:	**blond**	/d/	**blonde**
	grand		**grande**
	petit	/t/	**petite**
	amusant		**amusante**
	français	/z/	**française**
	anglais		**anglaise**
	américain	/n/	**américaine**
	canadien		**canadienne**

Section 7. Allô!

 Allez à la page 168.

Section 8. Créa-dialogue

 Allez à la page 168.

Nom ______________________________

Classe ____________________ Date ____________

CASSETTE WORKSHEET Leçon 20 La voiture de Roger

Section 1 Dialogue: La voiture de Roger

A. ***Compréhension orale***

Dans la rue, il y a une voiture rouge.
C'est une petite voiture. C'est une voiture de sport.

Dans la rue, il y a aussi un café.
Au café, il y a un jeune homme.
Il s'appelle Roger.
C'est le propriétaire de la voiture rouge.

Une jeune fille entre dans le café.
Elle s'appelle Véronique.
C'est l'amie de Roger.
Véronique parle à Roger.

ROGER: Tiens, bonjour Véronique! Ça va?
VÉRONIQUE: Oui, ça va. Dis, tu as une nouvelle voiture, n'est-ce pas?
ROGER: Oui, j'ai une nouvelle voiture.
VÉRONIQUE: Est-ce qu'elle est grande ou petite?
ROGER: Oh, c'est une petite voiture.
VÉRONIQUE: De quelle couleur est-elle?
ROGER: C'est une voiture rouge.
VÉRONIQUE: Est-ce que c'est une voiture italienne?
ROGER: Oui, c'est une voiture italienne. Mais, dis donc, Véronique, tu es vraiment très curieuse!
VÉRONIQUE: Et toi, tu n'es pas assez curieux!
ROGER: Ah bon? Pourquoi?
VÉRONIQUE: Pourquoi? . . . Regarde la contractuelle là-bas!
ROGER: Ah, zut alors!

B. ***Écoutez et répétez.***

Section 2 Les couleurs

C. ***Écoutez et répétez.***

 Allez à la page 172.

Section 3 De quelle couleur?

D. ***Compréhension orale***

a. ____ rouge **b.** ____ jaune **c.** ____ vert(e) **d.** ____ blanc (blanche)

e. ____ gris(e) **f.** ____ noir(e) **g.** ____ marron **h.** ____ orange

CASSETTE WORKSHEET Leçon 20 (cont.)

Section 4 Qu'est-ce que tu préfères?

E. ***Questions et réponses***

▶ —Est-ce que tu préfères la voiture rouge ou la voiture grise?
—Je préfère la voiture rouge.
(Je préfère la voiture grise.)

▶

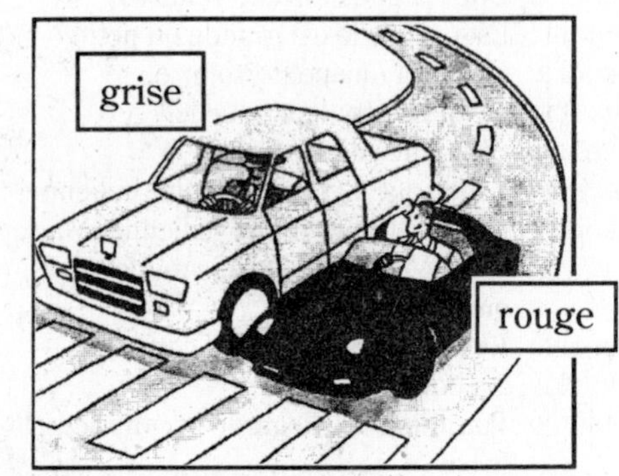

1.

2.

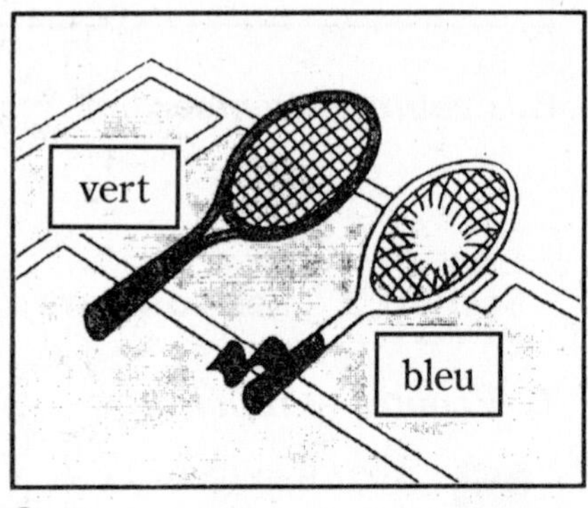

3.

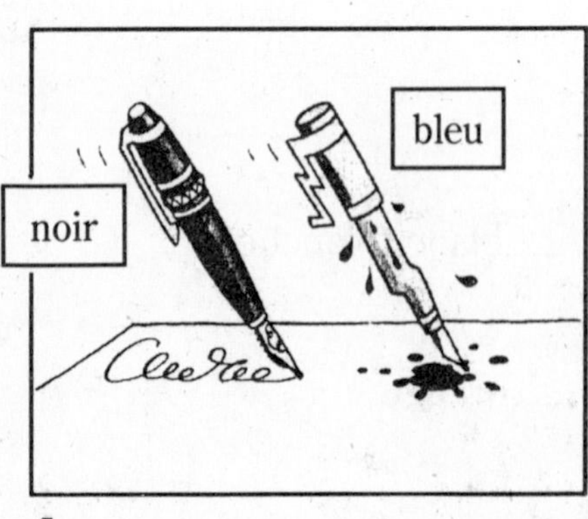

4.

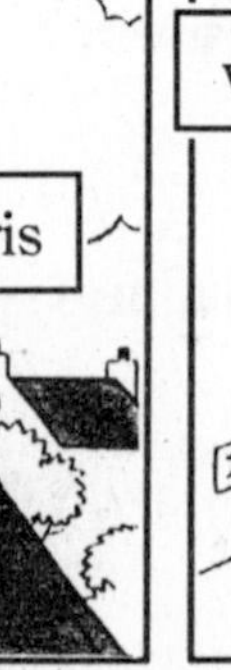

5.

verte et rouge
noire et jaune

6.

Nom ____

CASSETTE WORKSHEET Leçon 20 (cont.)

Section 5 Descriptions

F. ***Écoutez et répétez.***

Allez à la page 173.

Section 6 Dialogue: C'est ta voiture?

G. ***Compréhension orale***

1.	C'est la voiture de Jean-Claude.	vrai	faux
2.	C'est une Citroën.	vrai	faux
3.	Elle marche très bien.	vrai	faux
4.	Elle n'est pas rapide.	vrai	faux
5.	Elle fait du 160 à l'heure *(160 kilometers per hour).*	vrai	faux
6.	Jean-Claude a son permis *(driver's license).*	vrai	faux

Section 7 Prononciation

H. ***Les lettres «ch»***

Écoutez: **chien**

The letters "**ch**" are usually pronounced like the English *"sh."*

Répétez: **chien chat chose marche**
chouette chocolat affiche
Michèle a un chat et deux chiens.

CASSETTE WORKSHEET Leçon 20 (cont.)

À votre tour!

Section 8. Allô!

 Allez à la page 178.

Section 9. Créa-dialogue

 Allez à la page 178.

UNITÉ 5

Nom ______________________

Classe ______________ Date ______________

DISCOVERING FRENCH - BLEU

WRITING ACTIVITIES Leçon 17 Le français pratique: Les personnes et les objets

A 1. Auto-portrait

Write a short paragraph describing yourself. Give the following information:

- your name
- your age
- two physical traits

2. Mes acteurs favoris

Describe your favorite actor and actress by completing the following chart. Use complete sentences.

	MON ACTEUR FAVORI	MON ACTRICE FAVORITE
• name	Il ______	Elle ______
• age (approx.)		
• physical traits (affirmative or negative)		

3. Communication

1. Your French friend Sophie has a new neighbor and you want to know more about him.

   Ask Sophie . . .
   - *his name*
   - *how old he is*
   - *if he is tall or short*
   - *if he is good-looking*

2. Your friend Christophe has just told you that one of his cousins—a girl—is going to visit him next week.

   Ask Christophe . . .
   - *her name*
   - *if she is blond or brunette*
   - *if she is pretty*

UNITÉ 5

WRITING ACTIVITIES Leçon 17 (cont.)

B/C **4. L'intrus** *(The intruder)*

The following sentences can be completed logically by three of the items A, B, C, and D. One item does not fit. It is the intruder. Cross it out.

	A	B	C	D
1. Dans le garage, il y a . . .	une voiture	un vélo	une chambre	un scooter
2. Dans le sac, il y a . . .	un disque	une porte	un walkman	un appareil-photo
3. Sur le bureau, il y a . . .	un ordinateur	une calculatrice	un téléphone	une chaise
4. Sur le mur *(wall)*, il y a . . .	une affiche	une montre	une photo	un poster
5. Sur la table, il y a . . .	un crayon	une radio	un stylo	une mobylette
6. Dans la chambre, il y a . . .	une moto	une table	deux chaises	une chaîne stéréo
7. Sous le lit, il y a . . .	un scooter	un livre	des compacts	un chat

5. Quatre listes

Complete each list with three items.

What I carry in my school bag:

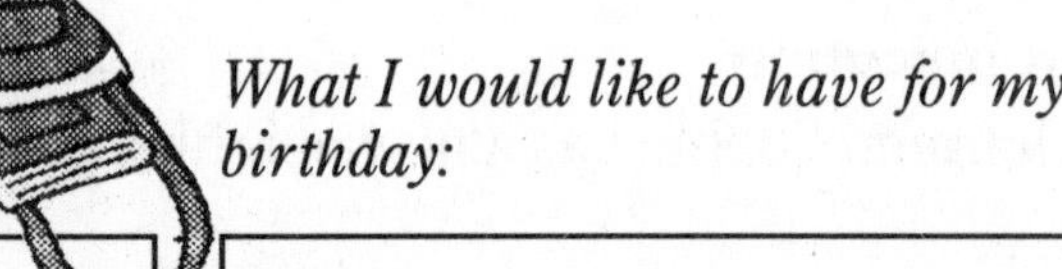

- ______________________________
- ______________________________
- ______________________________

What I would like to have for my birthday:

- ______________________________
- ______________________________
- ______________________________

What I would take on a trip to Paris:

- ______________________________
- ______________________________
- ______________________________

What I would want to have if I were lost on a desert island:

- ______________________________
- ______________________________
- ______________________________

UNITÉ 5

WRITING ACTIVITIES Leçon 17 (cont.)

6. Leurs possessions *(Their belongings)*

Look at the illustrations and describe four things that each of the following people own. Be sure to use **un** or **une,** as appropriate.

1. Isabelle a *(has)* un vélo, ____________________________________.
2. Mademoiselle Dumas a ____________________________________.
3. Julien et Frédéric ont *(have)* ____________________________________
____________________________________.
4. Monsieur Renoir a ____________________________________
____________________________________.

UNITÉ 5

WRITING ACTIVITIES Leçon 17 (cont.)

D 7. Ma chambre

Make a floor plan of your room, indicating the position of the door, the window(s), and the various pieces of furniture. Label everything in French.

8. Où sont-ils?

Describe the cartoon by completing the sentences with the appropriate expressions of location.

1. Le policier est ______________ la voiture.
2. L'homme est ______________ la voiture.
3. Le chien est ______________ la voiture.
4. Le chat est ______________ la voiture.
5. Le vélo est ______________ la voiture.

Nom ______________________________

Classe ____________________ Date ____________

WRITING ACTIVITIES Leçon 18 Vive la différence!

A 1. Au café

A group of friends is at a café. Read what everyone is ordering. Then say if they are hungry or thirsty, using the appropriate forms of **avoir faim** or **avoir soif.**

▶ Hélène commande *(orders)* un jus de tomate. Elle a soif.

1. Nous commandons une pizza. ____________
2. Je commande une limonade. ____________
3. Tu commandes un steak-frites. ____________
4. Patrick commande un sandwich. ____________
5. Vous commandez un jus de raisin. ____________
6. Pauline et Sophie commandent un soda. ____________

B 2. Au choix *(Your choice)*

Complete the sentences with one of the suggested nouns. Be sure to use **un** or **une,** as appropriate.

▶ Éric mange une pizza (un sandwich) . (sandwich? pizza?)

1. Nathalie commande ____________ . (glace? soda?)
2. Sophie écoute ____________ . (cassette? disque?)
3. J'écris *(write)* avec ____________ . (crayon? stylo?)
4. Pour mon anniversaire, je voudrais ____________ . (vélo? radiocassette?)

UNITÉ 5

WRITING ACTIVITIES Leçon 18 (cont.)

C 3. Quel article?

Complete the following sentences with the suggested articles, as appropriate.

(un, une, des)

1. Dans le garage, il y a ______ voiture et ______ bicyclettes.
2. Dans ma chambre, il y a ______ chaises et ______ lit.
3. Thomas a ______ cassettes et ______ magnétophone.
4. Isabelle est ______ copine. Paul et Marc sont ______ copains.

(le, la, l', les)

5. ______ élèves et ______ professeur sont dans la classe.
6. ______ ordinateur est sur ______ bureau.
7. ______ livres sont sur ______ table.
8. Où sont ______ cassettes et ______ disques?

D 4. Pourquoi pas?

Sometimes we do not do certain things because we do not have what we need. Read about what the following people do not do. Then explain why by saying that they do not have one of the things in the box.

une télé	**une voiture**	*une radio*
une raquette	une montre	**un livre**

▶ Monsieur Dumont ne voyage pas. *Il n'a pas de voiture.*

1. Claire ne regarde pas le match de foot. ______________________
2. Paul ne joue pas au tennis. ______________________
3. Henri n'écoute pas le concert. ______________________
4. Sophie n'étudie pas. ______________________
5. Jean n'est pas ponctuel *(punctual)*. ______________________

UNITÉ 5

Nom ______________________________

WRITING ACTIVITIES Leçon 18 (cont.)

E 5. Qu'est-ce que tu préfères?

Indicate your preferences by choosing one of the items in parentheses.
(Note: * = a feminine singular noun; ** = a plural noun)

▶ (soda ou limonade*?) Je préfère la limonade (le soda).

1. (théâtre ou cinéma?) ______________________
2. (musique* ou sports**?) ______________________
3. (gymnastique* ou volley?) ______________________
4. (français ou maths**?) ______________________
5. (pizza* ou spaghetti**?) ______________________
6. (carottes** ou salade*?) ______________________

F 6. Quel jour?

Say on which days of the week you do the following things.

▶ J'ai une classe de maths le mardi et le jeudi.

1. J'ai une classe de français ______________________.
2. J'ai une classe de musique ______________________.
3. Je dîne au restaurant ______________________.
4. Je fais les courses *(go shopping)* ______________________.

	LUNDI	MARDI	MERCREDI	JEUDI	VENDREDI	SAMEDI
8 h 30 à 9 h 30	Histoire	Allemand		Sciences économiques		Français
9 h 30 à 10 h 30	Anglais	Français	Anglais	Sciences physiques	Allemand	Français
10 h 30 à 11 h 30	Sport	Français	Sciences économiques	(13 h 30) Maths	Latin	Latin
11 h 30 à 12 h 30	Français	Latin	Maths	(13 h 30)	Sciences physiques	Histoire ou Civilisation
13 h 00 à 14 h 00						
14 h 00 à 15 h 00	Sciences physiques	Maths		Allemand		
15 h 00 à 16 h 00	Géographie	Maths		Histoire		
16 h 00 à 17 h 00	Civilisation	Anglais				

UNITÉ 5

Nom ______________________________

WRITING ACTIVITIES Leçon 18 (cont.)

7. Communication: En français!

1. You want to organize a party but you need help with the music. You phone your friend Mélanie.
   - *Tell her that you do not have a stereo.* ______________________________
   - *Ask her if she has a tape recorder.* ______________________________
   - *Ask her if she has cassettes.* ______________________________
2. You have invited Stéphanie to your house.
   - *Ask her if she is thirsty.* ______________________________
   - *Ask her if she likes orange juice.* ______________________________
   - *Ask her if she wants to watch TV.* ______________________________

Nom ______________________________

Classe ____________________ Date ____________

WRITING ACTIVITIES Leçon 19 Le copain de Mireille

A 1. Frères et soeurs

The following brothers and sisters are like each other. Describe the sisters, according to the model.

▶ Alain est blond. Monique est blonde.

1. Marc est petit. Yvonne ______.
2. Philippe est grand. Françoise ______.
3. Jean-Claude est timide. Stéphanie ______.
4. Pierre est intelligent. Alice ______.
5. Paul est sympathique. Juliette ______.
6. Jérôme est beau. Hélène ______.
7. Julien est mignon. Céline ______.
8. Patrick est sportif. Catherine ______.

2. Cousin, cousine

Describe two cousins of yours, one male, one female. Write four sentences for each person. (Your sentences may be affirmative or negative.)

▶ Il n'est pas très grand.

Mon cousin s'appelle ______.

1. ______
2. ______
3. ______
4. ______

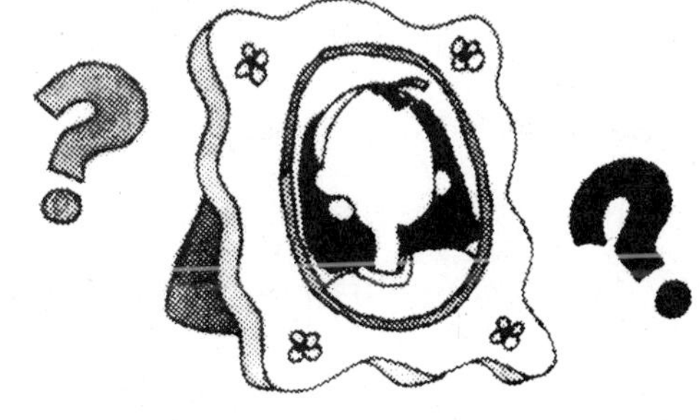

Elle est assez mignonne.

Ma cousine s'appelle ______.

1. ______
2. ______
3. ______
4. ______

UNITÉ 5

WRITING ACTIVITIES Leçon 19 (cont.)

A/B 3. Descriptions

Complete the following descriptions with **le, la,** or **les** and the appropriate forms of the adjectives in parentheses.

▶ Les livres sont intéressants. (intéressant)

1. ____ cassette est ______________. (intéressant)
2. ____ livres sont ______________. (amusant)
3. ____ table est ______________. (grand)
4. ____ chambre est ______________. (petit)
5. ____ chiens sont ______________. (gentil)

4. Quelle nationalité?

Read where the people live and give their nationalities. (Be sure to give the appropriate form of the adjective.)

▶ Madame Li habite à Hong Kong. Elle est chinoise.

1. Anne et Marie habitent à Québec. Elles ______________.
2. Madame Suárez habite à Mexico. Elle ______________.
3. Mon cousin habite à Zurich. Il ______________.
4. Silvia et Maria habitent à Rome. Elles ______________.
5. Peter et Jim habitent à Liverpool. Ils ______________.
6. M. et Mme Sato habitent à Kyoto. Ils ______________.
7. Delphine et Julie habitent à Paris. Elles ______________.
8. John et Mike habitent à Boston. Ils ______________.

WRITING ACTIVITIES Leçon 19 (cont.)

C 5. Les voisins

Sandrine is talking about her neighbors. Write what she says using the words in parentheses. Follow the model.

▶ (fille / amusant) Catherine est une fille amusante.

1. (garçon / timide) Charles ____________________.
2. (amie / gentil) Véronique ____________________.
3. (homme / sympathique) M. Dupont ____________________.
4. (femme / intelligent) Mme Bérard ____________________.

A/B/C 6. Commérages *(Gossip)*

Jean-Paul likes to talk about other people. Write what he says, using the suggested words.

▶ Philippe / avoir / amie / japonais

Philippe a une amie japonaise.

1. Frédéric / inviter / fille / anglais

____

2. Jacques et Olivier / dîner avec / amies / canadien

____

3. Bernard / téléphoner à / copine / mexicain

____

4. Le professeur / avoir / élèves / bête

____

5. Jean-Pierre / avoir / livres / intéressant

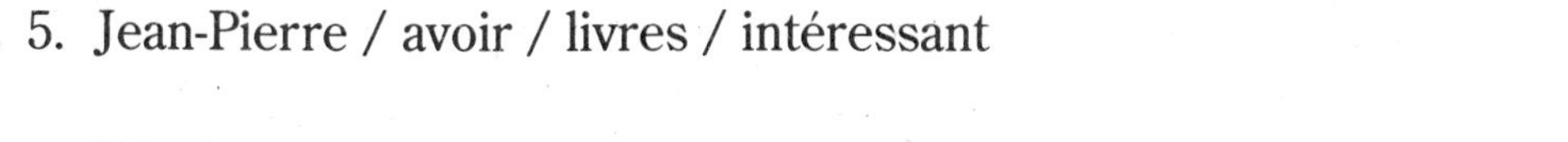

____

Tu connais la dame?
Oui, c'est Madame Vallée.

UNITÉ 5

WRITING ACTIVITIES Leçon 19 (cont.)

7. Communication

Write a short letter in French in which you describe yourself and two of your best friends.

UNITÉ 5

Nom ______________________________

Classe ____________________ Date ______________

WRITING ACTIVITIES **Leçon 20** La voiture de Roger

A 1. Drapeaux de pays francophones *(Flags of French-speaking countries)*

Color the flags according to the instructions.

B L E U	B L A N C	R O U G E

France

N O I R	J A U N E	R O U G E

Belgique

O R A N G E	B L A N C	V E R T

Côte d'Ivoire

2. De quelle couleur?

Describe the colors of the following items. (Use your imagination, if necessary.)

▶ Mon jean est ______bleu______.

1. Mon tee-shirt est ______________.
2. Mon crayon est ______________.
3. Ma chambre est ______________.
4. Ma bicyclette est ______________.
5. Mon chien est ______________.
6. La voiture de ma famille est ______________.

UNITÉ 5

WRITING ACTIVITIES Leçon 20 (cont.)

B 3. Descriptions

Complete the following descriptions by writing in the appropriate form of one of the adjectives from the box.

bon	**mauvais**	grand	**beau**	petit

▶ San Francisco est une belle (grande) ville *(city)*.

1. New York est une ______________ ville.
2. J'habite dans une ______________ ville.
3. Ma famille a une ______________ voiture.
4. J'ai une ______________ chambre.
5. Les Red Sox sont une ______________ équipe *(team)*.
6. Les Cowboys sont une ______________ équipe.
7. Le président est un ______________ président.

4. Le Rallye cycliste

A group of friends is bicycling together. Each one has a different bicycle. Describe the bicycles using the suggested adjectives.

▶ Éric a un vélo anglais. (anglais)

▶ Isabelle a un grand vélo. (grand)

1. Philippe a ______________________________. (italien)
2. Thomas a ______________________________. (rouge)
3. Claire a ______________________________. (petit)
4. Hélène a ______________________________. (vert)
5. Marc a ______________________________. (joli)
6. Laure a ______________________________. (japonais)

Nom ____

WRITING ACTIVITIES Leçon 20 (cont.)

C 5. Panne sèche *(Out of ink)*

Nathalie had planned to stress certain words by writing them in red ink. She realized—too late—that her red pen had dried up. Complete her assignment by filling in the missing words: **c'est, il est,** or **elle est.**

1. Voici Jean-Pierre.

   __________ un copain.

   __________ canadien.

   __________ un garçon sympathique.

2. Voici Madame Leblanc.

   __________ une voisine.

   __________ une personne intéressante.

   __________ très intelligente.

3. Regarde la voiture là-bas.

   __________ une voiture française.

   __________ une Renault.

   __________ petite et rapide.

4. J'ai un scooter.

   __________ rouge.

   __________ italien.

   __________ un bon scooter.

WRITING ACTIVITIES Leçon 20 (cont.)

D 6. Opinions personnelles

Here is a list of activities. Choose three activities you like and one activity you do not like. Explain why, using adjectives from the box.

ACTIVITÉS:

- danser
- chanter
- nager
- jouer au foot
- jouer au basket
- voyager
- visiter les musées
- organiser des boums
- inviter des copains
- étudier
- parler français
- travailler à la maison

chouette	**pénible**
super	**facile**
extra	**difficile**
drôle	

▶ *J'aime organiser les boums. C'est chouette!*

▶ *Je n'aime pas visiter les musées. C'est pénible.*

1. ______________________________________
2. ______________________________________
3. ______________________________________
4. ______________________________________

7. Communication: La voiture familiale *(The family car)*

Write a short description of your family car—or the car of someone you know. You may want to answer the following questions—in French, of course!

- *What make is it?* ______________________
- *Is it an American car?* ______________________

  (if not, what is it?) ______________________
- *What color is it?* ______________________
- *Is it large or small?* ______________________
- *Is it a good car?* ______________________

UNITÉ 5

Nom ______________________________

Classe ____________________ Date ____________

READING AND CULTURE ACTIVITIES Unité 5

A. En France

1. You would go to this place if you had a problem with your . . .
- ☐ bicycle
- ☐ watch
- ☐ car
- ☐ computer

ASTORIA

Agent Citroën

Voitures neuves et occasions
Mécanique - Carrosserie - Dépannage

→ consultez l'Annuaire Electronique

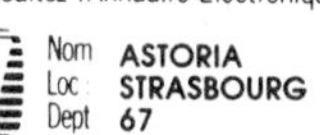

Nom ASTORIA
Loc STRASBOURG
Dept 67

Nouvelle Citröen XM
La route maitrisée

2. This is an ad for . . .
- ☐ a book
- ☐ a cassette
- ☐ a concert
- ☐ a TV program

UN LIVRE QUI N'A PAS FINI
DE FAIRE JAZZER.
JAZZ
LES INCONTOURNABLES
jazz
filipacchi

3. According to this ad, which of the following items could you buy at this store?
- ☐ A tape recorder.
- ☐ A typewriter.
- ☐ A computer.
- ☐ A movie camera.

THOMSON

machines à laver
réfrigérateurs
congélateurs
cuisinières
lave-vaisselle
téléviseurs
magnétophones
électrophones
transistors
hi-fi

SDRM 67, quai Paul Doumer - B.P. 130 - 92402 Courbevoie

READING AND CULTURE ACTIVITIES Unité 5 (cont.)

30 chambres plein centre ville, à 100 m de la gare et du lac

T.V. - Téléphone
Insonorisation

Wir sprechen Deutsch
We speak English

41, av. Romains
74000 ANNECY
Tel. 50 57 14 89

4. The following ad was placed by Parmelan, which is the name of . . .

- ☐ a hotel
- ☐ a travel agency
- ☐ a phone company
- ☐ a TV store

le magazine de l'informatique pour tous

5. You would buy this magazine if you were interested in . . .

- ☐ music
- ☐ photography
- ☐ history
- ☐ computers

LIBRAIRIE • PAPETERIE • DISQUES

GIBERT JOSEPH

achat vente **4000M² à PARIS** *neuf occasion*

LIBRAIRIE UNIVERSITAIRE ET GENERALE
DISQUES
26, BOULEVARD Saint-Michel
LIBRAIRIE SCOLAIRE
SERVICE ACHAT OCCASION
5, rue Racine
PAPETERIE
30, BOULEVARD Saint-Michel
M RER : ODEON • CLUNY-SORBONNE • LUXEMBOURG

6. According to the ad, this would be the place to go if you wanted to buy . . .

- ☐ used records
- ☐ secondhand typewriters
- ☐ stereo equipment
- ☐ old clothes

READING AND CULTURE ACTIVITIES Unité 5 (cont.)

B. Articles à vendre

You are in France and have gone to the local supermarket. There, on the board, you see the following announcements for items for sale.

OCCASION EXCEPTIONNELLE
vends
Appareil-photo OLYMPUS AM 100
avec Flash intégré
Prix: 350 F
Téléphoner à Sophie Lebihan
49.22.61.32

- What is Sophie selling? ______________________________

  What price is she asking? ______________________________
- How can you reach her? ______________________________

À VENDRE
Vélo tout terrain
10 vitesses
Excellente condition
Prix: à débattre
Téléphoner à Didier Muller
entre 16 heures et 19 heures
88.22.61.32

- What is Didier selling? ______________________________

  What price is he asking? ______________________________
- When can you reach him? ______________________________

READING AND CULTURE ACTIVITIES Unité 5 (cont.)

C. Le club des Correspondants

You have been looking at a French youth magazine and noticed the following requests for pen pals.

Le club des Correspondants

Garçon français, 16 ans, brun, yeux bleus, sympathique mais un peu timide, voudrait correspondre avec Américaine ou Anglaise parlant le français. Aime le sport, le ciné et la moto. Joindre photo. Réponse assurée.
Olivier Lambesq
25, place Gambetta
24100 Bergerac

Jeune Française, 15 ans, sportive (tennis, basket, ski) désire correspondre avec étudiants américains ou anglais du même âge pour échanger posters et cassettes de rock et de rap.
Écrire à:
Dominique Loiseau
32, rue du Dragon
75006 Paris

J'aime la danse, le cinéma et la musique. J'ai 16 ans et je suis française. Je voudrais correspondre avec fille ou garçon de mon âge, de préférence porto-ricain ou mexicain, pour échanger cassettes de musique latine ou de guitare espagnole.
Carole Gaune
45, boulevard de la Mer
76200 Dieppe, France

Jeune Américain, 16 ans, voudrait correspondre avec jeunes Français du même âge parlant l'anglais. Aime le ciné, la musique classique et la moto. Joindre photo. Réponse assurée.
Patrick Smith
1329 Cole Street
San Francisco, CA 94117

Je m'appelle Julie, et j'ai douze ans. Je voudrais correspondre avec un garçon canadien de 13 à 15 ans, parlant anglais, pour échanger cassettes. J'aime le jazz, le rock et le rap.
Julie Cartier
25, rue Colbert
63000 Clermont-Ferrand.

Mots croisés

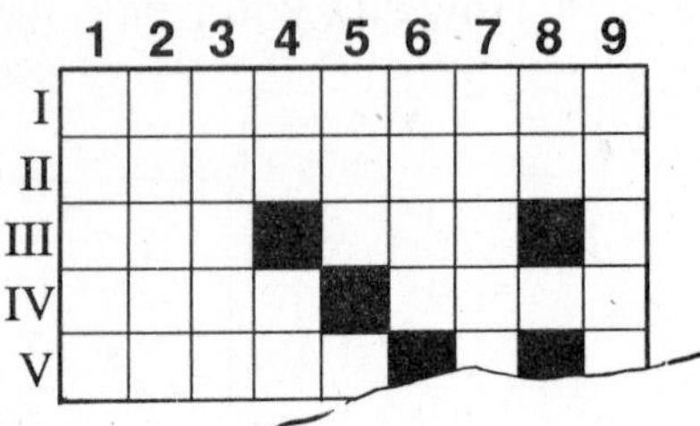

- Which of the young people like music?

  ____

  Which one does not mention music? ______________________________
- Which ones want to trade things? ______________________________

  What do they want to trade? ______________________________
- Which ones mention sports? ______________________________
- Would you like to correspond with any of these young people?

  Why or why not? ______________________________

COMMUNICATIVE EXPRESSIONS AND THEMATIC VOCABULARY

Unité 5 Le monde personnel et familier

▶ CULTURAL CONTEXT: **People and their possessions**

COMMUNICATIVE EXPRESSIONS

Asking what things people have
Est-ce que tu as . . . ?
Oui, j'ai . . .
Non, je n'ai pas (de) . . .

Asking what there is
Qu'est-ce qu'il y a?
Est-ce qu'il y a . . . ?
Il y a . . .
Il n'y a pas (de) . . .

Asking where something is
Où est . . . ?
Il/Elle est | **dans . . .** | **sur . . .** | **sous . . .** | **devant . . .** | **derrière . . .**

Asking if something works
Est-ce qu'il/elle marche?

Saying that you know or do not know
Je sais.
Je ne sais pas.

Giving an opinion on an activity
C'est . . . **chouette**, **difficile**, **drôle**, **extra**, **facile**, **faux**, **pénible**, **super**, **vrai**, **bien**, **mal**

VOCABULARY

People

des gens	**une personne**
un camarade	**une camarade**
un élève	**une élève**
un étudiant	**une étudiante**
un homme	**une femme**
un professeur	
un voisin	**une voisine**

Objects and things

un objet — **une chose**

un appareil-photo	**un sac**	**une affiche**	**une montre**
un compact	**un scooter**	**une auto**	**une moto**
un crayon	**un stylo**	**une bicyclette**	**une radio**
un disque	**un téléphone**	**une calculatrice**	**une radiocassette**
un livre	**un vélo**	**une cassette**	**une raquette**
un magnétophone	**un walkman**	**une chaîne stéréo**	**une télé**
un ordinateur		**une guitare**	**une voiture**
		une mobylette	

COMMUNICATIVE EXPRESSIONS AND THEMATIC VOCABULARY

VOCABULARY *(continued)*

In a room

une chambre | **un bureau** | **une chaise**
une fenêtre | **un lit** | **une table**
une porte

Description of people

- *physical features*

beau, belle | **grand** | **joli**
blond | **jeune** | **petit**
brun

- *personality traits*

amusant | **intéressant** | **sportif, sportive**
bête | **méchant** | **sympathique**
gentil, gentille | **mignon, mignonne** | **timide**
intelligent

- *nationalities*

américain | **espagnol** | **japonais**
anglais | **français** | **mexicain**
canadien, canadienne | **italien, italienne** | **suisse**
chinois

Colors

De quelle couleur est . . . ?

blanc, blanche | **noir**
bleu | **orange**
gris | **rose**
jaune | **rouge**
marron | **vert**

Other descriptions

bon, bonne | **mauvais**

Verbs

avoir | **marcher**
avoir faim
avoir soif

Other words and expressions

assez | **si** *(yes)* | **le lundi** | **alors**
très | | **le weekend** | **dis!**
| | | **dis donc!**

UNITÉ 5

UNITÉ 6
En ville

LISTENING ACTIVITIES
Leçons 21–24

WRITING ACTIVITIES
Leçons 21–24

READING AND CULTURE ACTIVITIES
Unité 6

POUR *COMMUNIQUER*

Communicative Expressions and Thematic Vocabulary

Nom ______________________________

Classe ______________________ Date ____________

CASSETTE WORKSHEET Leçon 21 Le français pratique: La ville et la maison

Section 1 La ville de Nathalie

A. ***Compréhension orale***

▶ Dans ma rue, il y a . . .

a. ☑ un hôtel

b. ☑ un magasin

(c.) ☐ un café

d. ☑ un restaurant

1. Dans ma rue, il y a . . .

a. ☐ une bibliothèque

b. ☐ un cinéma

c. ☐ un magasin

d. ☐ un supermarché

4. Dans ma ville, il y a aussi . . .

a. ☐ un supermarché

b. ☐ un hôpital

c. ☐ un centre commercial

d. ☐ une piscine

2. Dans mon quartier, il y a . . .

a. ☐ une église

b. ☐ une école

c. ☐ un hôpital

d. ☐ un café

5. Il y a aussi . . .

a. ☐ un stade

b. ☐ une plage

c. ☐ un parc

d. ☐ un musée

3. Dans ma ville, il y a . . .

a. ☐ une bibliothèque

b. ☐ une église

c. ☐ un théâtre

d. ☐ un musée

CASSETTE WORKSHEET Leçon 21 (cont.)

Section 2 Qu'est-ce que c'est?

B. *Questions et réponses*

▶ — Qu'est-ce que c'est?
— **C'est un cinéma.**

Section 3 Monologue: La ville de Tours

C. *Compréhension orale*

KEY

A. Bibliothèque municipale
B. Château de Tours
C. Cathédrale
D. Quartier du Vieux Tours
E. Restaurant Buré
F. Lycée Descartes
G. Rue Nationale et les Nouvelles Galeries
H. Hôtel de ville
I. Avenue de Grammont et le Café de l'Univers
J. Jardin des Prébendes
K. Piscine municipale

Nom ____

CASSETTE WORKSHEET Leçon 21 (cont.)

D. *Compréhension orale*

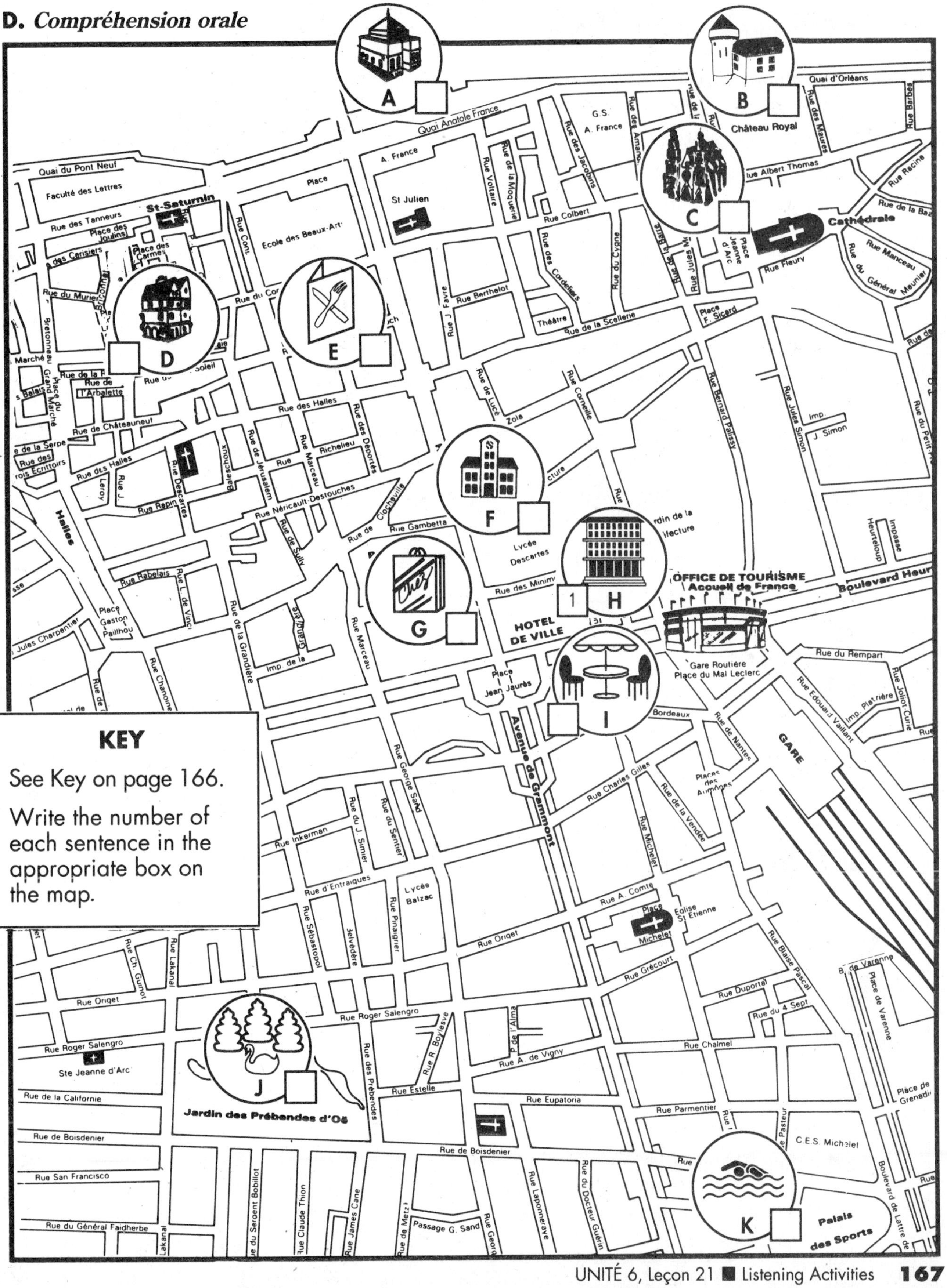

KEY

See Key on page 166.

Write the number of each sentence in the appropriate box on the map.

CASSETTE WORKSHEET Leçon 21 (cont.)

Section 4 Pardon. Excusez moi!

E. ***Compréhension orale***

1. Le Café de l'Univers?
a. ☐ C'est tout droit.
b. ☐ C'est là-bas à droite.
c. ☐ C'est là-bas à gauche.

2. Le Grand Hôtel?
a. ☐ C'est loin.
b. ☐ Ce n'est pas très loin.
c. ☐ C'est à côté *(next door)*.

3. Un restaurant?
a. ☐ Là-bas, vous tournez à gauche.
b. ☐ Là-bas, vous tournez à droite.
c. ☐ Là-bas, vous allez tout droit.

4. La cathédrale?
a. ☐ Vous continuez tout droit.
b. ☐ Vous tournez à droite et vous continuez tout droit.
c. ☐ Vous tournez à gauche et vous continuez tout droit.

Section 5 La maison d'Olivier

F. ***Compréhension orale***

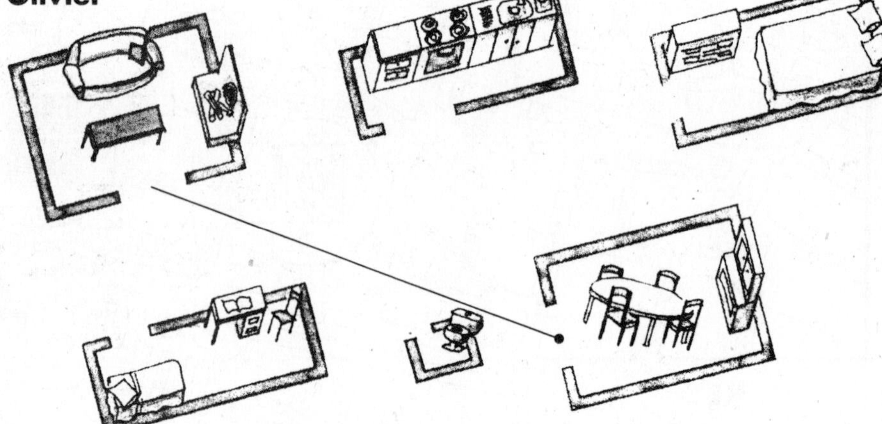

Section 6. La bonne réponse

 Allez à la page 196.

Section 7. Créa-dialogue

 Allez à la page 196.

Section 8. Où est-ce?

 Allez à la page 196.

UNITÉ 6

Nom ______________________________

Classe ____________________ Date ____________

CASSETTE WORKSHEET Leçon 22 Weekend à Paris

Section 1 Weekend à Paris

A. ***Compréhension orale***

Aujourd'hui c'est samedi.
Les élèves ne vont pas en classe.
Où est-ce qu'ils vont alors?
Ça dépend!

Thomas va au café.
Il a un rendez-vous avec une copine.

Florence et Karine vont aux Champs-Élysées.
Elles vont regarder les magasins de mode.
Après, elles vont aller au cinéma.

Daniel va chez son copain Laurent.
Les garçons vont jouer au ping-pong.
Après, ils vont aller au musée des sciences de la Villette.
Ils vont jouer avec les machines électroniques.

Béatrice a un grand sac et des lunettes de soleil.
Est-ce qu'elle va à un rendez-vous secret?
Non! Elle va au Centre Pompidou.
Elle va regarder les acrobates.
Et après, elle va écouter un concert.

Et Jean-François? Qu'est-ce qu'il va faire aujourd'hui?
Est-ce qu'il va visiter le Centre Pompidou?
Est-ce qu'il va regarder les acrobates?
Est-ce qu'il va écouter un concert?
Hélas, non!
Il va rester à la maison.
Pourquoi? Parce qu'il est malade.
Pauvre Jean-François!
Il fait si beau dehors!

Section 2 Où allez-vous?

B. ***Compréhension orale***

a. ____ au stade
b. ____ au café
c. __1__ à l'école
d. ____ au musée
e. ____ au centre commercial
f. ____ au restaurant
g. ____ au lycée
h. ____ au supermarché

Section 3 Où est-ce que tu vas?

C. ***Compréhension orale***

a. ____ la bibliothèque
b. ____ l'hôtel
c. ____ la piscine
d. ____ le cinéma

Tu vas au café?
Non, je vais à la plage.

UNITÉ 6

CASSETTE WORKSHEET Leçon 22 (cont.)

Section 4 Où vont-ils?

D. *Questions et réponses*

▶ —Est-ce qu'il va au restaurant ou au stade?
—**Il va au restaurant.**

Section 5 Qu'est-ce que vous allez faire?

E. *Compréhension orale*

a. ____

b. ____

c. ____

d. __1__

e. ____

f. ____

g. ____

h. ____

i. ____

Nom ______________________________

CASSETTE WORKSHEET Leçon 22 (cont.)

Section 6 Tu vas nager?

F. *Questions et réponses*

▶ —Tu vas nager?
—**Oui, je vais nager.**
(Non, je ne vais pas nager.)

Section 7 Dialogue: Julien travaille

G. *Compréhension orale*

1.	Julien reste avec ses amis.	vrai	faux
2.	Julien va à la piscine.	vrai	faux
3.	Julien va nager.	vrai	faux
4.	Julien va travailler.	vrai	faux
5.	Quand les copains arrivent à la piscine, Julien n'est pas là.	vrai	faux

Nom ___________________________________

CASSETTE WORKSHEET Leçon 22 (cont.)

Section 8 Prononciation

H. ***Les semi-voyelles* /w/ *et* /j/**

Écoutez: **oui** **très bien**

In French, the semi-vowels /**w**/ and /**j**/ are pronounced very quickly, almost like consonants.

Répétez: /w/ **oui chouette Louise**

/wa/, /wɛ̃/ **moi toi pourquoi voiture loin**
Chouette! La voiture de Louise n'est pas loin.

/j/ **bien chien radio piano Pierre Daniel violon pied étudiant**
Pierre écoute la radio avec Daniel.

Section 9. Allô!

 Allez à la page 208.

Section 10. Créa-dialogue

 Allez à la page 208.

Nom ________________________________

Classe ______________________ Date ____________

CASSETTE WORKSHEET Leçon 23 Au Café de l'Univers

Section 1 Au Café de l'Univers

A. ***Compréhension orale***

Où vas-tu après les classes?
Est-ce que tu vas directement chez toi?
Monique, elle, ne va pas directement chez elle.
Elle va au Café de l'Univers avec ses copines Anne-Marie et Estelle.
Elle vient souvent ici avec elles.

À la table de Monique la conversation est toujours tres animée.
De quoi parlent les filles aujourd'hui?

Est-ce qu'elles parlent de l'examen d'histoire? du problème de maths? de la classe de sciences?
Non!

Est-ce qu'elles parlent du weekend prochain? des vacances?
Non plus!

Est-ce qu'elles parlent du nouveau copain de Marie-Claire? de la cousine de Pauline? des amis de Véronique?
Pas du tout!

Aujourd'hui, les filles parlent d'un sujet beaucoup plus important! Elles parlent du nouveau prof d'anglais! (C'est un jeune professeur américain. Il est très intéressant, très amusant, très sympathique . . . et surtout il est très mignon!)

Nom ____________________

CASSETTE WORKSHEET Leçon 23 (cont.)

Section 2 Quels sports est-ce que vous pratiquez?

B. *Compréhension orale*

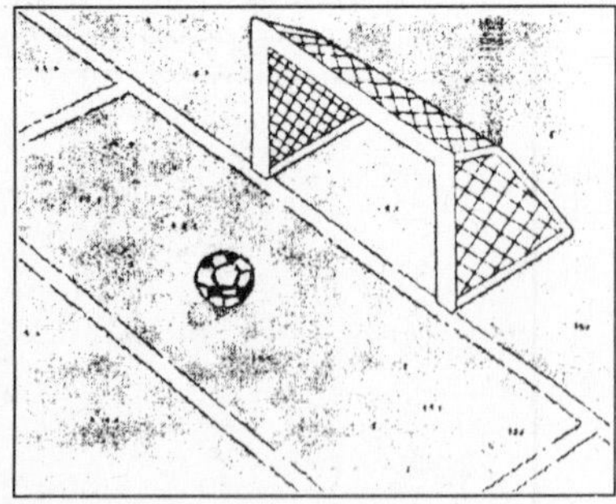

a. ____

b. ____

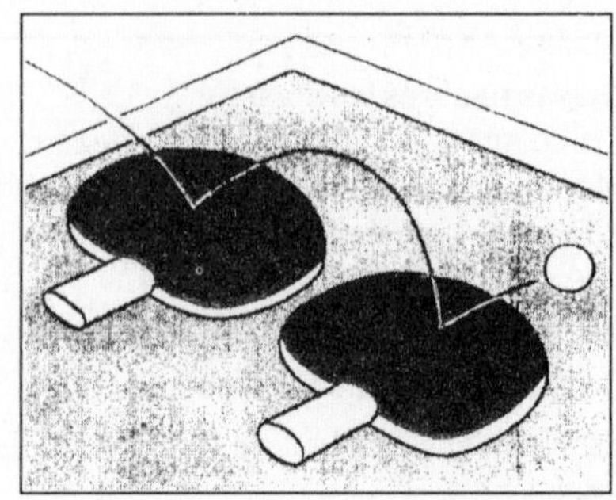

c. __1__

d. ____

e. ____

Section 3 Tu veux jouer au volley?

C. *Compréhension orale*

a. ____

b. ____

c. ____

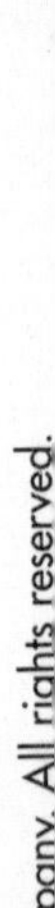

UNITÉ 6

Nom ______________________________

CASSETTE WORKSHEET Leçon 23 (cont.)

Section 4 Est-ce que Paul joue au tennis?

D. *Questions et réponses*

▶ —Est-ce que Paul joue au tennis ou au ping-pong?
—Il joue au ping-pong.

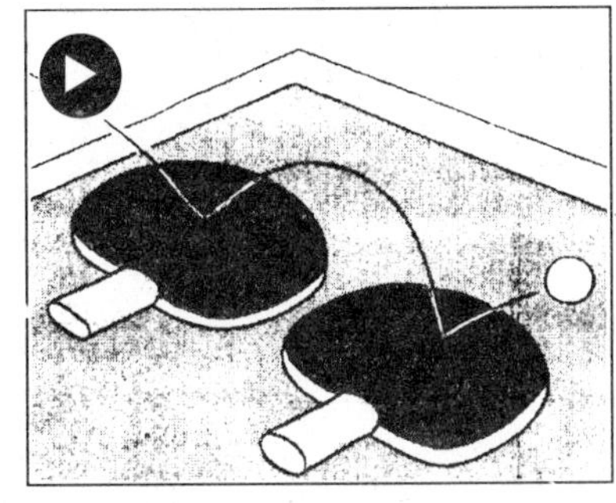

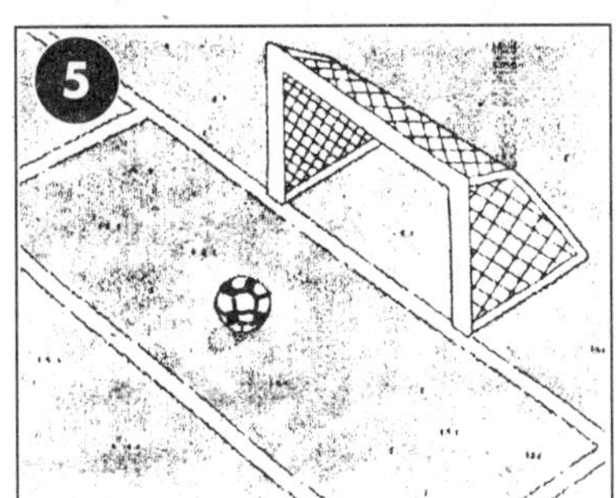

Section 5 De quel instrument est-ce que tu joues?

E. *Compréhension orale*

a. ____ le piano **b.** __1__ la flûte **c.** ____ la guitare **d.** ____ la batterie

e. ____ le violon **f.** ____ le saxo **g.** ____ la clarinette

UNITÉ 6

Nom ___________________________________

CASSETTE WORKSHEET Leçon 23 (cont.)

Section 6 Dialogue: Interview avec Éric

F. *Compréhension orale*

1. Éric aime la musique.	vrai	faux
2. Il aime le rock et le jazz.	vrai	faux
3. Il joue de la clarinette.	vrai	faux
4. Il joue dans un orchestre.	vrai	faux
5. L'orchestre joue dans des boums.	vrai	faux

Section 7 Prononciation

G. *Les voyelles* /ø/ *et* /œ/

Écoutez: **deux** **neuf**

The letters "**eu**" and "**oeu**" represent vowel sounds that do not exist in English but that are not very hard to pronounce.

Répétez:

/ø/ **deux eux je veux**
je peux un peu jeux
il pleut
Tu peux aller chez eux.

/œ/ **neuf soeur heure**
professeur jeune
Ma soeur arrive à neuf heures.

À votre tour!

Section 8. Conversation

 Allez à la page 218.

Section 9. Créa-dialogue

 Allez à la page 218.

Nom ______________________________

Classe ____________________ Date ____________

CASSETTE WORKSHEET Leçon 24 Mes voisins

Section 1 Mes voisins

A. ***Compréhension orale***

Bonjour!
Je m'appelle Frédéric Mallet.
J'habite à Versailles avec ma famille.
Nous habitons dans un immeuble de six étages.
Voici mon immeuble et voici mes voisins.
Monsieur Lacroche habite au sixième étage avec sa femme. Ils sont musiciens. Lui, il joue du piano et elle, elle chante. Oh là là, quelle musique!
Mademoiselle Jolivet habite au cinquième étage avec son oncle et sa tante.
Paul, mon meilleur ami, habite au quatrième étage avec sa soeur et ses parents.
Mademoiselle Ménard habite au troisième étage avec son chien Pomme, ses deux chats Fritz et Arthur, son perroquet Coco et son canari Froufrou. (Je pense que c'est une personne très intéressante, mais mon père pense qu'elle est un peu bizarre.)
Monsieur et Madame Boutin habitent au deuxième étage avec leur fils et leurs deux filles.
Et qui habite au premier étage?
C'est un garçon super-intelligent, super-cool et très sympathique! Et ce garçon . . . c'est moi!

Section 2 La famille

B. ***Écoutez et répétez.***

Allez à la page 223.

Section 3 La famille de Frédéric

C. ***Questions et réponses***

▶ —Qui est Éric Vidal?
—C'est le cousin de Frédéric.

CASSETTE WORKSHEET Leçon 24 (cont.)

Section 4 C'est ma maison

D. ***Écoutez et écrivez.***

▶ Eh bien, voilà. C'est ___ma___ maison.

1. Et ça, c'est la maison des voisins. C'est __________ maison.
2. Ça, c'est __________ voiture. Et ça, c'est leur voiture.
3. Voici __________ mobylette.
4. Et voilà la mobylette de mon frère. C'est __________ mobylette.
5. Voici __________ living.
6. Voici __________ chambre.
7. Et voici la chambre de mes parents. C'est __________ chambre.
8. Voici la chambre de ma soeur. C'est __________ chambre.
9. Ah, mais ça, ce n'est pas son walkman. C'est __________ walkman!

CASSETTE WORKSHEET Leçon 24 (cont.)

Section 5 C'est ta voiture?

E. ***Écoutez et écrivez.***

1. — C'est ____________ voiture?

— Eh bien, oui, c'est ____________ voiture.

2. — C'est ____________ voiture?

— Euh, oui, c'est ____________ voiture.

3. — C'est ____________ stylo?

— Non, ce n'est pas ____________ stylo!

4. — C'est ____________ maison?

— Oui, c'est ____________ maison.

— C'est ____________ maison.

5. — C'est ____________ sandwich!

— Non, ce n'est pas ____________ sandwich. C'est ____________ sandwich!

— Mais non, ce n'est pas ____________ sandwich.

C'est ____________ sandwich!

6. — Salut, Richard!

— Salut, Sophie!

— C'est ____________ copain?

— Non, c'est le copain de ____________ cousine.

— Ah, bon, dommage!

Nom ______________________________

CASSETTE WORKSHEET Leçon 24 (cont.)

Section 6 Dialogue: C'est ta famille?

F. *Compréhension orale*

a. _____ la grand-mère d'Olivier

b. _____ la mère d'Olivier

c. _____ la soeur d'Olivier

d. _____ la tante Alice

e. _____ le mari de tante Alice

f. _____ l'oncle Édouard

g. _____ le père d'Olivier

h. _____ les cousins d'Olivier

i. _____ Olivier

1.

2.

3.

4.

5.

Section 7 Prononciation

G. *Les voyelles /o/ et /ɔ/*

Écoutez: **vélo** **téléphone**

The French vowel /o/ is pronounced with more tension than in English. It is usually the last sound in a word.

Répétez: /o/ **vélo radio nos vos eau**
château chaud
Nos vélos sont au château.

The French vowel /ɔ / occurs in the middle of a word. Imitate the model carefully.

Répétez: /ɔ/ **téléphone école Nicole notre**
votre copain prof dommage
Comment s'appelle votre prof?

Section 8. Allô!

Allez à la page 228.

Section 9. Créa-dialogue

Allez à la page 228.

Nom ______________________________

Classe ____________________ Date ____________

WRITING ACTIVITIES Leçon 21 Le français pratique: La ville et la maison

A/B 1. Bienvenue à Bellerive-du-Lac *(Welcome to Bellerive-du-Lac)*

Imagine that you are spending your vacation in the small French town of Bellerive-du-Lac. The various facilities that the town has to offer are represented on an information panel. List as many of these facilities as you can.

BIENVENUE À BELLERIVE-DU-LAC INFORMATION

À Bellerive, il y a . . .

(1) un hôtel

(2) ____________

(3) ____________

(4) ____________

(5) ____________

(6) ____________

(7) ____________

(8) ____________

(9) ____________

A/B 2. Mon quartier

Name three different places of interest in the area where you live. Describe each one briefly.

▶ Dans mon quartier, il y a un restaurant français. Il s'appelle Chez Tante Louise. C'est un assez bon restaurant.

1. ____________

2. ____________

3. ____________

WRITING ACTIVITIES Leçon 21 (cont.)

C/D 3. Où est-ce?

Imagine that you are living in a French town. Someone is asking you for directions. Help the person out, according to the suggestions.

▶ — Pardon, où est l'hôtel Beau-Rivage?

— C'est tout droit !

1. — S'il vous plaît, où est l'hôpital Velpeau?

   — C'est ____________________ !

2. — Excusez-moi, où est la bibliothèque municipale?

   — C'est ____________________ !

3. — Pardon, où sont les toilettes?

   — C'est ____________________ !

4. — S'il vous plaît, où est le garage?

   — C'est ____________________ !

D 4. Ma maison

Draw a floor plan of your house or apartment. Label each room. (If you prefer, you can draw the floor plan of your dream house.)

UNITÉ 6

Nom ______________________

Classe ______________________ Date ______________

WRITING ACTIVITIES Leçon 22 Weekend à Paris

A 1. La tour Eiffel

Fit the six forms of **aller** into the Eiffel Tower. Then fill in the blanks to the left with the corresponding subject pronouns.

1. ________
2. ________
3. ________
4. ________
5. ________
6. ________

A/B 2. Le weekend

On weekends, people go to different places. Read what the following people like to do. Then say where each one is going by choosing an appropriate place from the list. Use the appropriate forms of **aller à.**

piscine	**restaurant**	**cinéma**	**musée**	**stade**
plage	**bibliothèque**	**concert**	**centre commercial**	

▶ Caroline aime nager. Elle va à la piscine.

1. Philippe et Jean-Louis aiment jouer au football. ______________
2. Mademoiselle Bellamy aime l'art moderne. ______________
3. Brigitte aime les westerns. ______________
4. Paul et Marc aiment la musique. ______________
5. J'aime regarder les magazines français. ______________
6. Tu aimes dîner en ville. ______________
7. Nous aimons nager. ______________
8. Vous aimez le shopping. ______________

UNITÉ 6

WRITING ACTIVITIES Leçon 22 (cont.)

B 3. Qu'est-ce qu'ils font?

Describe what the following people are doing. Use the suggested words to form complete sentences.

▶ Jacqueline / parler à / le garçon français

Jacqueline parle au garçon français.

1. Marc / parler à / le professeur

____

2. Le professeur / parler à / les élèves

____

3. Le guide / parler à / les touristes

____

4. Nathalie / téléphoner à / le garçon canadien

____

5. Hélène / téléphoner à / l'étudiant français

____

6. Jean-Pierre / être à / le cinéma

____

7. Juliette / étudier à / la bibliothèque

____

8. Le taxi / arriver à / l'aéroport

____

Nom ______________________________

WRITING ACTIVITIES Leçon 22 (cont.)

C 4. Les voisins de Mélanie

Mélanie is selling tickets to the school fair and hopes her neighbors will buy some. Indicate that Mélanie is visiting the houses in the illustration. Use the expression **chez.**

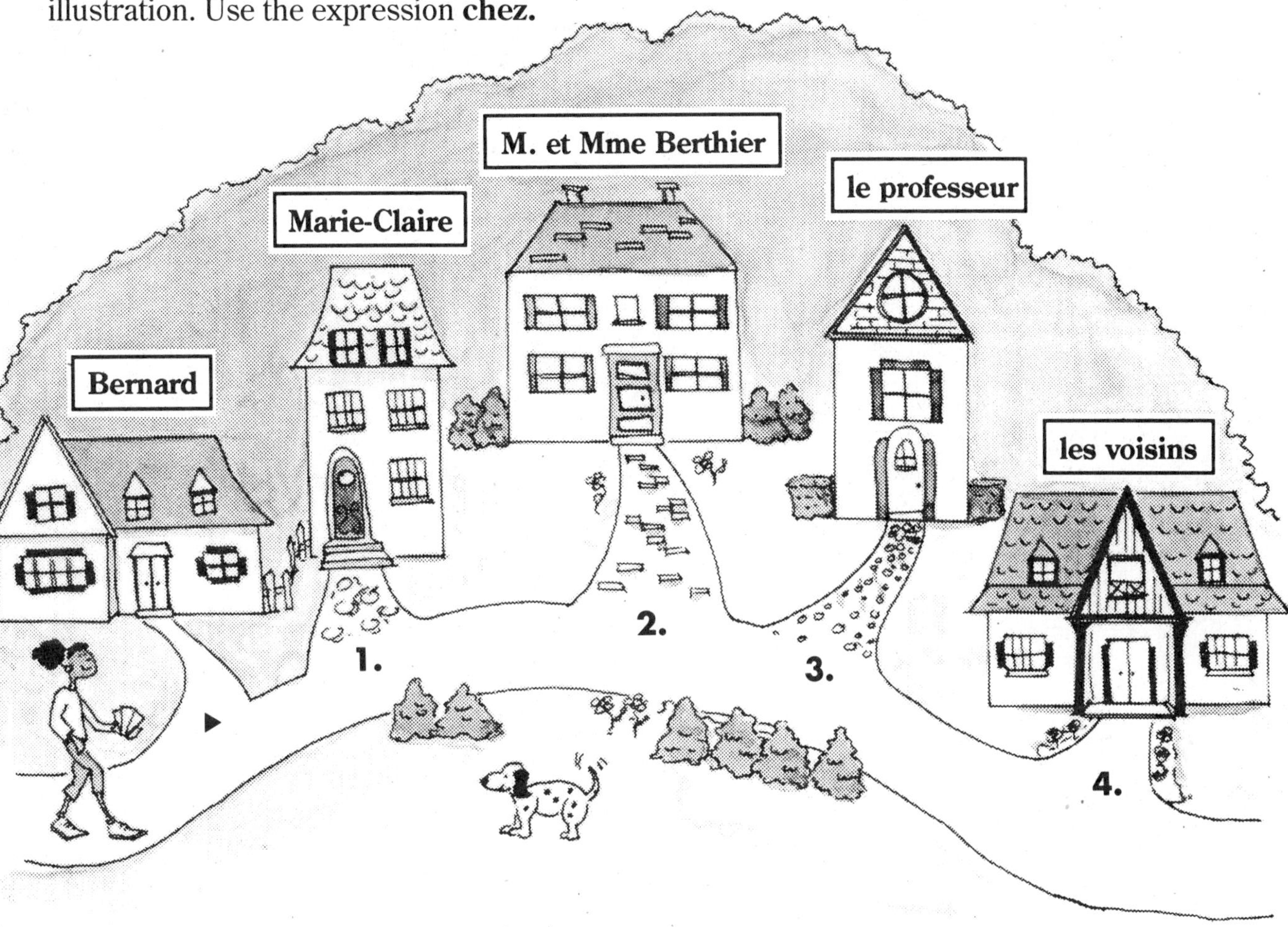

▶ Mélanie va chez Bernard.

1. Elle va ______________________________.
2. Elle va ______________________________.
3. Elle va ______________________________.
4. Elle va ______________________________.

Nom ______________________

WRITING ACTIVITIES Leçon 22 (cont.)

D 5. Qu'est-ce qu'ils vont faire?

The following people are going out. Describe what each one is going to do, using the construction **aller** + infinitive.

▶ Je vais faire une promenade à vélo.

1. Nous ______________________.
2. Vous ______________________.
3. Tu ______________________.
4. Sylvie ______________________.
5. M. et Mme Dumaine ______________________.

6. Communication: Le weekend

Write a short paragraph about your weekend plans. Describe four things that you are going to do and two things you are not going to do.

OUI!

- ______________________
- ______________________
- ______________________
- ______________________

NON!

- ______________________
- ______________________

Nom ______________________________

Classe ____________________ Date ____________

WRITING ACTIVITIES Leçon 23 Au Café de l'Univers

A 1. La boum de Catherine

Catherine is organizing a party. Say who is coming and who is not, using the appropriate forms of **venir.**

▶ Claire a un examen demain. *Elle ne vient pas.*

1. Philippe et Antoine aiment les boums. ____________
2. Je dois étudier. ____________
3. Nous aimons danser. ____________
4. Tu acceptes l'invitation. ____________
5. Vous n'êtes pas invités. ____________
6. Thomas est malade *(sick)*. ____________

A/B 2. D'où viennent-ils?

It is dinner time and everyone is going home. Say which places each person is coming from.

▶ Éric *vient du cinéma*.

1. 2. 3. 4. 5.

1. Nathalie ____________.
2. Les élèves ____________.
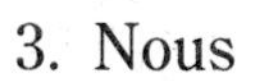
3. Nous ____________.
4. Monsieur Loiseau ____________.
5. Vous ____________.

WRITING ACTIVITIES Leçon 23 (cont.)

B 3. À la Maison des Jeunes

La Maison des Jeunes is a place where young people go for all kinds of different activities. Say what the following people are doing, using **jouer à** or **jouer de,** plus the activity illustrated.

▶ Nous jouons au ping-pong.

1. Diane ________________.
2. Stéphanie et Claire ________________.
3. Vous ________________.
4. Tu ________________.
5. Marc et Antoine ________________.
6. Ma cousine ________________.

C 4. Conversations

Complete the following mini-dialogues, using stress pronouns to replace the underlined nouns.

▶ —Tu dînes avec Jean-Michel?

—Oui, je dîne avec lui.

1. —Tu étudies avec ta copine?

   —Oui, ________________.

2. —Tu travailles pour Monsieur Moreau?

   —Oui, ________________.

3. —Tu vas chez Vincent et Thomas?

   —Oui, ________________.

4. —Tu voyages avec Hélène et Alice?

   —Oui, ________________.

UNITÉ 6

WRITING ACTIVITIES Leçon 23 (cont.)

5. L'orage *(The storm)*

Because of the storm, everyone is staying home today. Express this by completing the sentences below with **chez** and the appropriate stress pronoun.

▶ Nous étudions chez nous.

1. Monsieur Beaumont reste ____________________.
2. Madame Vasseur travaille ____________________.
3. Je regarde une vidéocassette ____________________.
4. Tu joues à Nintendo ____________________.
5. Vous dînez ____________________.
6. Vincent et Philippe jouent aux échecs ____________________.
7. Cécile et Sophie étudient ____________________.
8. Jean-Paul regarde la télé ____________________.

D 6. Qu'est-ce que c'est?

Identify the following objects more specifically.

▶ C'est une raquette de tennis.

1. C'est une raquette ____________________.

2. C'est un ballon ____________________.

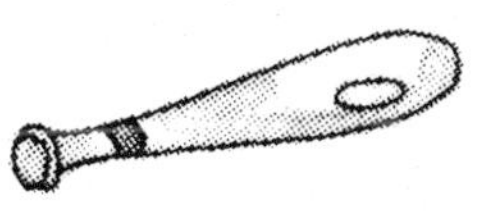

3. C'est une batte ____________________.

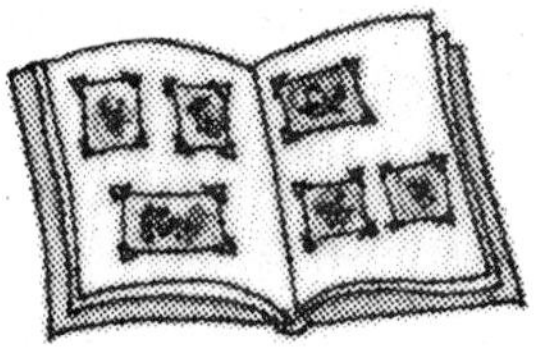

4. C'est un album ____________________.

5. C'est un livre ____________________.

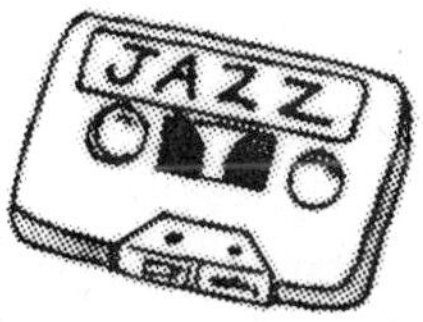

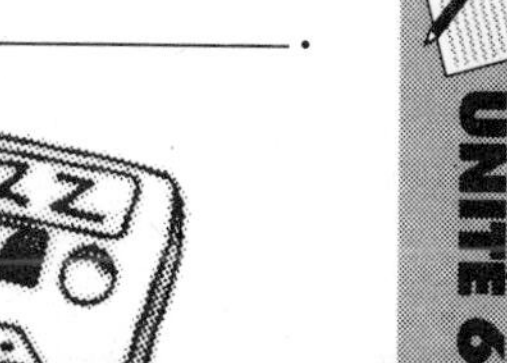

6. C'est une cassette ____________________.

WRITING ACTIVITIES Leçon 23 (cont.)

7. Communication

1. Et vous?

Describe your leisure activities.

Say . . .

- *which sports you play* ______________________________
- *which games you play* ______________________________
- *which instrument(s) you play* ______________________________

2. Lettre à Jérôme

Your friend Jérôme is going to spend Saturday with you.

Ask him . . .

- *at what time he is coming*
- *if he plays tennis*
- *if he has a tennis racket*
- *if he likes to play chess*

Tell him that you are going to have dinner at your cousins'.

Ask him . . .

- *if he wants to go to their place too*
- *what time he has to go home*

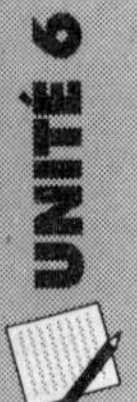

Nom ______________________________________

Classe ________________________ Date __________

DISCOVERING FRENCH – *BLEU*

WRITING ACTIVITIES Leçon 24 Mes voisins

A 1. La consigne *(The check room)*

The following objects have been left at the check room, tagged with their owner's names. Identify each item.

Stéphanie ▶ *C'est la guitare de Stéphanie.*

Jean-Pierre 1. ______________________________

Isabelle 2. ______________________________

M. Camus 3. ______________________________

Raphaël 4. ______________________________

Mme Vénard 5. ______________________________

2. En famille

Look at the family tree and explain the relationships between the following people.

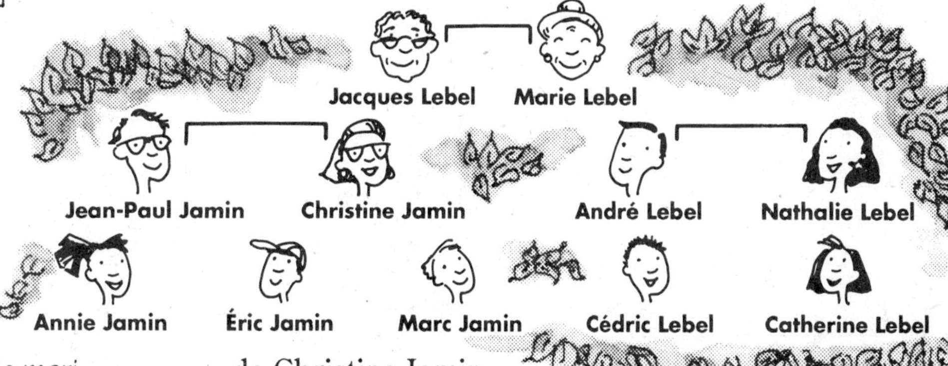

▶ Jean-Paul Jamin est *le mari* de Christine Jamin.

1. Nathalie Lebel est __________ d'André Lebel.
2. Jacques et Marie Lebel sont __________ de Cédric.
3. Marie Lebel est __________ de Christine Jamin.
4. Éric et Marc sont __________ de Christine Jamin.
5. Cédric est __________ d'Éric.
6. Catherine est __________ de Marc.
7. Catherine est __________ d'André et Nathalie Lebel.
8. Jean-Paul Jamin est __________ de Cédric et de Catherine.
9. Nathalie Lebel est __________ d'Annie Jamin.

UNITÉ 6

WRITING ACTIVITIES Leçon 24 (cont.)

B 3. En vacances

The following people are spending their vacations with friends or family. Complete the sentences below with **son, sa,** or **ses,** as appropriate.

1. Guillaume voyage avec ______ soeur et ______ parents.
2. Juliette visite Paris avec ______ frère et ______ cousines.
3. Paul va chez ______ ami Alain.
4. Sandrine est chez ______ amie Sophie.
5. En juillet, Jean-Paul va chez ______ grands-parents. En août, il va chez ______ tante Marthe. En septembre, il va chez ______ amis anglais.
6. Hélène va chez ______ grand-père. Après (*afterwards*), elle va chez ______ oncle François.

B/C 4. Pourquoi pas?

The following people are not engaged in certain activities because they do not have certain things. Complete the sentences with **son, sa, ses, leur,** or **leurs** and an appropriate object from the box. Be logical.

radio	**voiture**	*ordinateur*	**mobylette**
stylos	raquettes	**livres**	

▶ Isabelle et Cécile n'étudient pas. Elles n'ont pas leurs livres.

1. Pierre et Julien ne jouent pas au tennis. Ils n'ont pas ______________________.
2. Philippe ne va pas en ville. Il n'a pas ______________________.
3. Alice et Claire n'écoutent pas le concert. Elles n'ont pas ______________________.
4. Madame Imbert ne travaille pas. Elle n'a pas ______________________.
5. Mes parents ne voyagent pas. Ils n'ont pas ______________________.
6. Les élèves n'écrivent pas (*are not writing*). Ils n'ont pas ______________________.

UNITÉ 6

Nom ____

WRITING ACTIVITIES Leçon 24 (cont.)

5. Le weekend

On weekends we like to do things with our friends and relatives. Complete the sentences below with the appropriate possessive adjectives.

▶ Nous faisons une promenade en voiture avec ___nos___ parents.

1. Isabelle et Francine vont au cinéma avec __________ cousins.
2. Je joue au tennis avec __________ copains.
3. Tu dînes chez __________ oncle.
4. Philippe et Marc vont au restaurant avec __________ copines.
5. Hélène fait une promenade à vélo avec __________ frère.
6. Nous téléphonons à __________ grand-mère.
7. Vous allez au musée avec __________ oncle.
8. Nous jouons aux cartes avec __________ amis.
9. Vous visitez un musée avec __________ soeur.

D 6. La course cycliste

Say how the following people finished the bicycle race.

Jean-Paul Claire Nicolas Philippe Stéphanie Hélène Thomas Marc

▶ Nicolas ___est sixième___.

1. Philippe ______________________.
2. Claire ______________________.
3. Marc ______________________.
4. Hélène ______________________.
5. Jean-Paul ______________________.
6. Thomas ______________________.
7. Stéphanie ______________________.

WRITING ACTIVITIES Leçon 24 (cont.)

7. Communication: La famille de mes amis

Think of two of your friends. For each one, write four sentences describing his/her family. (If you wish, you can describe the families of imaginary friends.)

▶ Mon copain s'appelle Tom.

Sa soeur s'appelle Wendy.

Son père travaille dans un magasin.

Sa mère travaille dans un hôpital.

Ses cousins habitent à Cincinnati.

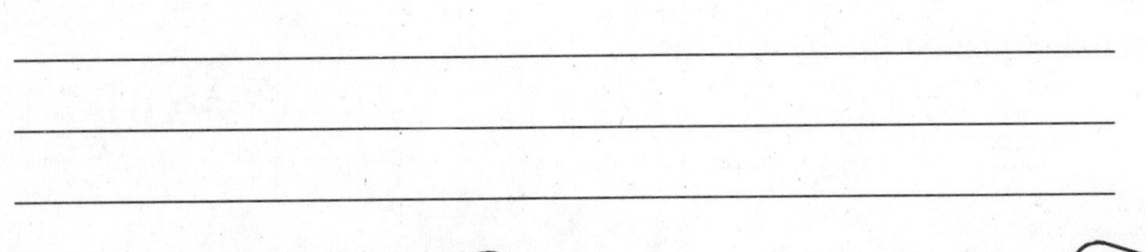

• Mon copain s'appelle ________.

____

____

____

____

• Ma copine s'appelle ________.

____

____

____

____

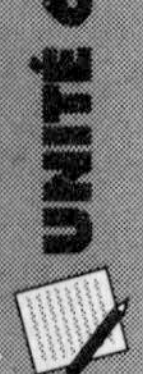

UNITÉ 6

Nom ______________________________

Classe ______________________ Date ______________

READING AND CULTURE ACTIVITIES Unité 6

A. En voyage

1. This ad is for . . .
- ☐ a vacation condo for sale
- ☐ a house for sale
- ☐ a house for rent
- ☐ a small hotel

Auberge pasta PIERRE

Cette belle d'autrefois
au coeur du village de Rawdon!
Salle à manger de 132 places
22 chambres, piscine extérieure
Bar, discothèque, terrasse
Grand salon avec foyer
Forfaits 4 saisons
3663, rue Queen, Rawdon
J0K 1S0, (514) 834-5417

2. This concert is going to be held . . .
- ☐ in a subway station
- ☐ in a school
- ☐ in a concert hall
- ☐ in a church

EGLISE de la MADELEINE
Place et métro Madeleine
Jeudi 29 novembre à 20h 30
MOZART
Concerto pour Clarinette en La M.
REQUIEM
Monique POURADIER DUTEIL, soprano
Sylvie OUSSENKO, mezzo-soprano
Francis BARDOT, ténor
Thierry de GROMARD, basse
Marie-Cécile COURCIER, clarinette
Chœurs de Montmorency
(chef des chœurs : Philippe BRANDEIS)
SINFONIETTA de PARIS
direction : Dominique FANAL
Locations
FNAC - VIRGIN MEGASTORE 60 Champs-Elysées, par téléphone au 42.33.43.00
et sur place le 28 et le 29 novembre à partir de 11h.

Nom ______________________________

READING AND CULTURE ACTIVITIES Unité 6 (cont.)

3. An attraction of this hotel is that it is located
- ☐ downtown
- ☐ near a beach
- ☐ near an airport
- ☐ near an amusement park

VEYRIER-DU-LAC

Les Acacias

HÔTEL - BAR RESTAURANT

Lac d'Annecy

Dans un cadre de verdure à 100 m de la plage.
Terrasse panoramique sur le lac.

Tél. 50 60 11 60

4. You would go to this place . . .
- ☐ to buy records
- ☐ to read books
- ☐ to listen to music
- ☐ to consult bus schedules

5. This map shows you how to get . . .
- ☐ to the downtown area
- ☐ to a large shopping mall
- ☐ to a hockey rink
- ☐ to a racetrack

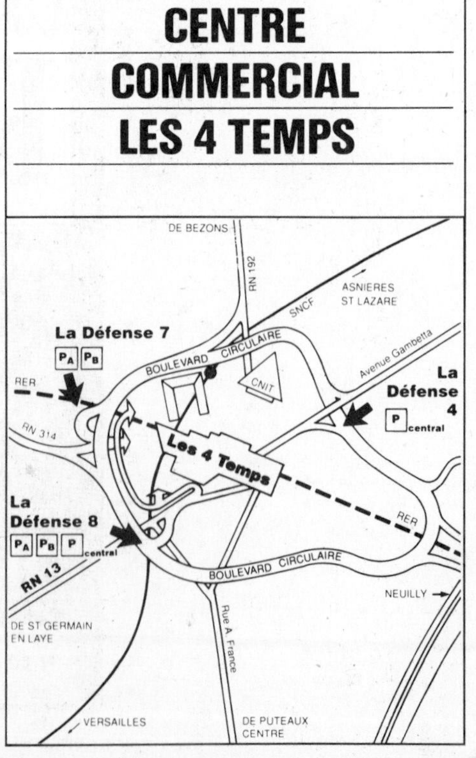

READING AND CULTURE ACTIVITIES Unité 6 (cont.)

Hotel de l'Abbaye

saint germain

★★★ 10, rue Cassette - 75006 PARIS
Tél. : (1) 45 44 38 11 - Adresse télég. : Abotel
R.C. Paris B 712 062 744

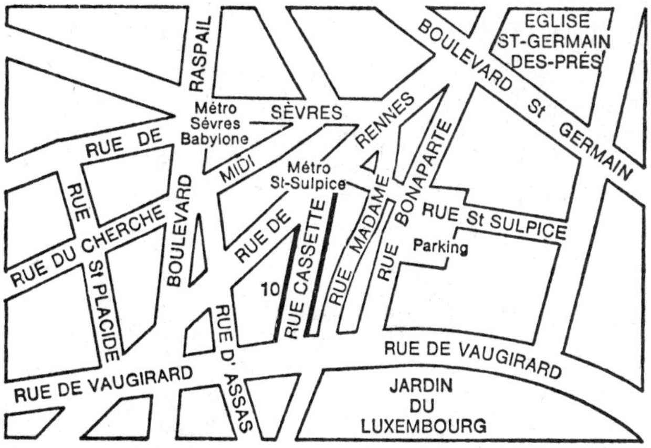

B. À l'hôtel de l'Abbaye

1. You are visiting France with your family and are looking for a hotel.

- What is the name of the hotel shown on the card? ____________________
- In which city is it located? ____________________
- On which street? ____________________
- If you wanted to make a reservation, which number would you call? ____________________

2. You have just made your reservation.

- Check the address of the hotel and find its location on the map. Mark the location with an "X."
- You and your family are planning to rent a car while in France. On the map, find and circle the nearest parking garage.
- Paris has a convenient subway system: **le métro.**

  How many subway stations are shown on the map? ____________________

  What is the name of the subway station closest to the hotel? ____________________
- The map shows one of the oldest churches in Paris. (It was built in the 12th century.) Find this church and draw a circle around it.

  What is its name? ____________________

  On which street is it located? ____________________
- The map also shows a large public garden where many people go jogging.

  What is the name of the garden? ____________________

  On which street is it located? ____________________

READING AND CULTURE ACTIVITIES Unité 6 (cont.)

C. En RER

Paris has a regular subway system called **le métro.** It also has a network of fast commuter trains called the **RER** which cross the city in about 12 minutes. If you want to go beyond the city limits, you must pay an extra fare.

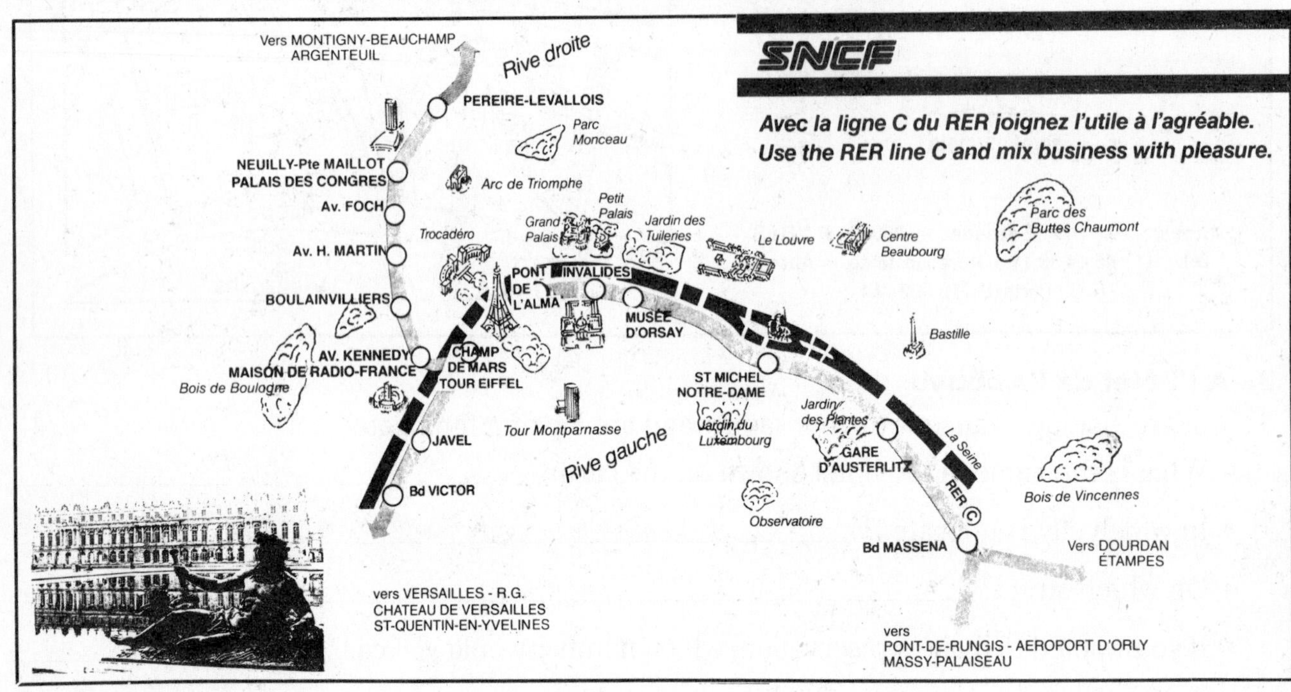

This map shows the C-line of the RER. Many famous monuments and places of interest are located along this line.

1. Look at the map and find at which stop you would get off to visit each of the following places.

La Tour Eiffel ______________________________

La Cathédrale Notre-Dame ______________________________

Le Grand Palais (un musée) ______________________________

Le Jardin des Tuileries ______________________________

Le Musée d'Orsay ______________________________

Le Palais des Congrès ______________________________

Le Louvre ______________________________

2. You can also use the C-line to get to places outside of Paris.

Which airport can you reach with this train? ______________________________

Which famous historical château can you visit? ______________________________

COMMUNICATIVE EXPRESSIONS AND THEMATIC VOCABULARY

Unité 6 En ville

▶ CULTURAL CONTEXT: **City life — the home, the family, and urban activities**

COMMUNICATIVE EXPRESSIONS

Asking a friend where he/she is going
Où est-ce que tu vas?
Où vas-tu?
Je vais | **à** *(+ place).*
| **chez** *(+ person).*

Asking a friend about what he/she is going to do
Qu'est-ce que tu vas faire?
Est-ce que tu vas . . . ?
Vas-tu . . . ?
Oui, je vais . . .
Non, je ne vais pas . . .

Asking for directions
Pardon, où est . . . ?
Excuse moi, où est . . . ?
C'est | **loin.** / **près** / **en haut** / **en bas**
Allez / **Tournez** / **C'est** | **à droite.** / **à gauche**
Continuez tout droit.

Asking a friend where he/she is coming from
D'où est-ce que tu viens?
D'où viens-tu?
Je viens de *(+ place).*

Pointing to people and saying who they are
C'est . . . **moi** / **toi** / **lui** / **elle** — **nous** / **vous** / **eux** / **elles**

Indicating ownership or relationship
C'est la voiture de Madame Dupont.
C'est le cousin de Marie.
C'est | **mon, ma . . .** / **ton, ta . . .** / **son, sa . . .** / **notre . . .** / **votre . . .** / **leur . . .**
Ce sont | **mes . . .** / **tes . . .** / **ses . . .** / **nos . . .** / **vos . . .** / **leurs . . .**

Ranking people or things
premier, première — **septième**
deuxième — **huitième**
troisième — **neuvième**
quatrième — **dixième**
cinquième — **vingtième**
sixième — **vingt-et-unième**

VOCABULARY

Verbs of motion
aller — **arriver** / **rentrer** / **rester** — **venir** / **revenir**

faire une promenade | **à pied** / **à vélo** / **en voiture**

How to go somewhere
à pied / **à vélo** — **en bus** / **en train** / **en voiture** — **en métro** / **en taxi**

Where to go in a city
• *towns and neighborhoods*
un endroit — **une adresse**

un quartier / **un village** — **une ville** — **un boulevard** — **une avenue** / **une rue**

UNITÉ 6

COMMUNICATIVE EXPRESSIONS AND THEMATIC VOCABULARY

VOCABULARY *(continued)*

• *public places and buildings*

un café	**un parc**	**une bibliothèque**
un centre commercial	**un restaurant**	**une école**
un cinéma	**un stade**	**une église**
un hôpital	**un supermarché**	**une piscine**
un hôtel	**un théâtre**	**une plage**
un musée		

• *events and happenings*

un concert	**un pique-nique**	**une boum**
un film	**un rendez-vous**	

The home and its description

un immeuble	**une maison**	**confortable**
un appartement		**moderne**
un garage	**une chambre**	
un jardin	**une cuisine**	
un salon	**une salle à manger**	
	une salle de bains	
	les toilettes	

The family

un parent	**une famille**	**un enfant**	**une enfant**	**un père**	**une mère**
un grand-parent		**un frère**	**une soeur**	**un grand-père**	**une grand-mère**
		un fils	**une fille**	**un oncle**	**une tante**
		un cousin	**une cousine**		

Sports, games, and musical instruments

un sport

le baseball	**le ping-pong**	**Je joue au foot.**
le basket(ball)	**le tennis**	
le foot(ball)	**le volley(ball)**	

un jeu

les échecs	**les cartes**	**Je joue** | **au Monopoly.**
le Monopoly	**les dames**	**aux échecs.**

un instrument de musique

le clavier	**la batterie**	**Je joue** | **du piano.**
le piano	**la clarinette**	**de la clarinette.**
le saxo(phone)	**la flûte**	
le violon	**la guitare**	

Other expressions

Pardon!	**Vas-y!**	**Vraiment?**
Excusez-moi!	**Va-t-en!**	**Tu es sûr?**
		Pas du tout!

UNITÉ 7
Le shopping

LISTENING ACTIVITIES
Leçons 25–28

WRITING ACTIVITIES
Leçons 25–28

READING AND CULTURE ACTIVITIES
Unité 7

Communicative Expressions and Thematic Vocabulary

Nom ____

Classe ____________________________ Date ________________

CASSETTE WORKSHEET Leçon 25 Le français pratique: L'achat des vêtements

Section 1 Qu'est-ce que vous cherchez?

A. *Compréhension orale*

a. ____

b. ____

c. ____

d. ____

e. ____

f. ____

g. ____

h. __1__

i. ____

j. ____

k. ____

l. ____

m. ____

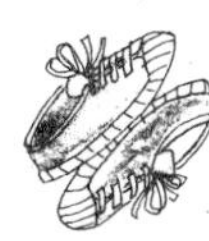

n. ____

o. ____

p. ____

CASSETTE WORKSHEET Leçon 25 (cont.)

Section 2 Vous désirez?

B. *Questions et réponses*

▶ —Vous désirez?
—Je cherche un tee-shirt. ▶

1 

2 

3 

4 

5 

Section 3 Dialogue: Aux Galeries Lafayette

C. *Compréhension orale*

a. ____ b. ____ c. ____

Section 4 Les nombres de 100 à 1000

D. *Écoutez et répétez.*

100	200	500	800
101	300	600	900
102	400	700	1000

CASSETTE WORKSHEET Leçon 25 (cont.)

Section 5 Combien coûte la veste?

E. *Questions et réponses*

▶ —Combien coûte la veste?
—**Elle coûte 500 francs.** ▶

1. 

2. 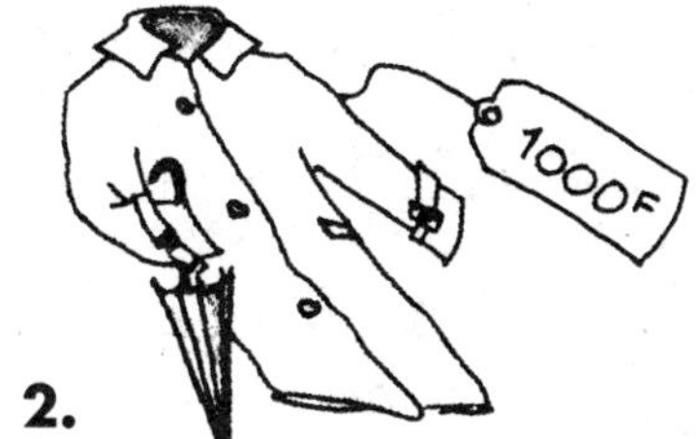

3. 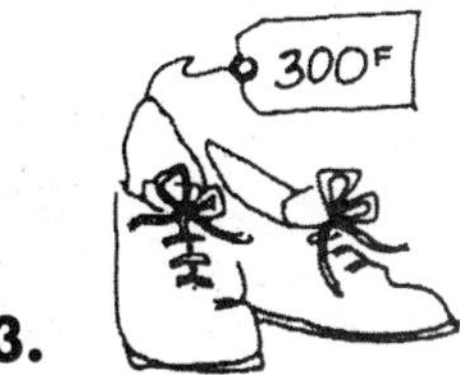

Section 6 Comment trouves-tu ma robe?

F. *Compréhension orale*

a. ____ 

b. ____ 

c. ____ 

d. ____ 

CASSETTE WORKSHEET Leçon 25 (cont.)

À votre tour!

Section 7. La bonne réponse

 Allez à la page 254.

Section 8. Créa-dialogue

 Allez à la page 254.

Section 9. Conversation dirigée

 Allez à la page 255.

Nom ______________________________

Classe ______________________ Date ______________

DISCOVERING FRENCH - *BLEU*

UNITÉ 7

CASSETTE WORKSHEET Leçon 26 Rien n'est parfait

Section 1 Rien n'est parfait

A. *Compréhension orale*

Cet après-midi, Frédéric et Jean-Claude vont acheter des vêtements. Ils vont acheter ces vêtements dans un grand magasin. Ce magasin s'appelle Le Bon Marché.

Frédéric et Jean-Claude regardent les pulls.

FRÉDÉRIC: Comment trouves-tu ce pull?
JEAN-CLAUDE: Quel pull?
FRÉDÉRIC: Ce pull bleu.
JEAN-CLAUDE: Il est chouette.
FRÉDÉRIC: C'est vrai, il est très chouette.
JEAN-CLAUDE: Il est aussi très cher.
FRÉDÉRIC: Combien est-ce qu'il coûte?
JEAN-CLAUDE: Six cents francs.
FRÉDÉRIC: Six cents francs! Quelle horreur!

Maintenant, Frédéric et Jean-Claude regardent les vestes.

FRÉDÉRIC: Quelle veste est-ce que tu préfères?
JEAN-CLAUDE: Je préfère cette veste jaune. Elle est très élégante et elle n'est pas très cher.
FRÉDÉRIC: Oui, mais elle est trop grande pour toi!
JEAN-CLAUDE: Dommage!

Frédéric est au rayon des chaussures. Quelles chaussures est-ce qu'il va acheter?

JEAN-CLAUDE: Alors, quelles chaussures est-ce que tu achètes?
FRÉDÉRIC: J'achète ces chaussures noires. Elles sont très confortables . . . et elles ne sont pas chères. Regarde, elles sont en solde.
JEAN-CLAUDE: C'est vrai, elles sont en solde . . . mais elles ne sont plus à la mode.
FRÉDÉRIC: Hélas, rien n'est parfait!

Section 2 Les verbes *acheter* et *préférer*

B. *Écoutez et répétez.*

 Allez à la page 258.

CASSETTE WORKSHEET Leçon 26 (cont.)

Section 3 **Comment trouves-tu ce pull?**

C. ***Écoutez et écrivez.***

▶ Dis Stéphanie! Regarde ___ce___ blouson.

1. Regarde __________ chapeau.

2. Qu'est-ce que tu penses de __________ chemise?

3. Regarde __________ chaîne!

4. Tu veux écouter __________ disque?

5. Regarde __________ voiture!

6. Regarde __________ sculpture!

7. Regardez __________ monument!

8. Eh! Regarde __________ fille là-bas!

9. Eh! Regarde __________ garçons.

Section 4 **Quel café?**

D. ***Compréhension orale***

a. ____ **b.** ____ **c.** ____ **d.** ____

CASSETTE WORKSHEET Leçon 26 (cont.)

Section 5 Quelle veste désirez-vous?

E. *Questions et réponses*

▶ —Quelle veste désirez-vous?
—Cette veste bleue.

1.

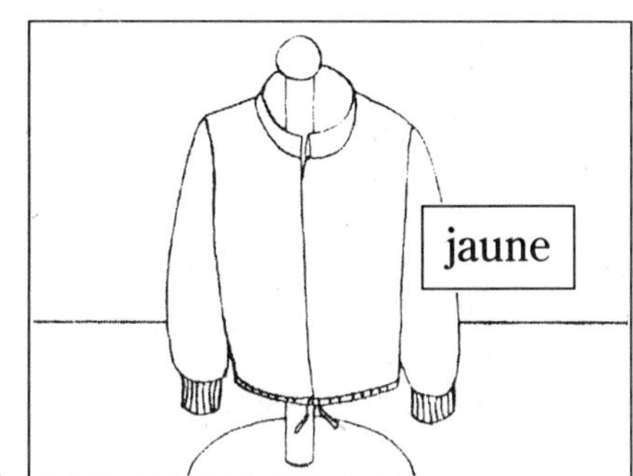

2.

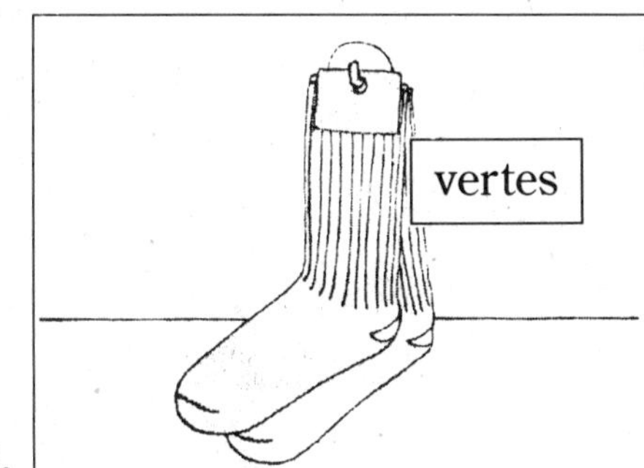

3.

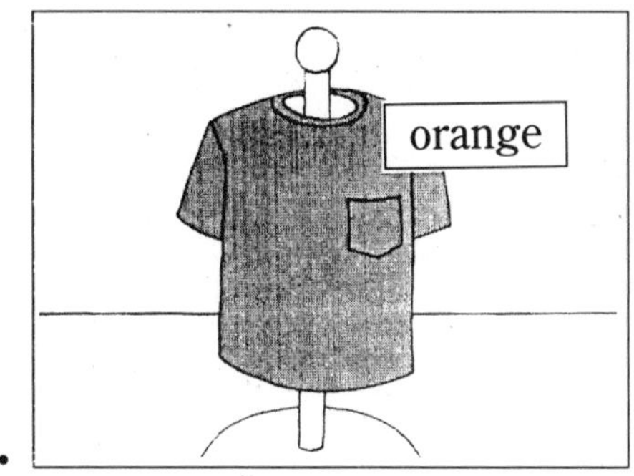

J'aime ce short-ci.
Eh bien, moi, je préfère ce short-là.

CASSETTE WORKSHEET Leçon 26 (cont.)

Section 6 Prononciation

F. ***Les lettres «e» et «è»***

Écoutez: **chemise** **chaussette** **chère**

Practice pronouncing "e" within a word:

- /ə/ (as in **je**) [. . . "e" + one consonant + vowel]

  Répétez: **chemise** **regarder** **Denise** **Renée** **petit** **venir**

Note that in the middle of a word the /ə/ is sometimes silent.

  Répétez: **achéter** **achétons** **améner** **samédi** **rarément** **avénue**

- /ɛ/ (as in **elle**) [. . . "e" + two consonants + vowel]

  Répétez: **chaussette** **veste** **quelle** **cette** **rester** **professeur** **raquette**

Now practice pronouncing "è" within a word:

- /ɛ/ (as in **elle**) [. . . "è" + one consonant + vowel]

  Répétez: **chère** **père** **mère** **achète** **amènent** **espère** **deuxième**

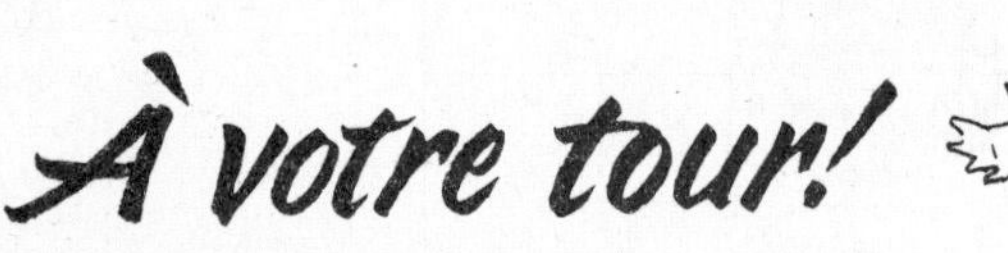

Section 7. La bonne réponse

 Allez à la page 264.

Section 8. Créa-dialogue

 Allez à la page 264.

Nom ______________________________

Classe ______________________ Date ____________

CASSETTE WORKSHEET LEÇON 27 Un choix difficile

Section 1 Un choix difficile

A. *Compréhension orale*

Delphine hésite entre une robe rouge et une robe jaune. Quelle robe est-ce qu'elle va choisir? Ah là là, le choix n'est pas facile.

VÉRONIQUE: Bon, alors, quelle robe est-ce que tu choisis?

DELPHINE: Eh bien, finalement je choisis la robe rouge. Elle est plus jolie que la robe jaune.

VÉRONIQUE: C'est vrai, elle est plus jolie . . . mais la robe jaune est moins chère et . . . elle est plus grande. Regarde. La robe rouge est trop petite pour toi.

DELPHINE: Mais non, elle n'est pas trop petite.

VÉRONIQUE: Bon, écoute, essaie-la!

Delphine sort de la cabine d'essayage.

DELPHINE: C'est vrai, la robe rouge est plus petite, mais ce n'est pas grave.

VÉRONIQUE: Pourquoi?

DELPHINE: Parce que j'ai un mois pour maigrir.

VÉRONIQUE: Et si tu grossis?

DELPHINE: Toi, tais-toi!

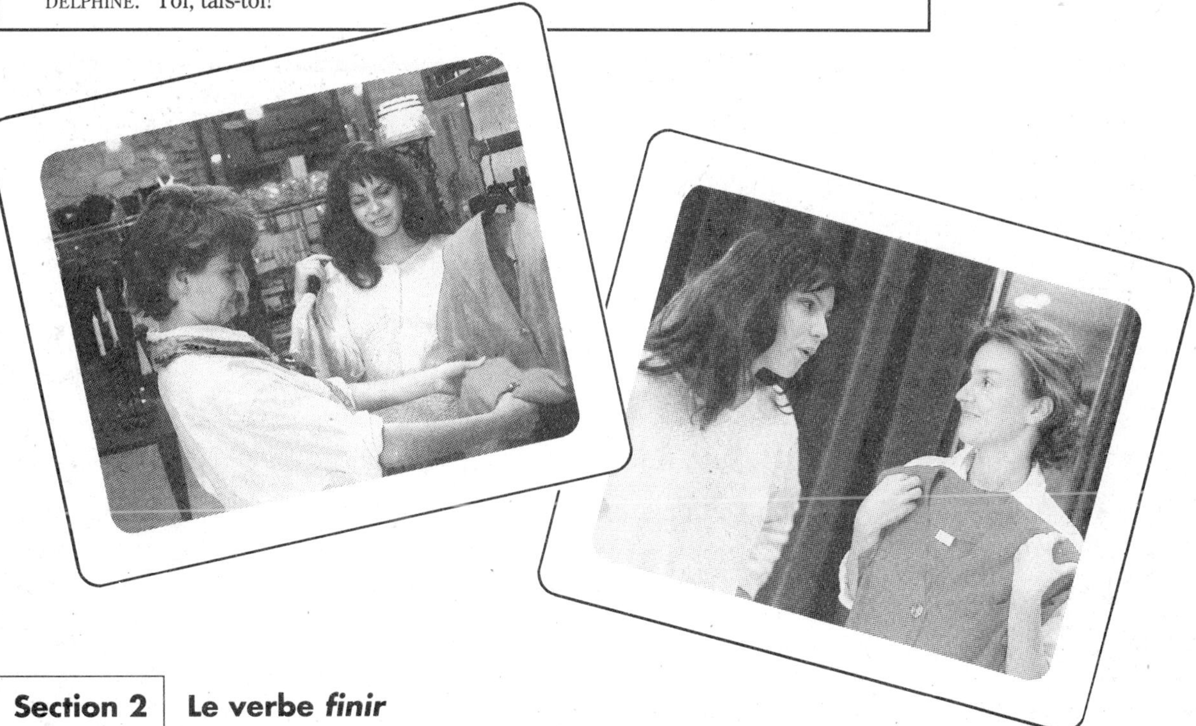

Section 2 Le verbe *finir*

B. *Écoutez et répétez.*

 Allez à la page 268.

Nom ______________________________

CASSETTE WORKSHEET Leçon 27 (cont.)

Section 3 **Comparaisons**

C. ***Compréhension orale***

▶ Les chaussures noires / ~~Les chaussures blanches~~ — sont plus confortables que — ~~les chaussures noires.~~ / les chaussures blanches.

1. Le chapeau vert / Le chapeau gris — est plus joli que — le chapeau vert. / le chapeau gris.

2. Le compact / La cassette — est moins cher (chère) que — le compact. / la cassette.

3. Le prof d'anglais / Le prof d'espagnol — est plus mignon que — le prof d'anglais. / le prof d'espagnol.

Nom ___________________________

CASSETTE WORKSHEET Leçon 27 (cont.)

Section 4 Comparaisons

D. ***Questions et réponses***

▶ —Est-ce que la veste bleue est plus chère ou moins chère que la veste jaune?
—**Elle est moins chère.**

▶

1.

2.

3.

CASSETTE WORKSHEET Leçon 27 (cont.)

Section 5 Prononciation

E. ***Les lettres «ill»***

Écoutez: **maillot**

In the middle of a word, the letters "**ill**" almost always represent the semi-vowel /j/ which is like the "**y**" of *yes*.

Répétez: **maillot travaillez oreille vieille**
fille famille juillet
En juillet, Mireille va travailler pour sa vieille tante.

At the end of a word, the sound /j/ is sometimes spelled **il.**

Répétez: **appareil-photo vieil travail**
Mon oncle a un vieil appareil-photo.

EXCEPTION: The letters **ill** are pronounced /il/ in the following words:

Répétez: **ville village mille Lille**

À votre tour!

Section 6. La bonne réponse

 Allez à la page 272.

Section 7. Créa-dialogue

 Allez à la page 272.

Nom ______________________________

Classe ____________________ Date __________

CASSETTE WORKSHEET Leçon 28 Alice a un job

Section 1 Dialogue: Alice a un job

A. *Compréhension orale*

Alice a un nouveau job. Elle travaille dans un magasin hifi. Dans ce magasin, on vend toutes sortes de choses: des chaînes stéréo, des mini-chaînes, des radiocassettes . . . On vend aussi des cassettes et des compacts. Un jour son cousin Jérôme lui rend visite.

JÉRÔME: Salut, ça va?
ALICE: Oui, ça va.
JÉRÔME: Et ce nouveau job?
ALICE: C'est super.
JÉRÔME: Qu'est-ce qu'on vend dans ton magasin?
ALICE: Eh bien, tu vois, on vend toutes sortes de matériel hifi . . . Moi, je vends des lecteurs compact-disc.
JÉRÔME: Tu es bien payée?
ALICE: Non, on n'est pas très bien payé, mais on a des réductions sur l'équipement stéréo et sur les compacts.
JÉRÔME: Qu'est-ce que tu vas faire avec ton argent?
ALICE: Je ne sais pas . . . J'ai envie de voyager cet été.
JÉRÔME: Tu as de la chance. Moi aussi, j'ai envie de voyager, mais je n'ai pas d'argent.
ALICE: Écoute, Jérôme, si tu as besoin d'argent, fais comme moi.
JÉRÔME: Comment?
ALICE: Cherche un job!

Section 2 Besoin ou envie?

B. *Compréhension orale*

		1	2	3	4	5	6
A	**besoin**						
B	**envie**						

CASSETTE WORKSHEET Leçon 28 (cont.)

Section 3 Qu'est-ce qu'on vend?

C. *Compréhension orale*

a. ____ b. ____ c. ____

Section 4 Qu'est-ce qu'on vend ici?

D. *Questions et réponses*

▶ —Qu'est-ce qu'on vend ici?
—On vend des chaussures.

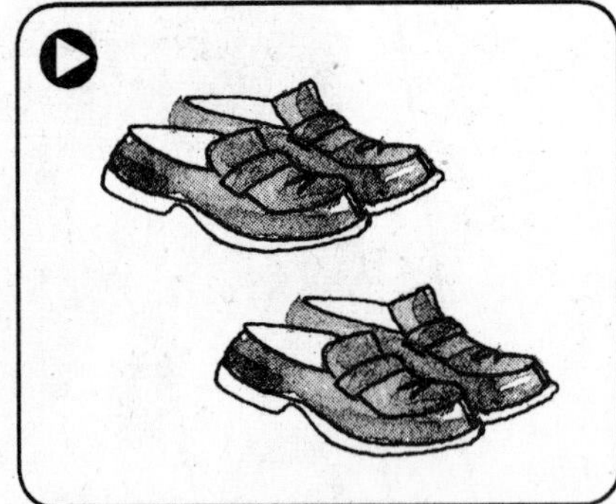

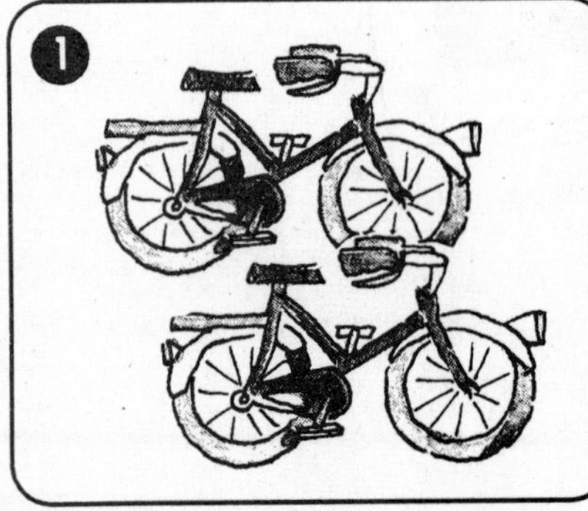

CASSETTE WORKSHEET Leçon 28 (cont.)

Section 5 On dîne?

E. *Compréhension orale*

a. ____ b. ____ c. 1

d. ____ e. ____ f. ____ g. ____

Section 6 On joue au tennis?

F. *Questions et réponses*

▶ —On joue au tennis?
—**D'accord! Jouons au tennis.**

Nom ____

CASSETTE WORKSHEET Leçon 28 (cont.)

Section 7 Le verbe *vendre*

G. *Écoutez et répétez.*

Allez à la page 280.

Section 8 Prononciation

H. *Les lettres «an» et «en»*

The letters "**an**" and "**en**" represent the nasal vowel /ɑ̃/. Be sure not to pronounce the sound "**n**" after the vowel.

Répétez:

/ɑ̃/ **enfant an manteau collants grand élégant**
André mange un grand sandwich.

/ɑ̃/ **enfant en argent dépenser attends entend vend envie**
Vincent dépense rarement son argent.

À votre tour!

Section 9. La bonne réponse

Allez à la page 284.

Section 10. Créa-dialogue

Allez à la page 284.

Nom ______________________________

Classe ____________________ Date ______________

UNITÉ 7

WRITING ACTIVITIES Leçon 25 Le français pratique: L'achat des vêtements

A/B **1. Une affiche de mode** *(A fashion poster)*

You are working in the ad department of a fashion designer. Complete the poster below with the names of the articles of clothing.

150 F

120 F

180 F

70 F

150 F

90 F

250 F

WRITING ACTIVITIES Leçon 25 (cont.)

2. Qu'est-ce que vous portez?

Describe in detail what you are wearing. Give the colors of each item of clothing. Then select two other people (one male and one female) and describe their clothes in the same manner.

▶ Aujourd'hui, je porte une chemise verte et jaune, un pantalon noir, . . .

1. Aujourd'hui, je porte ______________________________

____

2. ______________ porte ______________________________

____

3. ______________ porte ______________________________

____

WRITING ACTIVITIES Leçon 25 (cont.)

3. Les valises *(Suitcases)*

Imagine you are planning for four trips. Make a list of at least four items of clothing that you will pack in each of the following suitcases.

1. un weekend à la plage

2. un weekend de ski

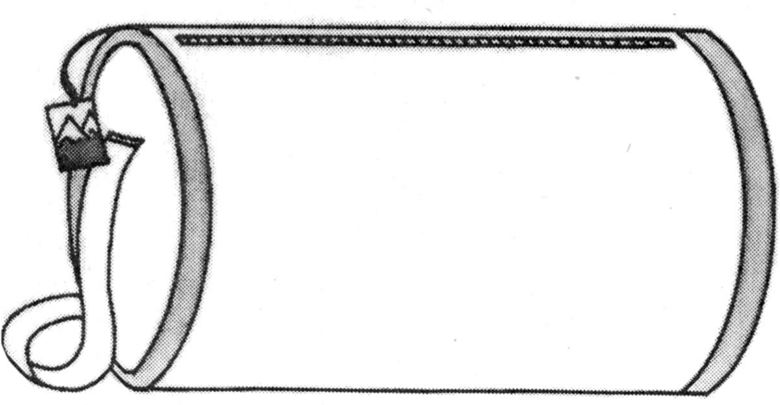

3. un mariage élégant

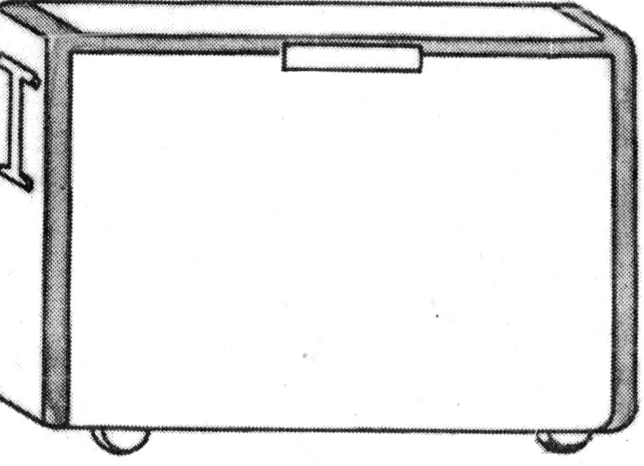

4. une semaine à Québec

WRITING ACTIVITIES Leçon 25 (cont.)

4. Conversations: Dans un magasin

Complete the dialogues on the basis of the illustrations. Use expressions from page 252 of your student text.

1. — Vous ______________________________ monsieur?
   — Je ______________________________.

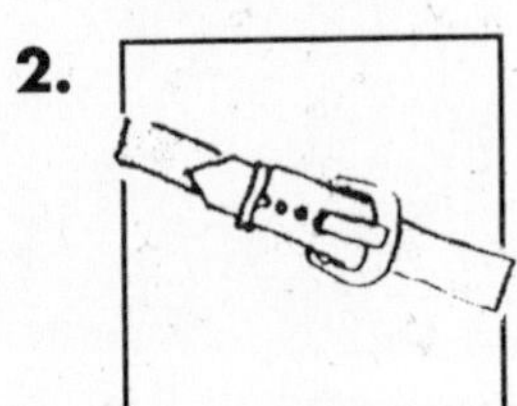

2. — Pardon, mademoiselle.
   Combien ______________________________?
   — ______________________________ francs.

3. — S'il vous plaît, monsieur, ______________________________
   ______________________________?
   — ______________________________.

4. — Est-ce que la robe est ______________________________?
   — Oh là là, non. Elle est très ______________________________.
   Elle coûte ______________________________ dollars.

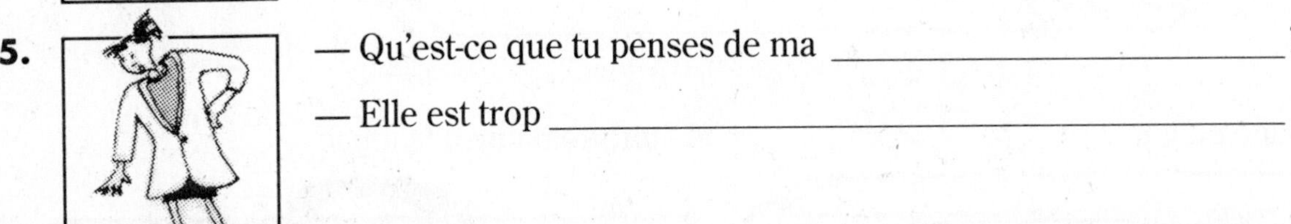

5. — Qu'est-ce que tu penses de ma ______________________________?
   — Elle est trop ______________________________.

6. — Comment ______________________________
   ______________________________?
   — Il est trop ______________________________.

Nom ______________________________

Classe ____________________ Date ____________

UNITÉ 7

WRITING ACTIVITIES Leçon 26 Rien n'est parfait!

A 1. Au centre commercial

Friends are shopping. Say what everyone is buying by completing the sentences with the appropriate forms of **acheter.**

1. Nous ______________ des vêtements.
2. Claire ______________ une ceinture.
3. Vous ______________ un walkman.
4. Virginie et Christine ______________ des compacts.
5. Tu ______________ une veste.
6. Marc ______________ un survêtement.
7. J' ______________ un sweat.
8. Mes copains ______________ des chaussures.

2. Une boum

Christine has invited her friends to a party. Some of them are bringing other friends. Others are bringing things for the party. Complete the sentences below with the appropriate forms of **amener** or **apporter.**

1. François ______________ des sandwichs.
2. Stéphanie ______________ un copain.
3. Nous ______________ des compacts.
4. Vous ______________ vos cousins.
5. Tu ______________ ta guitare.
6. Nous ______________ des copines.
7. Vous ______________ une cassette vidéo.
8. Marc et Roger ______________ leur soeur.

WRITING ACTIVITIES Leçon 26 (cont.)

B 3. Dans la rue

Olivier and Béatrice are walking in town. Olivier is pointing out various people and commenting on various things he sees. Complete his questions, as in the model.

▶ Tu connais ces filles ?

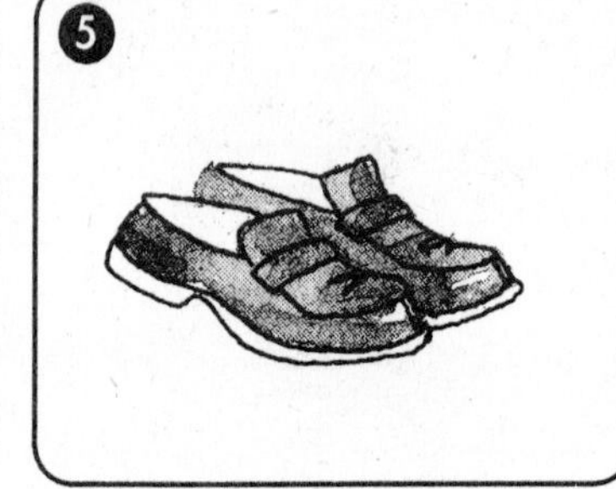

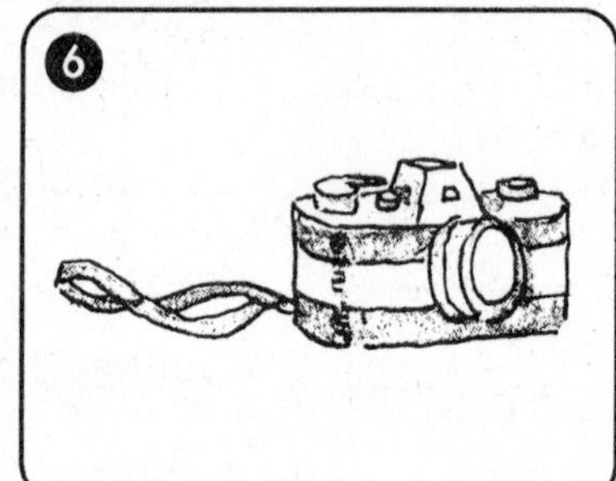

1. Qui sont ______________________________?
2. Regarde ______________________________!
3. Veux-tu aller dans ______________________________?
4. Regarde ______________________________!
5. Comment trouves-tu ______________________________?
6. Combien coûte ______________________________?

Nom ___________________________________

WRITING ACTIVITIES Leçon 26 (cont.)

B/C 4. Conversations

Complete the following mini-dialogues.

▶ — Quelle cravate préfères-tu?

— Je préfère cette cravate jaune.

1. —__________ imperméable vas-tu acheter?

   — Je vais acheter __________________ beige.

2. —__________ cassettes vas-tu écouter?

   — Je vais écouter __________________ de jazz.

3. —__________ blousons préfères-tu?

   — Je préfère __________________ bleus.

4. —__________ veste vas-tu porter pour la boum?

   —__________________ verte.

D 5. Qu'est-ce qu'ils mettent?

Read what the following people are doing or are going to do. Then complete the second sentence with the verb **mettre** and one of the items in the box. Be logical!

la table	**la télé**	**un maillot de bain**
la radio	**un survêtement**	**des vêtements élégants**

1. Julien va nager. Il __________________.
2. Vous allez dîner. Vous __________________.
3. Nous allons écouter le concert. Nous __________________.
4. Tu vas regarder le match de foot. Tu __________________.
5. Je vais faire du jogging. Je __________________.
6. Mes cousins vont à un mariage. Ils __________________.

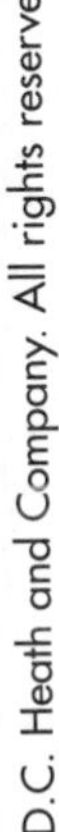

WRITING ACTIVITIES Leçon 26 (cont.)

6. Communication

Some French friends have invited you to a picnic.

Write a short paragraph saying . . .

- *what clothes you are going to wear to the picnic*
- *what items you are going to bring to the picnic*
- *whom you are going to bring along*

Nom ______________________________

Classe ______________________ Date ______________

WRITING ACTIVITIES Leçon 27 Un choix difficile

A 1. Au Bon Marché

The people below are shopping at Le Bon Marché. Say what each one is choosing, using the appropriate form of **choisir.**

1. Tu ______________________________.
2. Vous ______________________________.
3. Je ______________________________.
4. Nous ______________________________.
5. M. Voisin ______________________________.
6. Mme Lamy ______________________________.
7. Isabelle et Marthe ______________________________.

2. Oui ou non?

Read about the following people. Then describe a LOGICAL conclusion by completing the second sentence with the *affirmative* or *negative* form of the verb in parentheses.

▶ Alice fait beaucoup de jogging. Elle ne grossit pas. (grossir?)

1. Nous étudions. ______________ à l'examen. (réussir?)
2. Vous êtes riches. ______________ des vêtements chers. (choisir?)
3. Marc regarde la télé. ______________ la leçon. (finir?)
4. Mes cousins mangent beaucoup. ______________. (maigrir?)
5. Vous faites beaucoup de sport. ______________. (grossir?)
6. Les élèves n'écoutent pas le prof. ______________ à l'examen. (réussir?)

WRITING ACTIVITIES Leçon 27 (cont.)

B 3. Descriptions

Roger is describing certain people and things. Complete each description with the appropriate forms of the underlined adjectives.

1. Isabelle a beaucoup de beaux vêtements.

   Aujourd'hui elle porte une ________ jupe, un ________ chemisier et des ________ chaussures.

   Elle va acheter un ________ imperméable et des ________ pulls.

2. Mes cousins habitent dans une vieille ville.

   Dans cette ville, il y a un très ________ hôtel.

   Il y a aussi des ________ maisons, un ________ musée et des ________ quartiers.

3. Cet été, je vais acheter une nouvelle veste.

   Je vais aussi acheter un ________ maillot de bain, des ________ pantalons et des ________ chemises.

   Si j'ai beaucoup d'argent *(money)*, je vais aussi acheter un ________ appareil-photo.

C 4. Fifi et Nestor

Look at the scene and complete the comparisons, using the adjectives in parentheses.

(grand)	▶ Fifi est moins grand que	Nestor.
(sympathique)	1. Fifi ________	Nestor.
(méchant)	2. Fifi ________	Nestor.
(grande)	3. Mme Paquin ________	Catherine.
(jeune)	4. Mme Paquin ________	Catherine.

WRITING ACTIVITIES Leçon 27 (cont.)

5. Opinions

Compare the following by using the suggested adjectives. Express your personal opinions.

▶ un imper / cher / un manteau

Un imper est moins (aussi, plus) cher qu'un manteau.

1. une chemise / chère / une veste
2. une moto / rapide / une voiture
3. un chat / intelligent / un chien
4. le Texas / grand / l'Alaska
5. la Californie / jolie / la Floride
6. les filles / sportives / les garçons
7. la cuisine italienne / bonne / la cuisine américaine
8. les Royals / bons / les Yankees

WRITING ACTIVITIES Leçon 27 (cont.)

6. Communication: En français!

Make four to six comparisons of your own involving familiar people, places, or things.

▶ Ma soeur est plus jeune que mon frère. Elle est aussi intelligente que lui.

▶ Notre maison est moins grande que la maison des voisins.

____

____

____

____

____

____

Nom ______________________

Classe ______________ Date ______________

UNITÉ 7

WRITING ACTIVITIES Leçon 28 Alice a un job

A 1. Où?

Say where one usually does the activities suggested in parentheses. Choose one of the places from the box. Be logical!

▶ (étudier) On étudie à l'école.

1. (nager) ______________
2. (dîner) ______________
3. (jouer au foot) ______________
4. (acheter des vêtements) ______________
5. (parler français) ______________
6. (parler espagnol) ______________

- au Mexique
- en France
- au stade
- à la piscine
- à l'école
- au restaurant
- dans les grands magasins

B 2. Jobs d'été

The following students have jobs as salespeople this summer. Say what each one is selling.

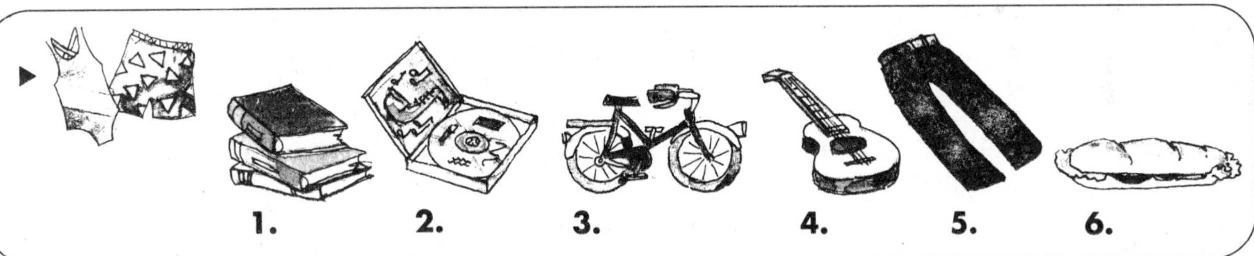

 vend des maillots de bain

1. Nous ______________.
2. Vous ______________.
3. Éric et Pierre ______________.
4. Tu ______________.
5. Je ______________.
6. Corinne ______________.

WRITING ACTIVITIES Leçon 28 (cont.)

3. Pourquoi?

Explain why people do certain things by completing the sentences with the appropriate form of the verbs in the box. Be logical!

• attendre	• répondre
• entendre	• vendre
• perdre	• rendre

1. Olivier ________________ son vélo parce qu'il a besoin d'argent.
2. Nous ________________ le match parce que nous ne jouons pas bien.
3. Vous ________________ correctement aux questions du prof parce que vous êtes de bons élèves.
4. Tu n' ________________ pas parce que tu n'écoutes pas.
5. Je ________________ souvent visite à mes voisins parce qu'ils sont sympathiques.
6. Martine et Julie ________________ leurs copains parce qu'elles ont un rendez-vous avec eux.

C 4. Oui ou non?

Tell a French friend to do or not to do the following things according to the situation. Be logical.

- ▶ (téléphoner) Ne téléphone pas à Sophie. Elle n'est pas chez elle.
- ▶ (inviter) Invite Jean-Paul. Il est très sympathique.

1. (acheter) ________________ cette veste. Elle est trop longue.
2. (choisir) ________________ ce tee-shirt. Il est joli et bon marché.
3. (attendre) ________________ tes copains. Ils vont venir dans cinq minutes.
4. (mettre) ________________ ce pantalon. Il est moche et démodé.
5. (aller) ________________ au cinéma. Il y a un très bon film.
6. (venir) ________________ chez moi. J'organise une boum.
7. (apporter) ________________ tes cassettes. Nous allons danser.
8. (manger) ________________ la pizza. Tu vas grossir.

Nom ______________________________

UNITÉ 7

WRITING ACTIVITIES Leçon 28 (cont.)

5. Au choix *(Your choice)*

Your friends have asked your advice. Tell them what to do, choosing one of the suggested options. If you wish, you may explain your choice.

▶ aller au théâtre ou au cinéma?

Allez au cinéma. C'est plus amusant (moins cher)!

(Allez au théâtre. C'est plus intéressant!)

1. regarder le film ou le match de baseball?

____

2. dîner à la maison ou au restaurant?

____

3. organiser une boum ou un pique-nique?

____

4. étudier le français ou l'espagnol?

____

6. Suggestions

It is Saturday. You and your friends are wondering what to do. Suggest that you do the following things together.

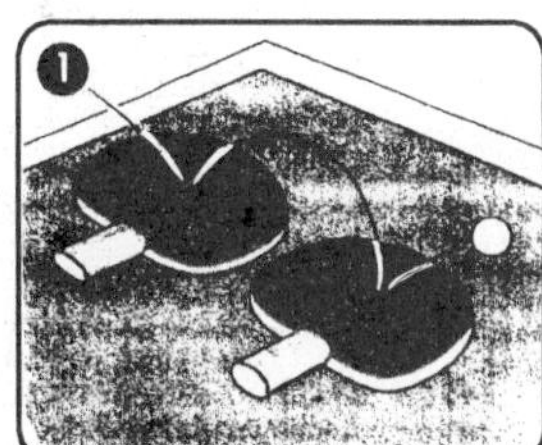

▶ Jouons au basket.

1. ______________________________
2. ______________________________
3. ______________________________
4. ______________________________
5. ______________________________
6. ______________________________

WRITING ACTIVITIES Leçon 28 (cont.)

7. Communication

Describe three things that you would like to do or buy, and say how much money you need to do so.

▶ *J'ai envie d'acheter un walkman.*

J'ai besoin de cinquante dollars.

1. ______________________________

____

2. ______________________________

____

3. ______________________________

____

Nom ______________________________

Classe ______________________ Date ____________

READING AND CULTURE ACTIVITIES Unité 7

A. Six boutiques

1.

PRIX SPECIAUX
JANVIER

Des exemples:

COSTUME pure laine 995 F
VESTE pure laine 790 F
BLAZER pure laine 775 F
PULLOVER laine d'agneau «Fabriqué en Ecosse» 255 F

ASTER hommes

2.

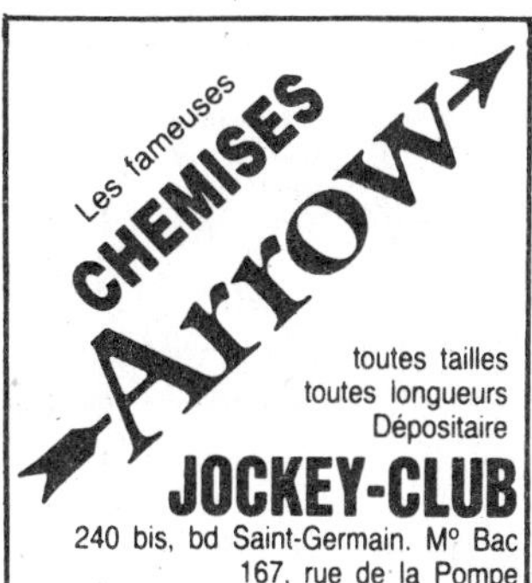

Les fameuses
CHEMISES
Arrow
toutes tailles
toutes longueurs
Dépositaire
JOCKEY-CLUB
240 bis, bd Saint-Germain. M° Bac
167, rue de la Pompe
Près avenue Bugeaud

3.

LUNETTES

EN VENTE CHEZ *TOUT POUR LA VUE*

4.

les cravates
JEAN
PATOU
sont en vente à
MADELIOS
PLACE DE LA MADELEINE - PARIS

5.

Chaussures
RALLYE

VILLE - SPORT - MONTAGNE
ARCUS - TECNICA

14, rue Royale, Annecy Tél. 50.45.09.88

6.

ouvre sa boutique

Maillots de bain, danse, jogging, ski
HOMMES - FEMMES - ENFANTS
4, rue de Sèvres PARIS 6e

- These six Paris shops are each advertising different things.
- Note that the ads have been numbered 1, 2, 3, 4, 5, and 6.
- Indicate where one would go to buy the following items by circling the number of the corresponding shop.

	BOUTIQUES					
a dress shirt	1	2	3	4	5	6.
a jacket	1	2	3	4	5	6
a swimsuit	1	2	3	4	5	6
an elegant tie	1	2	3	4	5	6
a man's suit	1	2	3	4	5	6
a pair of new glasses	1	2	3	4	5	6
a ballet leotard	1	2	3	4	5	6
a pair of walking shoes	1	2	3	4	5	6

READING AND CULTURE ACTIVITIES Unité 7 (cont.)

B. Les soldes

COLLECTION AUTOMNE - HIVER

-30% à -50%

BOUTIQUE HOMME	BOUTIQUE FEMME	BOUTIQUE SPORTSWEAR
CHEMISES à 49 Fr.	TUNIQUES à 69 Fr.	JEANS à 129 Fr.
PULLS à 99 Fr.	PULLS à 59 Fr.	SWEAT SHIRTS à 99 Fr.
VESTES " NEW LOOK " à 399 Fr.	PANTALONS à 69 Fr.	PANTALONS NEWMAN à 149 Fr.
PANTALONS LAINAGES à 99 Fr.	JUPES LAINAGE à 99 Fr.	BLOUSONS à 199 Fr.
PANTALONS (forme large) à 199 Fr.	ENSEMBLES à 199 Fr.	CHEMISES à 99 Fr.

353 , Rue de Vaugirard , PARIS 15 éme

OUVERT DE 9 H 30 à 19 H 30 - SANS INTERRUPTION

1. As you were walking down the Boulevard Saint-Michel in Paris, you were handed this flyer announcing a special sale. Read it carefully and answer the following questions.

- Comment s'appelle la boutique? ______________________________
- Quelle est l'adresse de la boutique? ______________________________
- À quelle heure est-ce que la boutique ouvre *(opens)*? ______________________________
- Combien coûtent les jeans? ______________________________

  Est-ce qu'ils sont chers ou bon marché? ______________________________

  (Note: $1 = approximativement 6 francs)

READING AND CULTURE ACTIVITIES Unité 7 (cont.)

2. You have decided to go shop at the Coroner. Imagine you have saved 500 francs to buy clothes. Make a list of what you are planning to buy and add up the total cost of your intended purchases.

Article	*Prix*
Prix total:	

3. You have tried on the items and they all fit well. You will buy all the things on your list. Write out a check for the total amount.

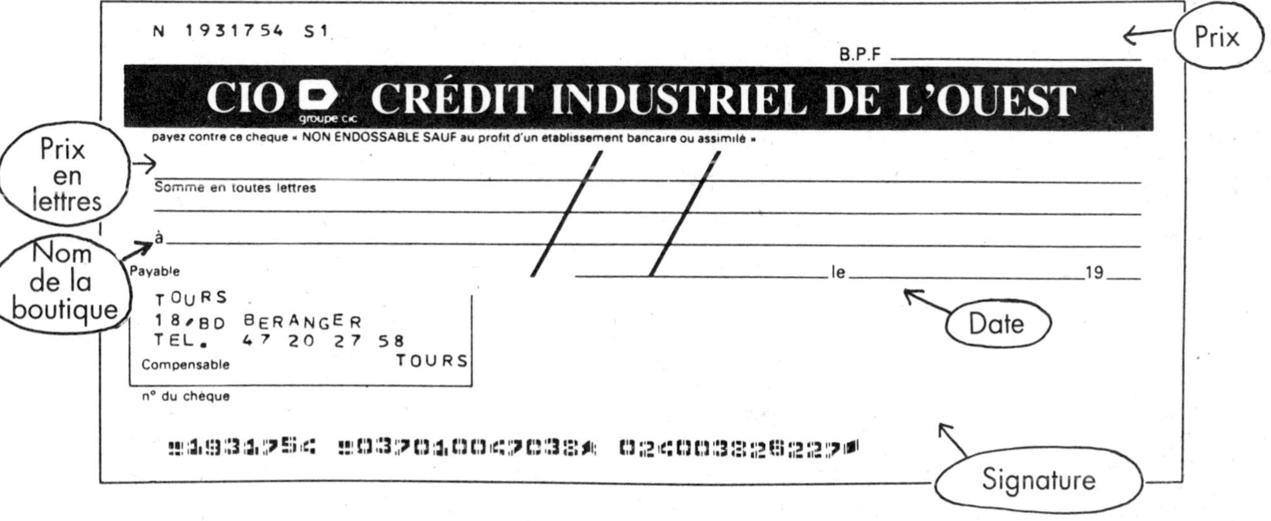

N 1931754 S1

B.P.F ____________________

CIO groupe CIC CRÉDIT INDUSTRIEL DE L'OUEST

payez contre ce cheque « NON ENDOSSABLE SAUF au profit d'un etablissement bancaire ou assimilé »

____

Somme en toutes lettres ____________________

à ____________________

Payable ____________________ le ____________________ 19____

TOURS
18/BD BERANGER
TEL. 47 20 27 58
Compensable TOURS

n° du chèque

⑈1931754⑆ ⑈037010047038⑉ 024003826227⑈

COMMUNICATIVE EXPRESSIONS AND THEMATIC VOCABULARY

Unité 7 Le shopping

▶ CULTURAL CONTEXT: **Buying clothes**

COMMUNICATIVE EXPRESSIONS

Telling a salesperson what you are looking for

Vous désirez?
Je cherche . . .
Je voudrais . . .

Asking how much an item costs

Combien coûte [ce pull]?
Combien coûtent [ces chaussures]?
Quel est le prix?

Asking a friend to give an opinion

Comment trouves-tu [cette chemise]?
Qu'est-ce que tu penses de [ce chapeau]?

Talking about specific items

Quel pantalon préfères-tu?
Je préfère ce pantalon bleu.

quel, quelle; quels, quelles
ce, cet, cette; ces

Making comparisons

Ce tee-shirt est	**plus joli que** **moins joli que** **aussi joli que**	**cette chemise.**
Le vélo rouge est	**meilleur que** **moins bon que** **aussi bon que**	**le vélo bleu.**

Indicating what you need and what you feel like having or doing

J'ai besoin de 5 dollars.
J'ai besoin de travailler.
J'ai envie d'une glace.
J'ai envie d'aller au café.

VOCABULARY

Clothing

les vêtements (m.)

un blouson
un chapeau
un chemisier
des collants
un imper(méable)
un jean
un manteau
un pantalon
un polo
un pull
des chaussettes (f.)
une chemise
une cravate
une jupe
une robe
une veste

les vêtements de sport

un jogging
un maillot de bain
un short
un survêtement
un sweat
un tee-shirt

COMMUNICATIVE EXPRESSIONS AND THEMATIC VOCABULARY

VOCABULARY *(continued)*

Clothing (cont.)

les chaussures (f.)

- **des baskets** (m.)
- **des tennis** (m.)
- **des bottes** (f.)
- **des sandales** (f.)

les accessoires (m.)

- **une ceinture**
- **des lunettes** (f.)
- **des lunettes** (f.) **de soleil**

Stores and shops

un magasin
un grand magasin
une boutique

Describing clothes

beau, belle
nouveau, nouvelle
vieux, vieille

bon marché
cher, chère
court
élégant
grand

joli
long, longue
moche
petit

à la mode
chouette
démodé
super

Money

l'argent (m.)
un billet
un prix

une pièce *(coin)*

pauvre
riche

combien?
combien de . . . ?

Some verbs

• *shopping*

acheter
chercher
porter
trouver
choisir
mettre *(to wear)*

• *earning and spending money*

coûter
dépenser
gagner
payer
vendre

• *other verbs*

apporter
penser

amener
préférer
espérer

finir
grossir
maigrir
réussir
réussir à un examen

attendre
entendre
perdre
rendre visite à
répondre à

avoir besoin
avoir envie

mettre *(to put, place, turn on)*

Numbers: 100–1000

cent
cent un
cent deux
cent dix

deux cents
deux cent cinquante
trois cents
sept cent soixante-quinze

mille

Other words and expressions

on
trop
eh bien!
à mon avis
c'est une bonne idée!

UNITÉ 8
Le temps libre

LISTENING ACTIVITIES
Leçons 29–32

WRITING ACTIVITIES
Leçons 29–32

READING AND CULTURE ACTIVITIES
Unité 8

POUR
COMMUNIQUER

Communicative Expressions and Thematic Vocabulary

Nom ______________________________

Classe ____________________ Date ____________

CASSETTE WORKSHEET Leçon 29 Le français pratique: Le weekend et les vacances

Section 1 Que faites-vous le weekend?

A. *Compréhension orale*

▶ Nathalie — d.

d. 

a. 

1. Olivier

2. François et André

3. Stéphanie, Dominique et Philippe

4. Henri et Laure

5. Monique

6. Jean-Paul

e. 

b. 

f. 

c. 

g.

Nom ______________________________

UNITÉ 8

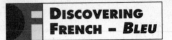

CASSETTE WORKSHEET Leçon 29 (cont.)

Section 2 Dialogue: Le weekend

B. *Compréhension orale*

		Conversation A	Conversation B
1	aller en ville		
2	aller à la campagne		
3	aller au cinéma		
4	rester à la maison		
5	faire un pique-nique		
6	faire les devoirs		
7	faire des achats		
8	faire du jogging		

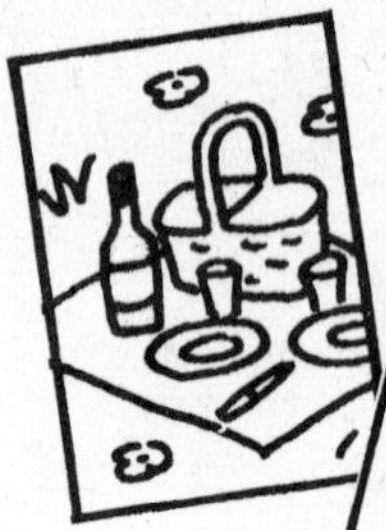
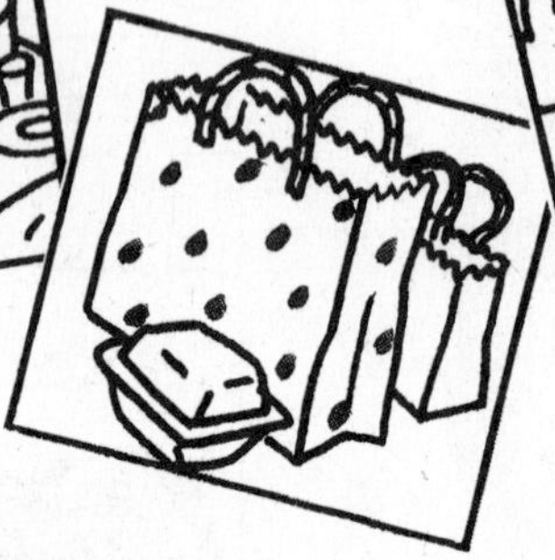
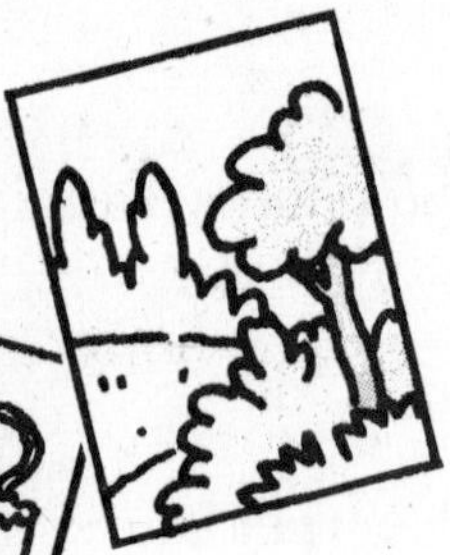
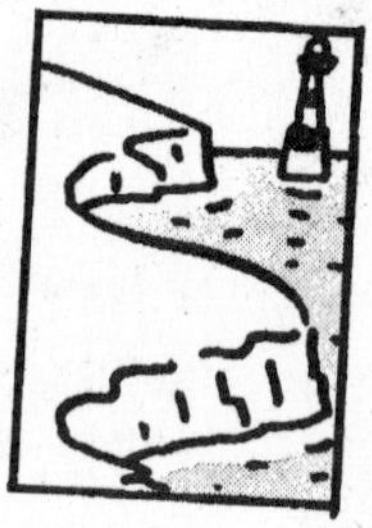
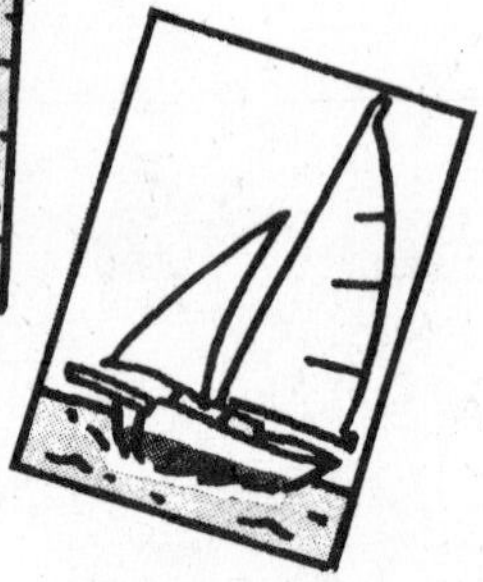
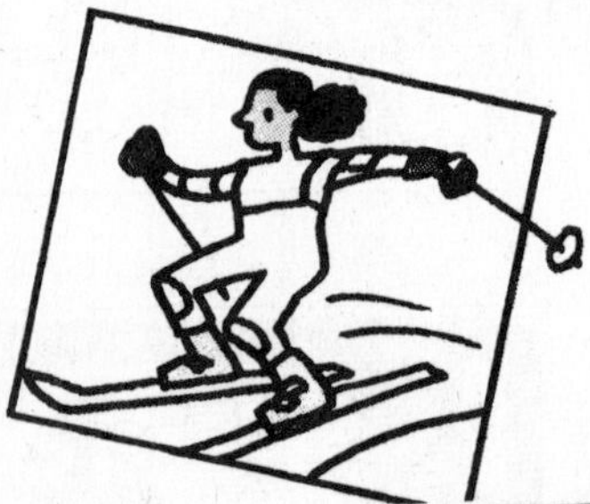
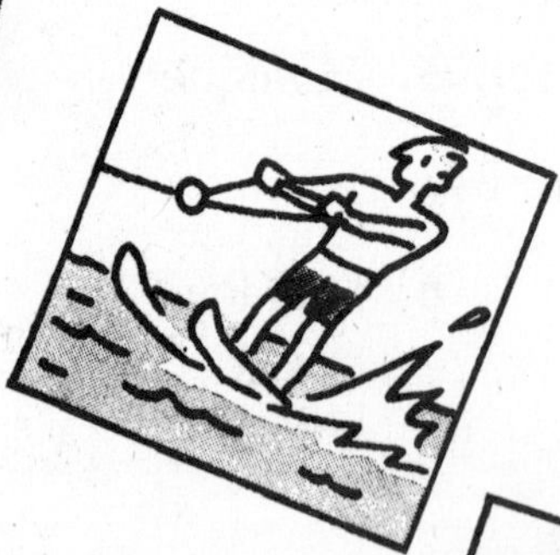
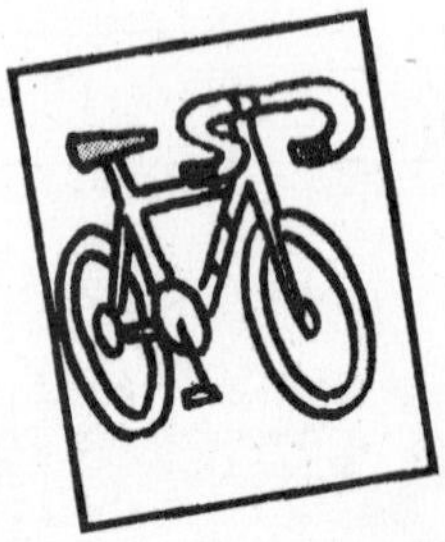
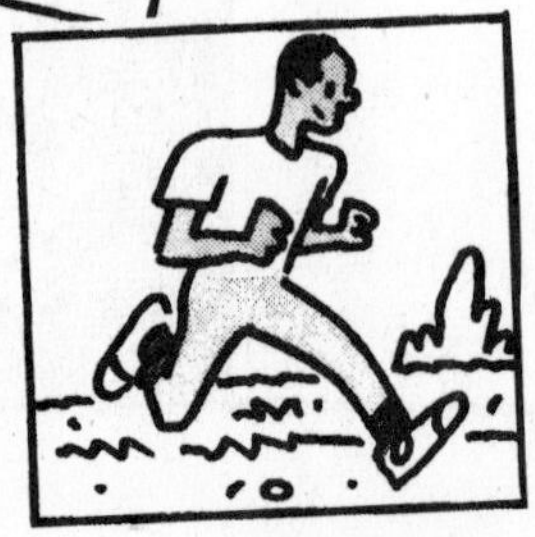
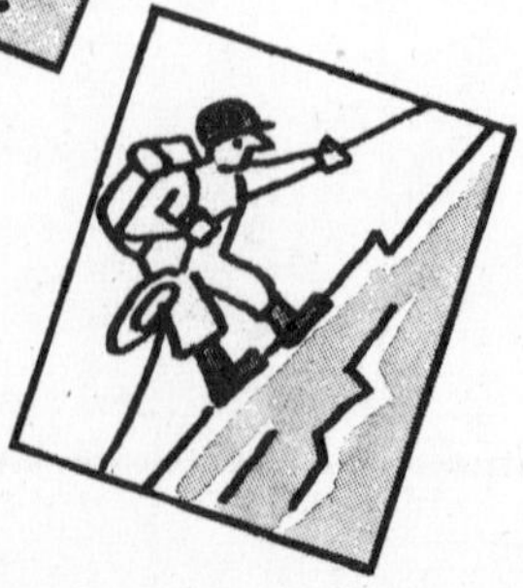

Nom ______________________________

CASSETTE WORKSHEET Leçon 29 (cont.)

Section 3 Samedi

C. *Questions et réponses*

▶ —Est-ce que tu vas nettoyer ta chambre samedi?
—**Oui, je vais nettoyer ma chambre.**
(Non, je ne vais pas nettoyer ma chambre.)

Section 4 Dialogue: Les vacances

D. *Compréhension orale*

		Conversation A	Conversation B
1	faire des promenades en bateau		
2	faire des promenades à vélo		
3	faire des promenades à pied		
4	faire de la planche à voile		
5	faire de l'alpinisme		
6	faire du ski nautique		

UNITÉ 8

CASSETTE WORKSHEET Leçon 29 (cont.)

Section 5 Qu'est-ce qu'il fait?

E. ***Questions et réponses***

▶ —Qu'est-ce qu'il fait? du vélo ou du jogging?
—Il fait du vélo.

À votre tour!

Section 6. Créa-dialogue

 Allez à la page 304.

Section 7. Conversation dirigée

 Allez à la page 304.

Nom ______________________________

Classe ____________________ Date ____________

CASSETTE WORKSHEET Leçon 30 Vive le weekend!

Section 1 Vive le weekend!

A. ***Compréhension orale***

Le weekend, nous avons nos occupations préférées. Certaines personnes aiment aller en ville et rencontrer leurs amis. D'autres préfèrent rester à la maison et bricoler. Qu'est-ce que les personnes suivantes ont fait le weekend dernier?

J'aime acheter des vêtements.	J'ai acheté des vêtements.
Tu aimes réparer ton vélo.	Tu as réparé ton vélo.
M. Lambert aime travailler dans le jardin.	Il a travaillé dans le jardin.
Nous aimons organiser des boums.	Nous avons organisé une boum.
Vous aimez jouer au foot.	Vous avez joué au foot.
Pluton et Philibert aiment rencontrer leurs amis.	Ils ont rencontré leurs amis.

B. ***Écoutez et répétez.***

Section 2 Qu'est-ce que tu as?

C. ***Écoutez et répétez.***

Allez à la page 308.

Section 3 Qu'est-ce que vous avez fait hier?

D. ***Compréhension orale***

		▶	▶	1	2	3	4	5	6	7	8	9	10	11	12	13	14
A	oui	✓															
B	non		✓														

CASSETTE WORKSHEET Leçon 30 (cont.)

Section 4 **Est-ce que tu as joué au tennis?**

E. *Compréhension orale*

a. ____

b. ____

c. ____

d. ____

e. ____

Nom ____________________

CASSETTE WORKSHEET Leçon 30 (cont.)

Section 5 Est-ce que tu as joué au tennis?

F. ***Questions et réponses***

▶ —Est-ce que tu as joué au tennis?
—Oui, j'ai joué au tennis. (Non, je n'ai pas joué au tennis.)

UNITÉ 8

Section 6 Mercredi après-midi

G. ***Compréhension orale***

Partie A. Mercredi

		Jean-Claude	Nathalie
1	Qui a passé l'après-midi dans les magasins?		
2	Qui a étudié tout l'après-midi?		
3	Qui a regardé les vêtements?		
4	Qui a acheté un compact?		
5	Qui a mangé un sandwich dans un café?		
6	Qui a étudié après le dîner?		
7	Qui a téléphoné à une copine?		
8	Qui a regardé un film à la télé?		

Partie B. Jeudi matin

Qu'est-ce que Jean-Claude a oublié? ____________________

Nom ________________________________

UNITÉ 8

CASSETTE WORKSHEET Leçon 30 (cont.)

Section 7 Prononciation

H. ***Les lettres «ain» et «in»***

Écoutez: **sa main semaine magasin magazine**

When the letters "**ain**", "**aim**", "**in**", and "**im**" are at the end of a word or are followed by a consonant, they represent the nasal vowel /ɛ̃/.

REMEMBER: Do not pronounce an /n/ after the nasal vowel /ɛ̃/.

Répétez: /ɛ̃/ **demain faim train main voisin cousin jardin magasin maintenant intelligent intéressant important**

When the letters "**ain**", "**aim**", "**in(n)**", and "**im**" are followed by a vowel, they do NOT represent a nasal sound.

Répétez: /ɛn/ **semaine américaine**

/ɛm/ **j'aime**

/in/ **voisine cousine cuisine magazine cinéma Corinne finir**

/im/ **timide dimanche Mimi centime**

Alain Minime a un rendez-vous important demain matin, avenue du Maine.

Section 8. Allô!

 Allez à la page 316.

Section 9. Créa-dialogue

 Allez à la page 316.

Nom ______________________________

Classe ______________________ Date ______________

CASSETTE WORKSHEET Leçon 31 L'alibi

Section 1 L'alibi

A. *Compréhension orale*

Êtes-vous bon détective? Pouvez-vous trouver la solution du mystère suivant?

Samedi dernier à deux heures de l'après-midi, il y a eu une panne d'électricité dans la petite ville de Marcillac-le-Château. La panne a duré une heure. Pendant la panne, un cambrioleur a pénétré dans la Banque Populaire de Marcillac-le-Château. Bien sûr, l'alarme n'a pas fonctionné et c'est seulement lundi matin que le directeur de la banque a remarqué le cambriolage: un million de francs.
Lundi après-midi, l'inspecteur Leflic a interrogé quatre suspects, mais chacun a un alibi.

SOPHIE FILOU:

Euh, . . . excusez-moi, Monsieur l'Inspecteur.
Ma mémoire n'est pas très bonne.
Voyons, qu'est-ce que j'ai fait samedi après-midi?
Ah oui, j'ai fini un livre.
Le titre du livre? Le crime ne paie pas!

MARC LAROULETTE:

Qu'est-ce que j'ai fait samedi?
J'ai rendu visite à mes copains.
Nous avons joué aux cartes.
C'est moi qui ai gagné!

PATRICK LESCROT:

Voyons, samedi dernier . . .
Ah oui . . . J'ai invité des amis chez moi.
Nous avons regardé la télé.
Nous avons vu le match de foot France-Allemagne.
Quel match! Malheureusement, c'est la France qui a perdu!
Dommage!

PAULINE MALIN:

Ce n'est pas moi, Monsieur l'Inspecteur!
Samedi j'ai fait un pique-nique à la campagne avec une copine.
Nous avons choisi un coin près d'une rivière.
Ensuite, nous avons fait une promenade à vélo.
Nous avons eu de la chance!
Il a fait un temps extraordinaire!

À votre avis, qui est le cambrioleur ou la cambrioleuse? Pourquoi?

UNITÉ 8

CASSETTE WORKSHEET Leçon 31 (cont.)

Section 2 Le verbe *voir*

B. ***Écoutez et répétez.***

Allez à la page 320.

Section 3 Qu'est-ce que vous avez fait?

C. ***Compréhension orale***

a. ____

b. ____

c. ____

d. ____

e. 1

f. ____

g. ____

Nom ____

CASSETTE WORKSHEET Leçon 31 (cont.)

Section 4 Est-ce qu'ils ont perdu?

D. *Questions et réponses*

▶ —Est-ce qu'ils ont perdu ou est-ce qu'ils ont gagné le match?
—Ils ont gagné le match.

Section 5 Dialogue: Pas de chance!

E. *Compréhension orale*

1. Hier Philippe a eu de la chance.	vrai	faux
2. Philippe n'a pas fait ses devoirs.	vrai	faux
3. Philippe a perdu son sac de classe dans l'autobus.	vrai	faux
4. Philippe a fait un match de tennis.	vrai	faux
5. Philippe a gagné son match.	vrai	faux
6. Philippe a fait une promenade à vélo.	vrai	faux
7. Philippe a eu un accident de vélo.	vrai	faux
8. Ce soir, Philippe va aller au concert.	vrai	faux

UNITÉ 8

Nom ______________________________

UNITÉ 8

CASSETTE WORKSHEET Leçon 31 (cont.)

Section 6 Prononciation

F. *Les lettres «gn»*

Écoutez: **espagnol**

The letters "**gn**" represent a sound similar to the "**ny**" in *canyon*. First, practice with words you know.

Répétez: **espagnol gagner mignon**
la montagne la campagne
un magnétophone

Now try saying some new words. Make them sound French!

Répétez: **Champagne Espagne** *(Spain)* **un signe**
la vigne *(vineyard)* **la ligne** *(line)* **un signal**
la dignité ignorer magnétique magnifique Agnès
Agnès Mignard a gagné son match. C'est magnifique!

Section 7. Allô!

 Allez à la page 326.

Section 8. Créa-dialogue

 Allez à la page 326.

Nom ______________________

Classe ______________________ Date ______________

CASSETTE WORKSHEET Leçon 32 Qui a de la chance?

Section 1 Dialogue: Qui a de la chance?

A. *Compréhension orale*

Vendredi après-midi

Anne et Valérie parlent de leurs projets pour le weekend.

ANNE: Qu'est-ce que tu vas faire samedi soir?
VALÉRIE: Je vais aller au cinéma avec Jean-Pierre.
ANNE: Tu as de la chance! Moi, je dois rester à la maison.
VALÉRIE: Mais pourquoi?
ANNE: Les amis de mes parents viennent chez nous ce weekend. Mon père insiste pour que je reste pour le dîner. Quelle barbe!
VALÉRIE: C'est vrai! Tu n'as pas de chance!

Lundi matin

Anne et Valérie parlent de leur weekend.

ANNE: Alors, tu as passé un bon weekend?
VALÉRIE: Euh non, pas très bon.
ANNE: Mais tu es sortie avec Jean-Pierre!
VALÉRIE: C'est vrai. Je suis allée au cinéma avec lui . . . Nous avons vu un très, très mauvais film! Après le film, j'ai eu une dispute avec Jean-Pierre. Et, en plus, j'ai perdu mon porte-monnaie . . . et je suis rentrée chez moi à pied! Et toi, tu es restée chez toi?
ANNE: Non.
VALÉRIE: Comment? Les amis de tes parents ne sont pas venus?
ANNE: Si, si, ils sont venus . . . avec leur fils!
VALÉRIE: Et alors?
ANNE: Eh bien, c'est un garçon très sympa et très amusant . . . Après le dîner, nous sommes allés au Zénith. Nous avons assisté à un concert de rock absolument extraordinaire. Après, nous sommes allés dans un café et nous avons fait des projets pour le weekend prochain.
VALÉRIE: Qu'est-ce que vous allez faire?
ANNE: Nous allons faire une promenade à la campagne dans la nouvelle voiture de sport de Thomas. (C'est le nom de mon nouveau copain!)
VALÉRIE: Toi, vraiment, tu as de la chance!

UNITÉ 8

Section 2 Où êtes-vous allé? Et qu'est-ce que vous avez fait?

B. *Compréhension orale*

a. ____

b. ____

c. ____

d. ____

e. ____

f. ____

g. ____

h. 1

i. ____

j. ____

UNITÉ 8

CASSETTE WORKSHEET Leçon 32 (cont.)

Section 3 Où est-ce qu'ils sont allés?

C. *Questions et réponses*

▶ —Où est-ce qu'ils sont allés hier? au club de gymnastique ou au restaurant?
—Ils sont allés au restaurant.

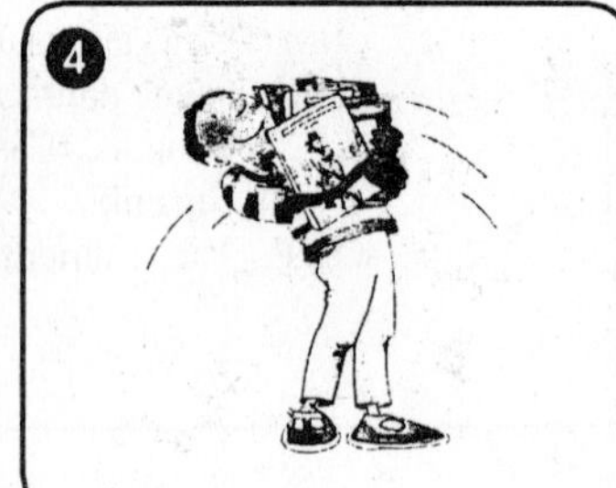

Section 4 Dialogue: Un bon weekend

D. *Compréhension orale*

1. Véronique a passé un bon weekend.	vrai	faux
2. Véronique est allée dans les magasins.	vrai	faux
3. Véronique est allée au théâtre.	vrai	faux
4. Véronique a rencontré son cousin Simon.	vrai	faux
5. Véronique est rentrée chez elle à minuit.	vrai	faux
6. Alice est restée chez elle.	vrai	faux
7. Alice est restée seule.	vrai	faux
8. Alice a passé la soirée avec Christophe.	vrai	faux

CASSETTE WORKSHEET Leçon 32 (cont.)

Section 5 Interview: La musique

E. ***Compréhension orale***

a. Paula Abdul b. Johnny Halliday c. Billy Idol d. Michael Jackson e. Prince	f. le disco g. le heavy metal h. le jazz i. le reggae j. le rock k. la musique pop

UNITÉ 8

1. —Qu'est-ce que vous venez écouter aujourd'hui?

—__________ .

2. —Et quelle sorte de musique est-ce que tu aimes?

—Ah, la musique de tous les jours, __________ .

3. —J'aime bien __________ et __________ .

4. —Quelle sorte de musique est-ce que vous aimez?

—Moi, j'aime bien __________ .

—Et moi, __________ , plutôt.

Les Rolling Stones
à Paris
Au Parc des Princes
le 23 juin

5. —Et est-ce que tu aimes les vedettes américaines?

—Oui, bien sûr.

—Lesquelles?

—J'aime bien __________ et __________ .

—Est-ce que tu vas souvent au concert?

—Une fois, de temps en temps, mais j'aime mieux écouter les compacts.

6. —Est-ce que tu vas souvent au concert?

—Quand je peux, de temps en temps; l'année dernière j'étais allé voir __________ au parc des Princes.

CASSETTE WORKSHEET Leçon 32 (cont.)

Section 6 Prononciation

F. ***Les lettres «qu»***

Écoutez: **un bouquet**

The letters "**qu**" represent the sound /k/. First, practice with words you know.

Répétez: **qui quand quelque chose quelqu'un quatre quatorze Québec Monique Véronique sympathique un pique-nique le ski nautique**

Now try reading some new words. Make them sound French!

Répétez: **un bouquet un banquet la qualité la quantité la conséquence une équipe** *(team)* **l'équipement fréquent la séquence**
Véronique pense que Monique aime la musique classique.

Section 7 Allô!

Allez à la page 336.

Section 8. Créa-dialogue

Allez à la page 336.

WRITING ACTIVITIES Leçon 29 Le français pratique: Le weekend et les vacances

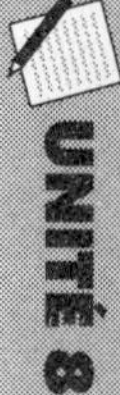

A/B 1. L'intrus *(The intruder)*

Each of the following sentences can be logically completed by three of the four suggested options. The option that does not fit is the intruder. Cross it out.

1. Je ne peux pas aller au cinéma avec toi. Je dois nettoyer . . .
   - ma chambre
   - la cuisine
   - les devoirs
   - le garage
2. Ce soir, je vais . . . mes copains.
   - inviter
   - téléphoner à
   - rencontrer
   - laver
3. Philippe est à la maison. Il . . . ses parents.
   - assiste à
   - parle avec
   - aide
   - prépare le dîner pour
4. Madame Halimi est dans le garage. Elle . . . sa voiture.
   - lave
   - répare
   - nettoie
   - rencontre
5. Frédéric est à la bibliothèque. Il . . .
   - étudie
   - choisit un livre
   - fait des achats
   - fait ses devoirs
6. Alice n'est pas chez elle. Elle assiste à . . .
   - une boutique
   - un concert
   - un récital
   - un match de foot
7. Nous allons à la campagne pour faire . . .
   - un pique-nique
   - les devoirs
   - une promenade à pied
   - une promenade à vélo
8. Marc va en ville. Il va . . .
   - faire de la voile
   - rencontrer des copains
   - voir un film
   - acheter des vêtements
9. On peut aller de Dallas à San Francisco . . .
   - en autocar
   - en voiture
   - en bateau
   - en avion
10. À la mer, on peut faire . . .
    - de l'alpinisme
    - de la voile
    - du ski nautique
    - de la planche à voile
11. À la montagne, on peut faire . . .
    - du ski
    - du ski nautique
    - de l'alpinisme
    - des promenades à pied
12. Cet été, je vais . . . un mois en France.
    - rester
    - passer
    - dépenser
    - voyager

WRITING ACTIVITIES Leçon 29 (cont.)

2. Les loisirs *(Leisure time activities)*

What do you think the following people are going to do during their leisure time? Complete the sentences logically.

▶ Béatrice va au centre commercial. Elle va faire des achats (acheter une robe . . .).

1. Philippe va au café. ______________________________
2. Valérie va au stade. ______________________________
3. Thomas et Christine vont au cinéma. ______________________________
4. Martin rentre chez lui. ______________________________
5. Cet été, Catherine va à la mer. ______________________________
6. Ce weekend, Isabelle va à la campagne. ______________________________
7. Pendant les vacances d'hiver, Jean-François va dans le Colorado. ______________________________
8. Pendant les grandes vacances, Daniel va à la montagne. ______________________________

3. Communication

In her last letter, your French pen pal Christine asked you several questions.

Answer them.

- En général, qu'est-ce que tu fais le weekend?
- Qu'est-ce que tu fais quand tu es chez toi le samedi?
- Qu'est-ce que tu vas faire le weekend prochain?
- Où est-ce que tu vas aller pendant les grandes vacances?

  Combien de temps est-ce que tu vas passer là-bas?

  Comment vas-tu voyager?

  Qu'est-ce que tu vas faire?

Nom ______________________________

Classe ____________________ Date ____________

WRITING ACTIVITIES **Leçon 30** Vive le weekend!

A 1. Pourquoi?

Read what the following people are doing and then explain why, using **avoir** and one of the expressions in the box.

▶ Alice mange une pizza. Elle a faim.

1. Je mets mon pull. ______________
2. Nous allons à la cafétéria. ______________
3. Tu ouvres *(open)* la fenêtre. ______________
4. Vous achetez des sodas. ______________
5. Robert fait un sandwich. ______________
6. Alice et Juliette vont au café. ______________

faim
soif
chaud
froid

B 2. Vive la différence!

People like to do similar things, but they do them differently. Explain this by completing the sentences below with the appropriate *passé composé* forms of the verbs in parentheses.

1. (visiter)

   À Paris, tu as visité Notre-Dame. Nous ______________ le musée d'Orsay. Ces touristes ______________ le Centre Pompidou.

2. (manger)

   Au restaurant, j'______________ des spaghetti. Tu ______________ une pizza. Mes cousins ______________ un steak-frites.

3. (travailler)

   L'été dernier, vous ______________ dans un restaurant. J'______________ dans un hôpital. Alain et Jérôme ______________ dans une station-service.

4. (acheter)

   Au centre commercial, Marie-Christine ______________ une veste. Tu ______________ des chaussures. Nous ______________ des lunettes de soleil.

Nom ______________________________

WRITING ACTIVITIES Leçon 30 (cont.)

3. Qu'est-ce qu'ils ont fait?

Last Saturday different people did different things. Explain what each one did by completing the sentences with the appropriate passé composé forms of the verbs in the box. Be logical.

acheter
assister
jouer
laver
nettoyer
rencontrer
travailler
visiter

1. Ma cousine ____________________ sa chambre.
2. Nous ____________________ à un match de foot.
3. Les touristes ____________________ le musée d'Art Moderne.
4. Pierre et Sébastien ____________________ leur voiture.
5. J' ____________________ mes copains au café.
6. Tu ____________________ au volley.
7. Vous ____________________ dans le jardin.
8. Catherine ____________________ des vêtements au centre commercial.

B/C 4. Et toi?

Say whether or not you did the following things last weekend.

1. ____

____

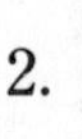

2.  ____

____

3.  ____

____

4.  ____

____

5. ____

____

6.  ____

____

WRITING ACTIVITIES Leçon 30 (cont.)

C 5. On ne peut pas tout faire. *(One cannot do everything.)*

Say that the people below did the first thing in parentheses but not the second one.

▶ (regarder / étudier)

Hier soir, Jean-Marc a regardé la télé.

Il n'a pas étudié.

1. (travailler / voyager)

   L'été dernier, nous ____________________.

   Nous ____________________.

2. (rencontrer / assister)

   Samedi, tu ____________________ tes copains en ville.

   Tu ____________________ au match de foot.

3. (nager / jouer)

   À la plage, vous ____________________.

   Vous ____________________ au volley.

4. (laver / nettoyer)

   J' ____________________ la voiture de ma mère.

   Je ____________________ ma chambre.

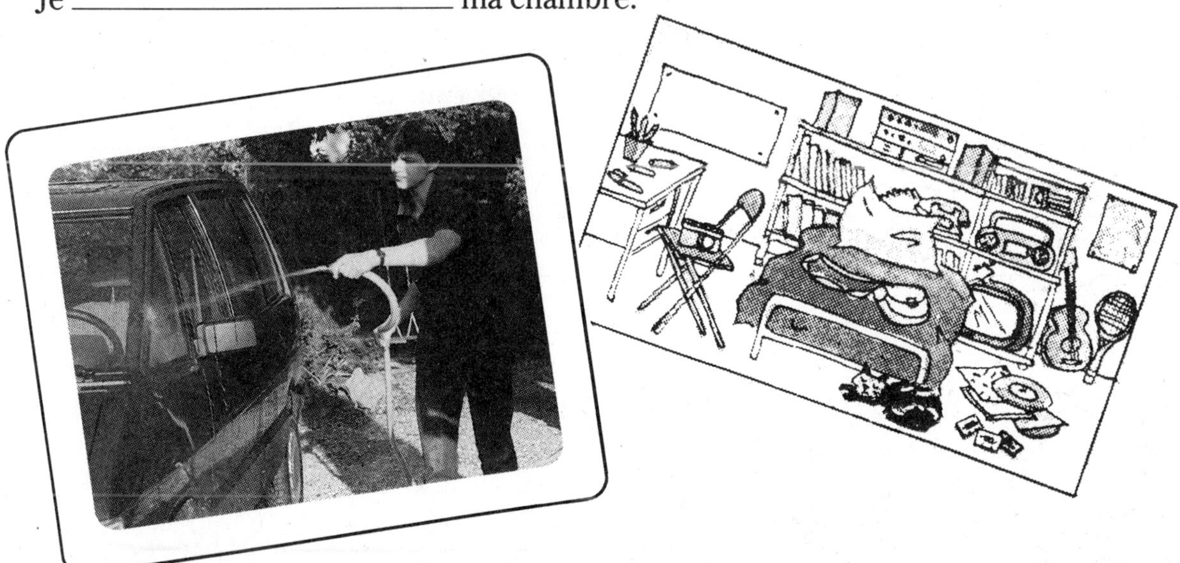

Nom ____

WRITING ACTIVITIES Leçon 30 (cont.)

D 6. Conversations

Complete each of the following mini-dialogues by writing in the question that was asked.

▶ (où / vous) — *Où est-ce que vous avez dîné* samedi soir?
—Nous avons dîné dans un restaurant vietnamien.

1. (à qui / tu) — ______________________________
—J'ai téléphoné à ma cousine.

2. (avec qui / Marc) — ______________________________ à la boum?
—Il a dansé avec Caroline.

3. (quand / vous) — ______________________________
—Nous avons visité Paris l'été dernier.

4. (où / Alice) — ______________________________
—Elle a rencontré Jean-Claude au Café de l'Univers.

7. Communication: Journal personnel *(Personal diary)*

Write a short paragraph in the passé composé saying what you did or did not do last weekend. You way want to use the expressions in the box as a guide.

étudier?	**travailler?**	**jouer: à quel sport?**	**téléphoner: à qui?**
inviter: qui?	**dîner: où?**	**regarder: quels programmes?**	**rencontrer: qui?**

____

____

____

____

____

____

____

____

Nom ______________________________

Classe ____________________ Date ______________

WRITING ACTIVITIES Leçon 31 L'alibi

A 1. Panorama

A group of friends in Normandy has gone on a bicycle ride along the cliffs. They have stopped at a turnout to rest and look at the view. Say what each one sees, using the appropriate forms of **voir.**

1. Alice __________ un petit village.
2. Nous __________ des bateaux.
3. Julien et Martin __________ la mer.
4. Tu __________ une belle maison.
5. Je __________ un car de touristes.
6. Vous __________ des campeurs.

B 2. Oui ou non?

Read about the following people and say what they did or did not do, using the passé composé of the verbs in parentheses, in the affirmative or negative form.

▶ Nous avons bien joué. Nous *n'avons pas perdu* le match. (perdre)

1. Marc n'est pas patient. Il ____________________ ses amis. (attendre)
2. Les élèves ont étudié. Ils ____________________ à l'examen. (réussir)
3. J'ai regardé la télé. Je ____________________ mes devoirs. (finir)
4. Éric n'écoute pas. Il ____________________ la question. (entendre)
5. Anne n'a pas bien joué. Elle ____________________ le match. (perdre)
6. Vous êtes végétariens. Vous ____________________ le steak-frites. (choisir)
7. Nous faisons beaucoup d'exercices. Nous ____________________. (maigrir)
8. Philippe est un bon élève. Il ____________________ à la question du prof. (répondre)

C 3. Et toi?

Say whether or not you did the following things yesterday evening.

▶ faire les devoirs? *J'ai fait les devoirs. (Je n'ai pas fait les devoirs.)*

1. mettre la table? ____________________
2. voir un film à la télé? ____________________
3. faire une promenade en ville? ____________________
4. être au cinéma? ____________________
5. avoir un rendez-vous? ____________________

Nom ____

WRITING ACTIVITIES Leçon 31 (cont.)

B/C 4. Pauvre Jérôme

Jérôme is not lucky. Describe what happened to him, by completing the following statements with the passé composé of the verbs in parentheses.

1. (vendre) Jérôme ______________________ sa moto.
2. (acheter) Il ______________________ une voiture.
3. (faire) Il ______________________ une promenade à la campagne.
4. (ne pas mettre) Il ______________________ sa ceinture de sécurité *(seatbelt)*.
5. (ne pas voir) Il ______________________ l'arbre *(tree)*.
6. (avoir) Il ______________________ un accident.
7. (être) Il ______________________ à l'hôpital.
8. (passer) Il ______________________ trois jours là-bas.
9. (vendre) Finalement, il ______________________ sa nouvelle voiture.

5. Communication

On a separate sheet of paper, describe several things that you did in the past month or so. You may use the following questions as a guide.

- As-tu vu un bon film? (Quel film? Où? Quand?)
- As-tu vu un match intéressant? (Quel match? Où? Avec qui?)
- As-tu eu un rendez-vous? (Avec qui? Où?)
- As-tu fait un voyage? (Où? Quand?)
- As-tu fait une promenade en voiture? (Où? Quand?)

Nom ____________________

Classe ____________________ Date ____________

WRITING ACTIVITIES Leçon 32 Qui a de la chance?

A 1. Où es-tu allé(e)?

Say whether or not you went to the following places in the past ten days. Use complete sentences.

1. au cinéma? ____________________
2. à la bibliothèque? ____________________
3. chez un copain ou une copine? ____________________
4. dans un restaurant mexicain? ____________________

2. Où sont-ils allés?

Read what the following people did last week and then say where they went, choosing a place from the box. Be logical.

à une boum	**à la campagne**	**au cinéma**
dans un restaurant italien	**à la mer**	**dans un magasin**

1. Pauline a vu un film. ____________________
2. Alain et Thomas ont fait de la voile. ____________________
3. Marc a acheté une veste. ____________________
4. Stéphanie a dansé. ____________________
5. Mes cousins ont fait une promenade à pied. ____________________
6. Mélanie et sa soeur ont mangé une pizza. ____________________

WRITING ACTIVITIES Leçon 32 (cont.)

UNITÉ 8

3. Voyages

The following people spent a month in France. Describe the things they did during their trip by using the passé composé of the verbs in parentheses. Be careful! Some of the verbs are conjugated with **être** and others with **avoir.**

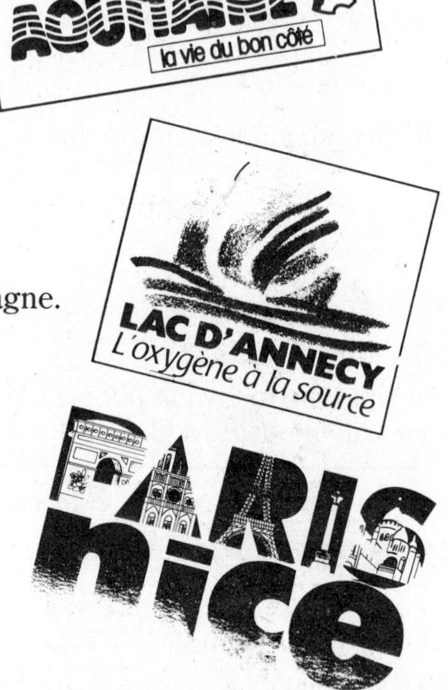

1. Nicolas (arriver / visiter / aller)

   Il ____________________ en France le 2 juillet.

   Il ____________________ Paris.

   Après, il ____________________ à Bordeaux.

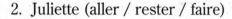

2. Juliette (aller / rester / faire)

   Elle ____________________ à Annecy en juin.

   Elle ____________________ quatre semaines là-bas.

   Elle ____________________ des promenades à la montagne.

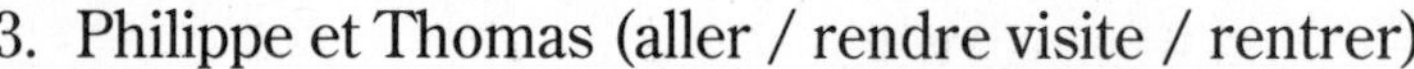

3. Philippe et Thomas (aller / rendre visite / rentrer)

   Ils ____________________ à Nice.

   Ils ____________________ à leurs cousins.

   Ils ____________________ chez eux le 15 août.

4. Hélène et Béatrice (venir / rencontrer / voyager)

   Elles ____________________ en France en juillet.

   Elles ____________________ des copains.

   Elles ____________________ avec eux.

WRITING ACTIVITIES Leçon 32 (cont.)

B 4. Vive les vacances!

Say that the people below never do the things mentioned in parentheses during their vacations.

▶ (travailler) — Monsieur Martin ne travaille jamais pendant les vacances.

1. (travailler) — Mes amis ______________________________.
2. (téléphoner à ses clients) — Le docteur Thibault ______________________________.
3. (aller à la bibliothèque) — Nous ______________________________.
4. (étudier) — Les élèves ______________________________.
5. (faire les devoirs) — Vous ______________________________.

C 5. Tant pis! *(Too bad!)*

Answer the following questions in the negative.

1. Philippe n'a pas faim. Est-ce qu'il mange quelque chose?

   Non, il ______________________________.

2. Julien n'est pas très généreux. Est-ce qu'il invite quelqu'un au restaurant?

   Non, il ______________________________.

3. Christine est fatiguée *(tired)*. Est-ce qu'elle fait quelque chose?

   Non, elle ______________________________.

4. Olivier est fauché *(broke)*. Est-ce qu'il achète quelque chose?

   Non, il ______________________________.

5. Alice est très entêtée *(stubborn)*. Est-ce qu'elle écoute quelqu'un?

   Non, elle ______________________________.

WRITING ACTIVITIES Leçon 32 (cont.)

6. Communication: Une page de journal *(A diary page)*
Write six sentences describing a recent trip . . . real or imaginary. You may want to answer the following questions — in French, of course!

- Where did you go?
- When did you arrive?
- How long did you stay?
- What/whom did you see?
- What did you visit?
- When did you come home?

Nom ______________________

Classe ______________ Date __________

READING AND CULTURE ACTIVITIES Unité 8

A. En vacances

1. On peut pratiquer les sports décrits dans cette annonce . . .
   - ☐ à la mer
   - ☐ à la montagne
   - ☐ dans une piscine
   - ☐ dans un stade

SPORTS

CERCLE NAUTIQUE MARTINIQUE

Ski nautique– Planche à voile–
parachute ascentionnel– Voiliers–
Locations Bateaux moteur avec ou sans permis

Tous les jours de 8h à 17h30 – Avant 8h sur R.V
Plage Hôtel Casino BATELIERE
Tél: 61 66 03 pour réservation

2. Les gens qui répondent à cette annonce vont . . .
   - ☐ faire une promenade à pied
   - ☐ aller à la campagne
   - ☐ rester dans un hôtel de luxe
   - ☐ faire une visite guidée en autocar

Visiter Montréal dans un autocar de luxe muni d'un toit vitré.

Découvrir Montréal, sa "Joie de vivre" et ses charmes par le service de tours guidés de Gray Line.

Tour de ville : 3 hres ; Adulte : 17$; Enfant : 8,50 $

INFORMATION • RÉSERVATION
(514) 934-1222

3. On peut pratiquer les activités décrites dans cette annonce . . .
   - ☐ à la mer
   - ☐ à la montagne
   - ☐ à la campagne
   - ☐ en ville

Sports

ALPINISME – ESCALADE
RANDONNEES
COMPAGNIE DES GUIDES
DE ST GERVAIS – VAL MONTJOIE

Promenade du Mont Blanc **50 78 35 37**
Du 15/6 au 30/6 de 15h30 à 19h.
Du 1/07 au 31/08:
de 10h à 12h et de 15h30 à 19h30.
Du 1/09 au 30/09 de 15h30 à 19h30.
Dimanches jours fériés de 16h à 19h30.
Ecole d'escalade de glace – Sorties Collectives – Stages – Randonnées en moyenne montagne.

UNITÉ 8

READING AND CULTURE ACTIVITIES Unité 8 (cont.)

4. Les touristes intéressés par cette annonce vont . . .
- ☐ visiter Paris
- ☐ visiter Rome
- ☐ voyager en train
- ☐ faire du camping

45 Rome par avion

Voyage Individuel d'avril à octobre 2 385 F

Hôtel standard

Départ de Paris le jour de votre choix. Retour à Paris le jour de votre choix (mais pas avant le dimanche suivant le départ).

Prix pour 2 jours à Rome (1 nuit) : 2 385 F. comprenant le voyage aérien en classe "vacances" (vols désignés), le logement en chambre double avec bains ou douche, le petit déjeuner.

Suppléments :
Chambre individuelle : 75 F par nuit.
Nuit supplémentaire : 235 F par nuit et par personne en chambre double avec petit déjeuner.
Vol "visite" : 300 F.

5. Pendant le voyage décrit dans cette annonce, qu'est-ce que les touristes *ne* vont *pas* faire?
- ☐ Faire une promenade en bateau.
- ☐ Voir des tulipes.
- ☐ Visiter Rotterdam.
- ☐ Voyager en avion.

28 Tulipe Express

Départ vendredi 2 mai 1 810 F

tout compris sauf boissons

Vendredi 2 mai : Départ de Paris gare du Nord vers 23 h en places assises de 2e classe.
Samedi 3 mai : Arrivée à Rotterdam tôt le matin. Visite du port en bateau. Petit déjeuner à bord. Visite de Rotterdam et promenade à pied dans le centre commercial. Visite de Delft (ville et faïencerie). Déjeuner à La Haye, découverte de la ville. Visite de Madurodam. Dîner à Amsterdam. Logement.
Dimanche 4 mai : Petit déjeuner. Visite d'Amsterdam et promenade en vedette sur les canaux. Déjeuner. Visite des champs de fleurs et de l'exposition florale du Keukenhof. Départ par train en places assises de 2e classe. Dîner libre. Arrivée à Paris-Nord vers 23 h.

Supplément chambre individuelle : **130 F.**
Supplément couchette à l'aller : se renseigner.

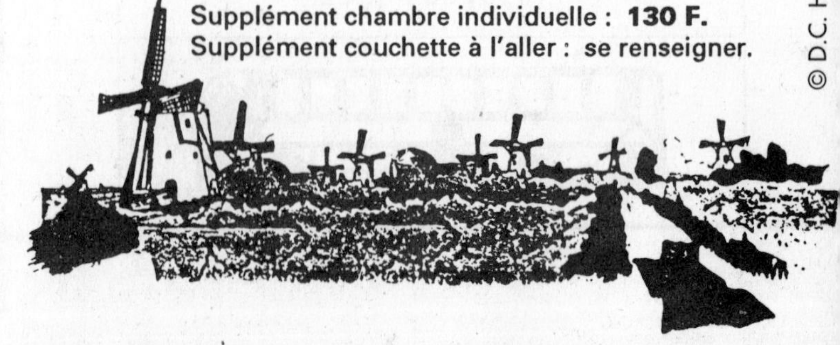

READING AND CULTURE ACTIVITIES Unité 8 (cont.)

B. À la télé ce soir

1. En France

20.40

CINÉMA OU TÉLÉVISION : TOUS LES SOIRS, UN FILM

CONAN LE BARBARE ★★★

AVENTURES. FILM DE JOHN MILIUS (ÉTATS-UNIS, 1981)

SCÉNARIO : JOHN MILIUS ET OLIVER STONE — DURÉE : 2 H 15

DIRECTEUR DE LA PHOTO : DUKE CALLAGHAN — MUSIQUE : BASIL POLEDOURIS

Conan .... Arnold Schwarzenegger
Thulsa Doom .... James Earl Jones
Le roi Ostric .... Max Von Sydow
Valeria .... Sandahl Bergman
Rexor .... Ben Davidson
La sorcière .... Cassandra Gaviola
La fille du roi .... Valérie Quennessen
Subotaï .... William Smith

Pour adultes et adolescents.

Conan (Arnold Schwarzenegger) et sa fameuse épée.

- Qu'est-ce qu'on peut voir à la télé ce soir? ____________________
- Comment s'appelle le film? ____________________
- Qui est l'acteur principal? ____________________
- Est-ce que c'est un film américain ou français?

  ____
- À quelle heure est le film? ____________________
- Regardez le texte sous la photo. Que veut dire «épée»? ____________________

READING AND CULTURE ACTIVITIES Unité 8 (cont.)

2. Au Canada

- Comment s'appelle ce film en français? ______________________________
- Quel est son titre anglais? ______________________________
- Qui est l'actrice principale? ______________________________
- Quel jour est-ce qu'on peut voir ce film? ______________________________
- À quelle heure est le film? ______________________________
- Regardez le petit texte.

  Le mot «cheminement» veut dire *path.* Peux-tu deviner *(guess)* l'équivalent anglais des mots suivants?

  l'esclavage = ________________

  la conquête = ________________

  la dignité = ________________

  une vedette = ________________

COMMUNICATIVE EXPRESSIONS AND THEMATIC VOCABULARY

Unité 8 Le temps libre

UNITÉ 8

▶ CULTURAL CONTEXT: Leisure time activities

COMMUNICATIVE EXPRESSIONS

Talking about what you did and where you went

Qu'est-ce que tu as fait?
J'ai voyagé.
Je n'ai pas travaillé.

Où est-ce que tu es allé(e)?
Je suis allé(e) à Québec.
Je ne suis pas allé(e) à Montréal.

Explaining why

Pourquoi est-ce que tu restes chez toi?
Je reste chez moi pour faire mes devoirs.

VOCABULARY

Leisure time and holidays

le weekend
les vacances
les grandes vacances
Noël
Pâques

Weekend activities

à la maison
aider
laver
nettoyer
préparer
réparer
faire les devoirs

en ville ou à la campagne
assister à un match
rencontrer [des amis]
voir un film
faire des achats
faire un pique-nique

Travel

aller | **à la mer**
| **à la montagne**

passer | **trois jours**
| **une semaine**
| **un mois**

rester à l'hôtel

voyager | **en avion** — **un avion**
| **en train** — **un train**
| **en autocar** — **un autocar, un car**
| **en bateau** — **un bateau**
| **en voiture** — **une voiture**

COMMUNICATIVE EXPRESSIONS AND THEMATIC VOCABULARY

VOCABULARY *(continued)*

Sports and outdoor activities

faire | **du jogging**	**l'alpinisme** (m.)	**la planche à voile**
de l'alpinisme	**le jogging**	**la voile**
de la voile	**le ski**	
	le ski nautique	
	le sport	

Expressions of time

maintenant	**avant**	**d'abord**
	après	**ensuite**
	pendant	**enfin**
		finalement

Other expressions of time

aujourd'hui	**hier**	**demain**
ce matin	**hier matin**	**demain matin**
cet après-midi	**hier après-midi**	**demain après-midi**
ce soir	**hier soir**	**demain soir**
samedi	**samedi dernier**	**samedi prochain**
ce weekend	**le weekend dernier**	**le weekend prochain**
cette semaine	**la semaine dernière**	**la semaine prochaine**
ce mois-ci	**le mois dernier**	**le mois prochain**

Expressions with ***avoir***

avoir chaud	**avoir froid**
avoir faim	**avoir soif**
avoir raison	**avoir tort**
avoir de la chance	

Someone, no one; something, nothing; often, never

quelqu'un	**ne . . . personne**
quelque chose	**ne . . . rien**
souvent	**ne . . . jamais**

UNITÉ 9
Les repas

LISTENING ACTIVITIES
Leçons 33–36

WRITING ACTIVITIES
Leçons 33–36

READING AND CULTURE ACTIVITIES
Unité 9

Communicative Expressions and Thematic Vocabulary

Nom ____________________

Classe ____________________ Date ____________

CASSETTE WORKSHEET Leçon 33 Le français pratique: Les repas et la nourriture

Section 1 Introduction: Où allez-vous quand vous avez faim?

A. *Compréhension orale*

a. ___

b. ___

c. ___

d. ___

e. ___

Section 2 Qu'est-ce que vous aimez manger?

B. *Compréhension orale*

a. ______ la glace à la vanille

b. ______ le jambon

c. ______ le pain, le beurre et la confiture

d. ______ le poisson, la sole et le thon

e. ______ les spaghetti et le fromage

f. ______ la viande, le poulet et le veau

g. ______ le yaourt

Nom ____________________

UNITÉ 9

CASSETTE WORKSHEET Leçon 33 (cont.)

Section 3 Vous préférez les frites ou les spaghetti?

C. *Compréhension orale*

	A	B
1.	les frites	les spaghetti
2.	le jus d'orange	le jus de pomme
3.	le fromage	le yaourt
4.	le gâteau	la glace

Section 4 Qu'est-ce que vous préférez?

D. *Questions et réponses*

▶ —Qu'est-ce que vous préférez? le gâteau ou la glace?
—Je préfère le gâteau.
(Je préfère la glace.)

▶  

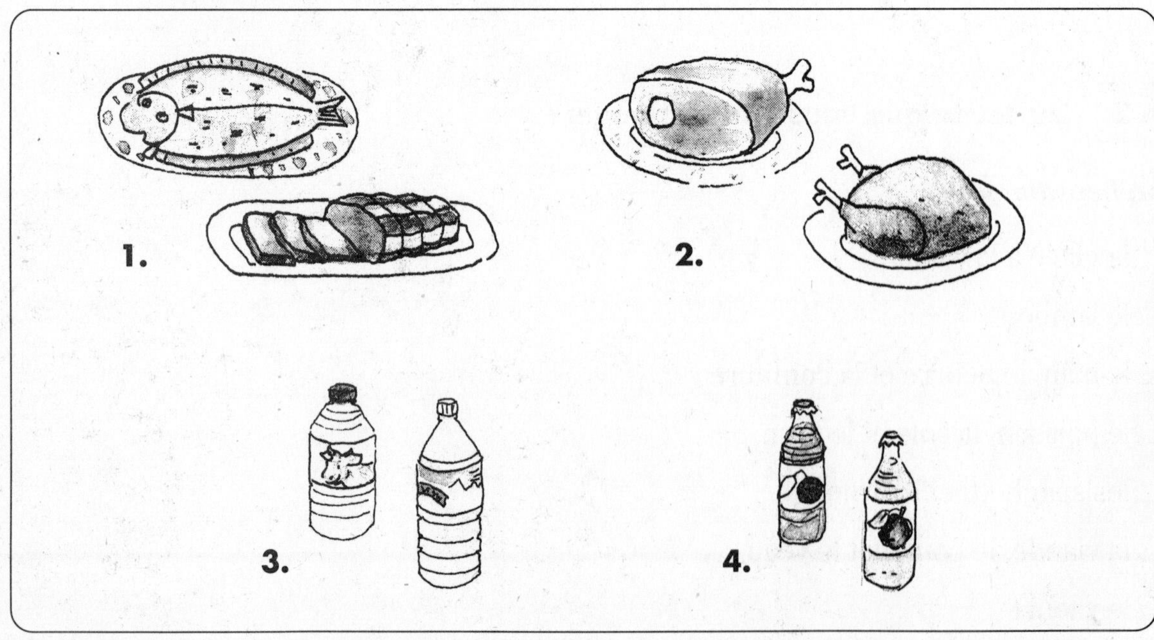

CASSETTE WORKSHEET Leçon 33 (cont.)

Section 5 Dialogue: Au marché

E. *Compréhension orale*

	A	B
1. des pommes:	un kilo	une livre
2. des haricots verts:	un kilo	une livre
3. des pamplemousses:	deux	dix

À votre tour!

Section 6. Créa-dialogue

 Allez à la page 356.

Section 7. Conversation dirigée

 Allez à la page 356.

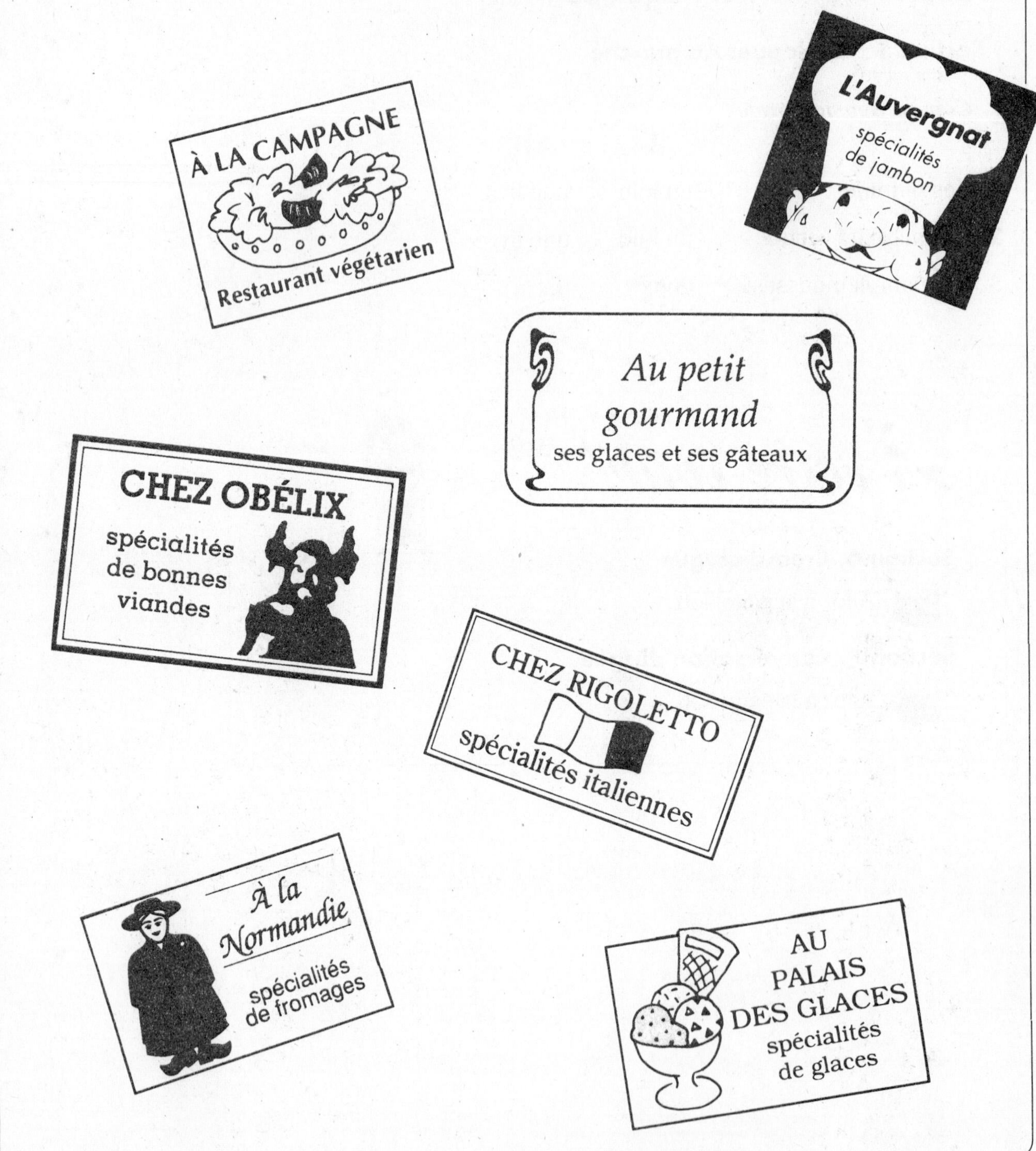
À LA CAMPAGNE
Restaurant végétarien
L'Auvergnat
spécialités
de jambon
Au petit
gourmand
ses glaces et ses gâteaux
CHEZ OBÉLIX
spécialités
de bonnes
viandes
CHEZ RIGOLETTO
spécialités italiennes
À la
Normandie
spécialités
de fromages
AU
PALAIS
DES GLACES
spécialités
de glaces

Nom ______________________________

Classe ____________________ Date ____________

CASSETTE WORKSHEET Leçon 34 À la cantine

Section 1 À la cantine

A. *Compréhension orale*

Il est midi et demi. Sophie va à la cantine. Elle rencontre Jean-Paul.

SOPHIE: Est-ce que tu veux déjeuner avec moi?
JEAN-PAUL: Ça dépend. Qu'est-ce qu'il y a aujourd'hui?
SOPHIE: Il y a du poisson!
JEAN-PAUL: Du poisson?
SOPHIE: Oui, du poisson.
JEAN-PAUL: Quelle horreur! Bon, aujourd'hui, je ne veux pas déjeuner.
SOPHIE: Il y a aussi du gâteau.
JEAN-PAUL: Du gâteau! Hm . . .
SOPHIE: Et de la glace!
JEAN-PAUL: Une minute . . . je vais prendre un plateau.

Section 2 Les verbes *vouloir* et *prendre*

B. *Écoutez et répétez.*

 Allez à la page 360.

Section 3 Voici du pain

C. *Compréhension orale*

		1	2	3	4	5	6	7
A	du							
B	de la							

CASSETTE WORKSHEET Leçon 34 (cont.)

Section 4 Je prends du beurre?

D. *Compréhension orale*

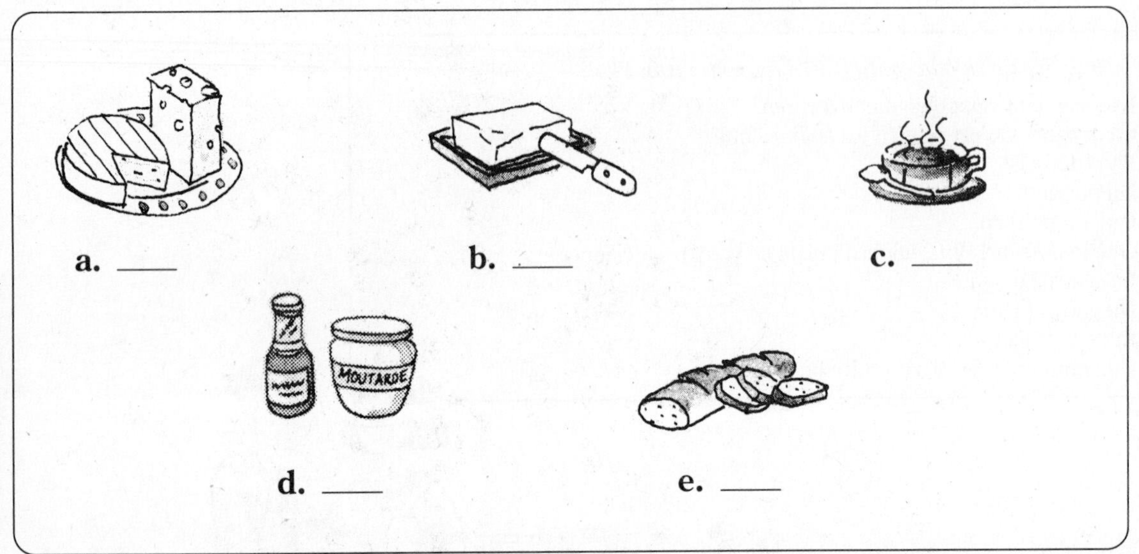

a. ____ b. ____ c. ____

d. ____ e. ____

Section 5 Tu veux du pain?

E. *Questions et réponses*

▶ —Tu veux du pain?
—Oui, donne-moi du pain, s'il te plaît. ▶ 

1. 2. 3. 4.

5. 6. 7.

CASSETTE WORKSHEET Leçon 34 (cont.)

Section 6 Dialogue: Le pique-nique

F. *Compréhension orale*

Scène 1

1. Madame Martin va faire les courses. vrai faux
2. Elle veut quelque chose de simple pour le pique-nique. vrai faux

Scène 2

3. Monsieur Martin et son fils achètent du pain. vrai faux
4. Ils achètent du beurre et du fromage. vrai faux
5. Ils achètent des yaourts. vrai faux
6. Ils achètent du jambon et du saucisson. vrai faux
7. Ils n'achètent pas de rosbif. vrai faux
8. Philippe a oublié la moutarde et le ketchup. vrai faux
9. Ils prennent de l'eau minérale. vrai faux
10. Ils ne prennent pas de jus d'orange. vrai faux

Scène 3

11. Madame Martin pense qu'ils ont acheté quelque chose de simple pour le pique-nique. vrai faux
12. Monsieur Martin pense qu'ils ont acheté quelque chose de simple pour le pique-nique. vrai faux

Section 7 Le petit déjeuner

G. *Compréhension orale*

	A	B	C	D
	Mme Aubin	**M. Aubin**	**Nathalie**	**Caroline**
1. du café				
2. du café au lait				
3. du chocolat				
4. du thé nature				
5. du pain				
6. du beurre				
7. de la confiture				
8. des biscottes				
9. des céréales avec du lait				

UNITÉ 9

CASSETTE WORKSHEET Leçon 34 (cont.)

Section 8 Prononciation

H. *Les lettres «ou» et «u»*

Écoutez: **la poule** **le pull**

The letters "**ou**" always represent the sound /u/.

Répétez: /u/ **vous nous poulet soupe**
fourchette couteau douzaine

The letter "**u**" always represents the sound /y/.

Répétez: /y/ **tu du une légume jus**
sucre bien sûr avenue musée

Now distinguish between the two vowel sounds:

Répétez: /u/ – /y/ **poule** *(hen)* – **pull**
roue *(wheel)* – **rue** **vous** – **vue** *(view)*
je joue – **le jus**
Vous buvez du jus de pamplemousse.
Je voudrais de la soupe, du poulet et du jus de raisin.

UNITÉ 9

À votre tour!

Section 9. Allô!

 Allez à la page 368.

Section 10. Créa-dialogue

 Allez à la page 368.

Nom ____

Classe ______________________________ Date ______________

CASSETTE WORKSHEET Leçon 35 Un client difficile

Section 1 Un client difficile

A. *Compréhension orale*

M. Ronchon a beaucoup d'appétit . . . mais pas beaucoup de patience. En fait, M. Ronchon est rarement de bonne humeur. Et quand il est de mauvaise humeur, c'est un client difficile. Aujourd'hui, par exemple, au restaurant . . .

M. RONCHON: Garçon!
GARÇON: J'arrive!

M. RONCHON: Qu'est-ce que vous avez comme hors d'oeuvre?
GARÇON: Nous avons du jambon et du saucisson.
M. RONCHON: Apportez-moi tout ça . . . avec du pain et du beurre, eh!
GARÇON: Bien, monsieur.

GARÇON: Et comme boisson, qu'est-ce que je vous apporte?
M. RONCHON: Donnez-moi de l'eau minérale . . . Dépêchez-vous! J'ai soif!

M. RONCHON: Apportez-moi du poulet et des frites . . . Dépêchez-vous! J'ai très faim!
GARÇON: Je vous apporte ça tout de suite.

M. RONCHON: Et apportez-moi aussi du fromage, ah . . . de la glace, oh . . . de la tarte aux pommes et de la tarte aux abricots . . . Mais, qu'est-ce que vous attendez?
GARÇON: Tout de suite, monsieur, tout de suite.

M. RONCHON: Mais qu'est-ce que vous m'apportez?
GARÇON: Je vous apporte l'addition!

UNITÉ 9

Section 2 Les services personnels

B. *Écoutez et répétez.*

Allez à la page 373.

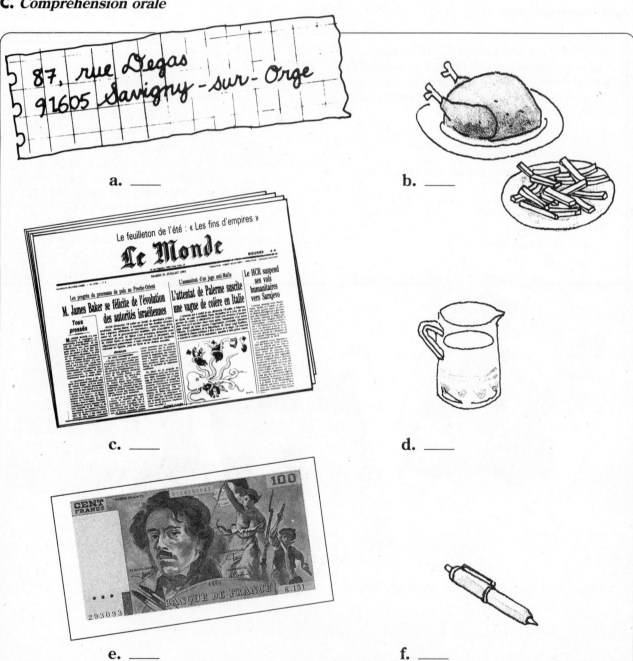

CASSETTE WORKSHEET Leçon 35 (cont.)

Section 3 **Apportez-moi du poulet . . .**

C. *Compréhension orale*

87, rue Degas
91605 Savigny-sur-Orge

a. ___

b. ___

Le feuilleton de l'été : « Les fins d'empires »
Le Monde
Les progrès du processus de paix au Proche-Orient
M. James Baker se félicite de l'évolution des autorités israéliennes
Tous pressés
L'assassinat d'un juge anti-Mafia
L'attentat de Palerme suscite une vague de colère en Italie
Le HCR suspend ses vols humanitaires vers Sarajevo

c. ___

d. ___

100
CENT FRANCS
BANQUE DE FRANCE

e. ___

f. ___

CASSETTE WORKSHEET Leçon 35 (cont.)

Section 4 **Qu'est-ce que tu veux?**

D. *Questions et réponses*

▶ —Qu'est-ce que tu veux? de l'eau minérale ou du jus d'orange?
—Donne-moi de l'eau minérale, s'il te plaît.
(Donne-moi du jus d'orange, s'il te plaît.)

▶ 

1.

2.

3.

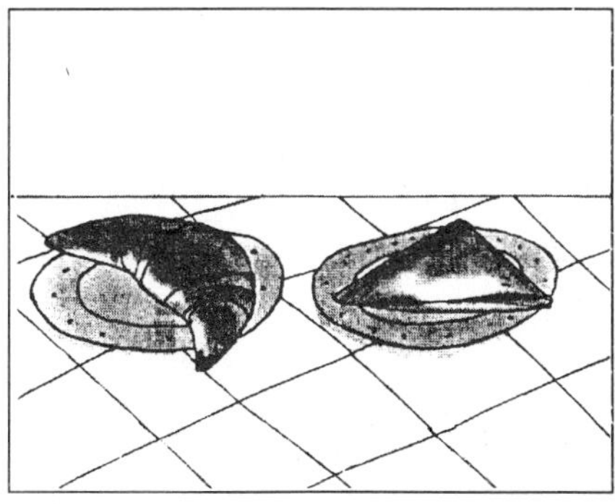

4.

CASSETTE WORKSHEET Leçon 35 (cont.)

Section 5 Les verbes *pouvoir* et *devoir*

E. ***Écoutez et répétez.***

 Allez à la page 376.

Section 6 Prononciation

UNITÉ 9

F. ***Les lettres «s» et «ss»***

Écoutez: **poison** **poisson**
Be sure to distinguish between "**s**" and "**ss**" in the middle of a word.

Répétez: /z/ **mauvaise cuisine fraise mayonnaise quelque chose magasin**

/s/ **poisson saucisson dessert boisson assiette pamplemousse**

/z/ – /s/ **poison – poisson désert – dessert**
Comme dessert nous choisissons une tarte aux fraises.

À votre tour!

Section 7. Allô!

 Allez à la page 378.

Section 8. Créa-dialogue

 Allez à la page 378.

Nom ______________________________

Classe ______________________ Date ______________

DISCOVERING FRENCH - *BLEU*

CASSETTE WORKSHEET Leçon 36 Pique-nique

Section 1 Dialogue: Pique-nique

A. ***Compréhension orale***

Florence et Jérôme organisent un pique-nique ce weekend. Ils préparent la liste des invités. Qui vont-ils inviter?

FLORENCE: Tu connais Stéphanie?
JÉRÔME: Oui, je la connais. C'est une copine.
FLORENCE: Je l'invite au pique-nique?
JÉRÔME: Bien sûr. Invite-la.
FLORENCE: Et son cousin Frédéric, tu le connais?
JÉRÔME: Oui, je le connais un peu.
FLORENCE: Je l'invite aussi?
JÉRÔME: Non, ne l'invite pas. Il est trop snob.
FLORENCE: Comment? Tu le trouves snob? Moi, je le trouve intelligent et sympathique. Et puis, il a une voiture et nous avons besoin d'une voiture pour transporter tout le monde . . .
JÉRÔME: Florence, tu es géniale . . . C'est vrai, Frédéric n'est pas aussi snob que ça . . . Téléphonons-lui tout de suite et invitons-le au pique-nique!

UNITÉ 9

Section 2 Le verbe *connaître*

B. ***Écoutez et répétez.***

Allez à la page 382.

Section 3 Tu le connais?

C. ***Questions et réponses***

		1	2	3	4	5
A	**le**					
B	**la**					
C	**les**					

CASSETTE WORKSHEET Leçon 36 (cont.)

Section 4 Tu connais Blanche-Neige?

D. ***Questions et réponses***

▶ —Tu connais Blanche-Neige?
—Oui, je la connais.
(Non, je ne la connais pas.)

1. Astérix
2. les Schtroumpfs
3. Batman
4. Oprah Winfrey
5. Bill Cosby
6. New Kids on the Block

Section 5 On va lui parler?

E. ***Compréhension orale***

		1	2	3	4
A	**lui**				
B	**leur**				

Section 6 Dialogue: Sur la plage

F. ***Compréhension orale***

1. Jean-Paul et Philippe sont à Deauville. vrai faux
2. À la plage, ils voient une fille. vrai faux
3. Jean-Paul ne la connaît pas. vrai faux
4. Jean-Paul va lui demander quelle heure il est. vrai faux
5. Jean-Paul va lui demander si elle est en vacances. vrai faux
6. Jean-Paul va l'inviter à aller au cinéma. vrai faux
7. Jean-Paul ne lui parle pas. vrai faux
8. C'est un nouveau garçon qui parle à la fille. vrai faux

CASSETTE WORKSHEET Leçon 36 (cont.)

Section 7 Prononciation

G. ***Les lettres «on» et «om»***

Écoutez: **lion** **lionne**

Be sure to distinguish between the nasal and non-nasal vowel sounds.

REMEMBER: Do not pronounce an /n/ or /m/ after the nasal vowel /ɔ̃/.

Répétez: /ɔ̃/ **mon ton son bon avion montrer répondre invitons blouson**

/ɔ̃n/ **téléphone Simone donner connais mayonnaise personne bonne**

/ɔ̃m/ **fromage promenade tomate pomme dommage comment**

/ɔ̃/ – /ɔ̃n/ **lion – lionne bon – bonne Simon – Simone**
Yvon – Yvonne
Monique donne une pomme à Raymond.
Simone connaît mon oncle Léon.

Section 8. Allô!

 Allez à la page 390.

Section 9. Créa-dialogue

 Allez à la page 390.

WRITING ACTIVITIES Leçon 33 Le français pratique: Les repas et la nourriture

A/B/C **1. L'intrus** *(The intruder)*

For each of the boxes, the item that does not fit the category is the intruder. Find it and cross it out.

FRUITS
poire
fromage
cerise
pamplemousse

LÉGUMES
fraises
carottes
haricots verts
pommes de terre

VIANDE
veau
rosbif
poulet
frites

DESSERTS
glace
gâteau
jambon
tarte

BOISSONS
lait
confiture
eau minérale
thé glacé

PRODUITS LAITIERS *(dairy products)*
yaourt
fromage
lait
poire

PETIT DÉJEUNER
pain
thon
beurre
confiture

UN REPAS VÉGÉTARIEN
riz
légumes
salade
saucisson

DANS LE RÉFRIGÉRATEUR
serviette
oeufs
thé glacé
beurre

REPAS
dîner
nourriture
petit déjeuner
déjeuner

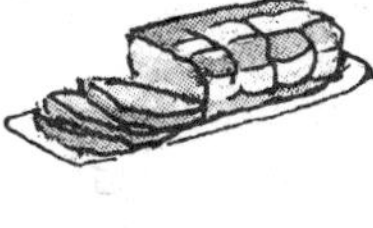

Nom ___

WRITING ACTIVITIES Leçon 33 (cont.)

2. Tes préférences

List the foods you like for each of the following courses.

1. Comme hors-d'oeuvre, j'aime ___.
2. Comme viande, j'aime ___.
3. Comme légumes, j'aime ___.
4. Comme fruits, j'aime ___.
5. Comme dessert, j'aime ___.

3. Au menu

Imagine you are working for a French restaurant. Prepare a different menu for each of the following meals.

MÉNU
PETIT DÉJEUNER

MÉNU
DÉJEUNER

MÉNU
DÎNER

WRITING ACTIVITIES Leçon 33 (cont.)

4. Le pique-nique

You have decided to organize a picnic for your French friends. Prepare a shopping list.

liste

Nom ______________________________

WRITING ACTIVITIES Leçon 33 (cont.)

5. Le mot juste

Complete each of the following sentences with a word from the box.
Be logical!

légumes	livre	verre	couteau
courses	viande	cuisine	petit déjeuner

1. Demain, je vais prendre le ____________ à huit heures et quart.
2. J'ai besoin d'un ____________ pour couper *(to cut)* mon steak.
3. Ma soeur a passé l'été au Mexique. Maintenant elle adore la ____________ mexicaine.
4. Alice est végétarienne. Elle ne mange jamais de ____________.
5. Voici un ____________ d'eau minérale.
6. Au supermarché j'ai acheté des fruits et des ____________.
7. Nous avons besoin de nourriture. Je vais faire les ____________.
8. S'il vous plaît, donnez-moi une ____________ de cerises.

UNITÉ 9

Nom ____

Classe ______________________ Date ______________

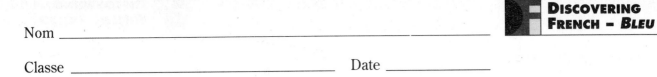

WRITING ACTIVITIES Leçon 34 À la cantine

A 1. Quand on veut . . .

Read about the following people. Then decide whether or not they want to do certain things. Complete the sentences with the appropriate affirmative or negative forms of **vouloir.**

▶ Nous sommes en vacances. Nous ne voulons pas étudier.

1. J'ai envie de voir un film. Je ______________ aller au cinéma.
2. Tu es timide. Tu ______________ parler en public.
3. Mes cousines ont envie de voyager cet été. Elles ______________ aller au Pérou.
4. Olivier est fatigué. Il ______________ aller au concert avec nous.
5. Nous avons faim. Nous ______________ déjeuner.
6. Stéphanie a besoin d'argent. Elle ______________ vendre son vélo.
7. Vous êtes très impatients. Vous ______________ attendre vos copains.
8. Mes petits cousins regardent un film. Ils ______________ aller au lit.

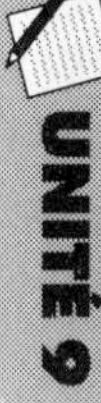

B 2. Quel objet?

In order to do certain activities, people must take along certain things. Write complete sentences to say what people are taking, using the appropriate form of **prendre** and one of the objects in the box. Be logical.

argent	appareil-photo	livres	raquette
maillot de bain	vélo	calculatrices	

▶ Paul va jouer au tennis. Il prend sa raquette.

1. Caroline va nager. ______________
2. Les élèves vont en classe. ______________
3. Je vais faire des achats. ______________
4. Tu veux prendre des photos. ______________
5. Vous faites une promenade à la campagne. ______________
6. Nous faisons des devoirs de maths. ______________

WRITING ACTIVITIES Leçon 34 (cont.)

C 3. «À la bonne auberge»

You are working as a waiter/waitress in a French restaurant named "À la bonne auberge." Explain the menu to your customers. Fill in the blanks with the appropriate *partitive articles.*

1. Comme hors-d'oeuvre, il y a __________ jambon et __________ soupe.
2. Comme viande, il y a __________ poulet et __________ rosbif.
3. Comme poisson, il y a __________ sole et __________ thon.
4. Après, il y a __________ salade et __________ fromage.
5. Comme dessert, il y a __________ glace et __________ tarte aux fraises.

4. À votre tour

Now it is your turn to be the client. The waiter is offering you the following choices. Tell him what you would like.

▶ soupe ou saucisson? Je voudrais du saucisson (de la soupe).

1. poisson ou viande? ______________________
2. veau ou poulet? ______________________
3. ketchup ou mayonnaise? ______________________
4. yaourt ou fromage? ______________________
5. gâteau ou tarte? ______________________
6. thé ou café? ______________________
7. eau minérale ou jus d'orange? ______________________

5. Les courses

Your brother is going shopping and is making a list. Tell him what to buy.

▶ 

1. 

2. 

3. 

4. 

5. 

6. 

7. 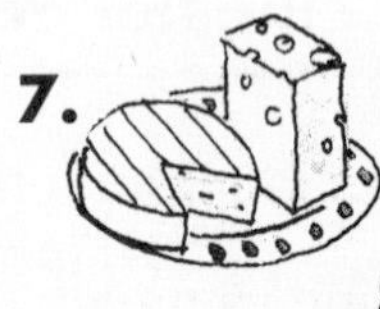

8.

▶ Achète du pain.

1. ______________________ 5. ______________________

2. ______________________ 6. ______________________

3. ______________________ 7. ______________________

4. ______________________ 8. ______________________

WRITING ACTIVITIES Leçon 34 (cont.)

D 6. Un végétarien

You are under doctor's orders not to eat meat. Imagine you are having lunch at a French restaurant. What will you answer when the waiter offers you the following foods?

▶ (la salade) Oui, je veux bien de la salade.

▶ (le rosbif) Non, merci. Je ne veux pas de rosbif.

1. (la soupe) ______________________
2. (le melon) ______________________
3. (le poulet) ______________________
4. (le jambon) ______________________
5. (le veau) ______________________
6. (la glace) ______________________

7. À la cantine

Look at the various items on Michel's cafeteria tray and answer the questions accordingly.

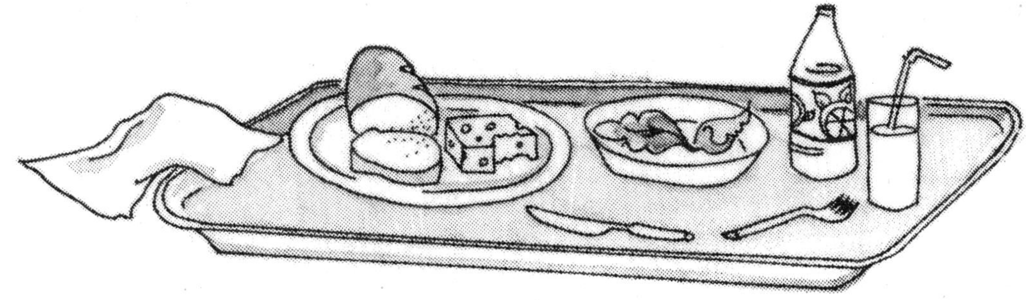

▶ Est-ce que Michel a pris de la soupe? Non, il n'a pas pris de soupe.

1. Est-ce que Michel a mangé du fromage? ______________________
2. Est-ce qu'il a mangé de la salade? ______________________
3. Est-ce qu'il a mangé de la viande? ______________________
4. Est-ce qu'il a pris de l'eau minérale? ______________________
5. Est-ce qu'il a pris du jambon? ______________________
6. Est-ce qu'il a mangé du pain? ______________________

WRITING ACTIVITIES Leçon 34 (cont.)

E 8. À la boum

Say what the guests are drinking at the party. Complete the sentences with the appropriate forms of **boire.**

1. Alain __________ du thé glacé.
2. Bruno et Guillaume __________ du soda.
3. Je __________ du soda, aussi.
4. Tu __________ de l'eau minérale.
5. Nous __________ de la limonade.
6. Vous __________ du jus de fruit.

9. Communication

A. Un repas

In a short paragraph, write about a recent meal (real or imaginary). Use words you know to describe . . .

- *where you ate*
- *what you had for each course*
- *what you drank*

▶ Samedi dernier, j'ai dîné dans un restaurant français.

Comme hors-d'oeuvre, j'ai pris du melon.

____

____

____

____

____

B. Le réfrigérateur

Check the contents of your refrigerator. List the names of the items that you know in French. Also list some of the things that are not in your refrigerator.

Dans mon réfrigérateur, il y a . . .	Il n'y a pas . . .
• du lait	• de jus de raisin
•	•
•	•
•	•
•	•
•	

UNITÉ 9

Nom ______________________________

Classe ______________________ Date ______________

WRITING ACTIVITIES Leçon 35 Un client difficile

A 1. D'accord ou pas d'accord?

Complete the mini-dialogues by answering the questions, using appropriate pronouns. Answer questions 1–3 affirmatively; answer questions 4 and 5 negatively.

1. —Tu m'invites chez toi?

   —D'accord, ______________________________ .

2. —Tu nous attends après la classe?

   —D'accord, ______________________________ .

3. —Tu me téléphones ce soir?

   —D'accord, ________________________ après le dîner.

4. —Tu m'attends?

   —Non, ________________________ . Je n'ai pas le temps.

5. —Tu nous invites au cinéma?

   —Non, ______________________________ .
   Je n'ai pas d'argent.

Nom ____________________

WRITING ACTIVITIES Leçon 35 (cont.)

B 2. S'il te plaît!

Ask your friends to do certain things for you, using the verbs in parentheses.

▶ J'ai besoin d'argent. (prêter)

S'il te plaît, prête-moi dix francs.

1. Je voudrais réparer mon vélo. (aider)

   S'il te plaît, ____________________.

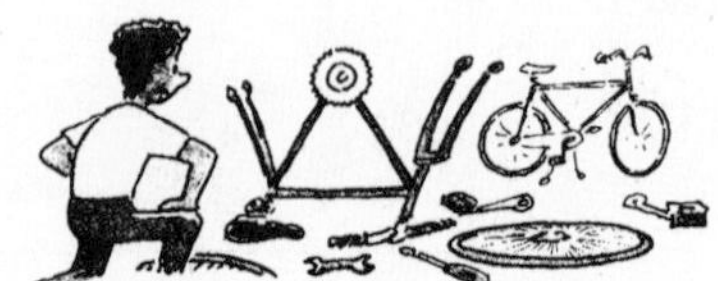

2. J'ai faim. (donner)

   S'il te plaît, ____________________ un sandwich.

3. Oh là là, j'ai très soif. (apporter)

   S'il te plaît, ____________________ un verre d'eau.

4. Je voudrais prendre des photos. (prêter)

   S'il te plaît, ____________________ ton appareil-photo.

5. Je voudrais téléphoner à ton copain. (donner)

   S'il te plaît, ____________________ son numéro de téléphone.

3. Petits services

Ask your French friend Vincent to . . .

- loan you his calculator ____________________
- give you his cousin's address *(l'adresse)* ____________________
- invite you to his party ____________________
- show you his photos ____________________
- wait for you after the class ____________________
- bring you a sandwich ____________________

WRITING ACTIVITIES Leçon 35 (cont.)

C 4. C'est impossible!

The following people cannot do certain things because they have to do other things. Express this by using the appropriate forms of **pouvoir** and **devoir,** as well as your imagination.

▶ Olivier *ne peut pas* aller au cinéma.
Il doit étudier (aider sa mère, . . .).

1. Nous ______________ jouer au basket avec vous.
   Nous ______________________________.
2. Je ______________ dîner chez toi.
   Je ______________________________.
3. Véronique et Françoise ______________ venir à la boum.
   Elles ______________________________.
4. Vous ______________ aller au concert.
   Vous ______________________________.
5. Jean-Marc ______________ rester avec nous.
   Il ______________________________.
6. Tu ______________ rencontrer tes copains.
   Tu ______________________________.

UNITÉ 9

WRITING ACTIVITIES Leçon 35 (cont.)

5. Communication: Un bon conseiller *(A good adviser)*

Imagine that you are a newspaper columnist and your readers write you for advice. Here are some of their problems. Write out your advice for each one, using the appropriate present-tense forms of **devoir** or **pouvoir** — and your imagination!

▶ «Je veux voyager cet été, mais je n'ai pas beaucoup d'argent. Qu'est-ce que je peux faire?»

Vous pouvez aller chez des amis à la mer.

Vous pouvez travailler pour gagner de l'argent et pour payer le voyage.

1. «Je n'ai pas de bonnes notes en français. Qu'est-ce que je dois faire?»

____

____

2. «Mon ami et moi, nous voulons faire une surprise à un copain pour son anniversaire. Qu'est-ce que nous pouvons faire?»

____

____

3. «Mes cousins vont en France pendant les vacances. Qu'est-ce qu'ils peuvent faire pendant leur voyage?»

____

____

4. «Avec une copine, nous voulons organiser une boum pour nos amis français. Qu'est-ce que nous devons faire?»

____

____

5. «En ce moment, j'ai des problèmes avec mon copain (ma copine). Qu'est-ce que je dois faire?»

____

____

Nom ______________________________ **DISCOVERING FRENCH – *BLEU***

Classe ______________________ Date __________

WRITING ACTIVITIES Leçon 36 Pique-nique

A 1. Connaissances

Complete the sentences below with the appropriate forms of **connaître.** Your answers could be affirmative or negative.

1. Je ______________ San Francisco.
2. Mes copains ______________ ma famille.
3. Ma copine ______________ mes cousins.
4. Ma famille et moi, nous ______________ bien nos voisins.

UNITÉ 9

B 2. Les photos d'Isabelle

While showing pictures of her friends, Isabelle makes comments about them. Complete her sentences with the appropriate direct object pronouns.

1. Voici Julien.

   Je __________ connais très bien. Je __________ rencontre souvent au café. Je __________ aide avec ses devoirs.

2. Voici Pauline.

   Je __________ trouve très intelligente. Je __________ aime beaucoup. Je __________ vois souvent le weekend.

3. Voici mes cousins.

   Je __________ vois pendant les vacances. Je __________ trouve un peu snobs.

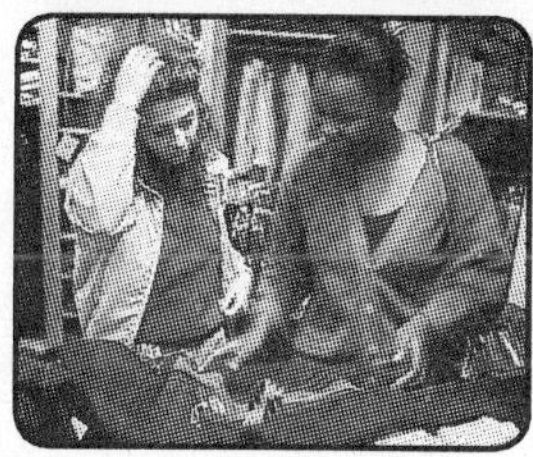

4. Voici mes copines.

   Je __________ trouve très sympathiques. Je __________ invite souvent chez moi.

Nom ___

3. Correspondance

Jean-François, your French pen pal, has written you a letter asking about your activities. Answer his questions affirmatively or negatively, using direct object pronouns.

▶ Tu regardes la télé? *Oui, je la regarde. (Non, je ne la regarde pas.)*

1. Tu regardes les matchs de foot? ___
2. Tu écoutes la radio? ___
3. Tu écoutes souvent tes compacts? ___
4. Tu prêtes tes cassettes? ___
5. Tu prends le bus pour aller à l école? ___
6. Tu invites souvent tes amis à la maison? ___
7. Tu aides ta mère? ___
8. Tu fais les courses? ___
9. Tu vois tes cousins? ___
10. Tu connais bien ton professeur de français? ___

UNITÉ 9

C 4. En colonie de vacances *(At camp)*

You are at a French summer camp. Your roommate is asking whether he/she can do the following things. Answer affirmatively or negatively, according to the way you feel.

▶ Je prends ta raquette? *Oui, prends-la.*
(Non, ne la prends pas.)

1. Je prends ton appareil-photo? ___
2. Je mets la radio? ___
3. Je mets le disque de rap? ___
4. Je nettoie la chambre? ___
5. Je fais le lit? ___
6. Je regarde les photos? ___

Nom ____________________

WRITING ACTIVITIES Leçon 36 (cont.)

D 5. Les cadeaux *(Presents)*

Imagine that you have bought the following presents. Decide which one you are giving to each of the following people and then write out your choices. If you wish, you may decide on other presents that are not illustrated.

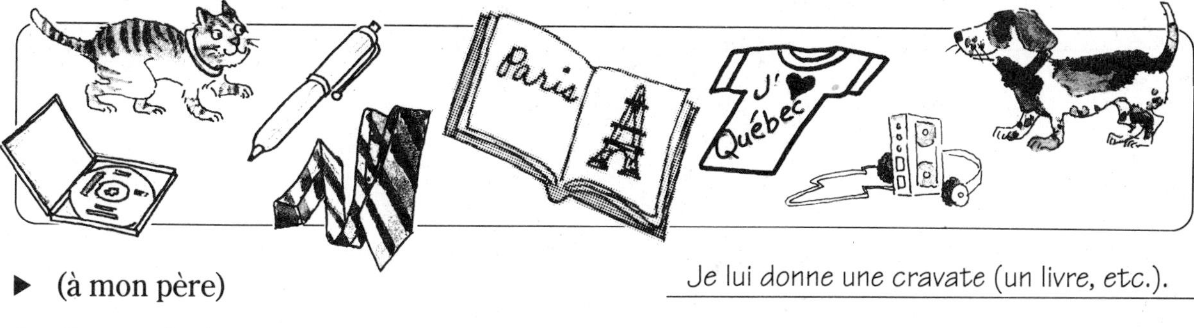

▶ (à mon père) *Je lui donne une cravate (un livre, etc.).*

1. (à ma mère) ____________________
2. (à mes grands-parents) ____________________
3. (à mes cousins) ____________________
4. (au professeur de français) ____________________
5. (à mon meilleur ami) ____________________
6. (à ma meilleure amie) ____________________

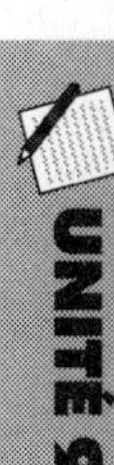

6. Les copains d'Hélène

Raphaël wants to know more about Hélène's friends. Complete Hélène's answers with the appropriate pronouns, direct **(le, la, l', les)** or indirect **(lui, leur).**

RAPHAËL	HÉLÈNE
▶ Tu téléphones souvent à Éric?	Oui, je *lui* téléphone assez souvent.
1. Tu connais bien Marthe?	Oui, je ________ connais assez bien.
2. Tu vois Éric et Olivier ce weekend?	Oui, je ________ vois samedi matin.
3. Tu téléphones à Catherine ce soir?	Oui, je ________ téléphone après le dîner.
4. Tu invites Cédric à ta boum?	Bien sûr, je ________ invite. C'est un très bon copain.
5. Tu rends souvent visite à tes copains canadiens?	Oui, je ________ rends visite assez souvent.
6. Tu parles souvent à tes cousins?	Bien sûr, je ________ parle tous les jours *(every day)*.
7. Tu aides ton frère?	Bien sûr. Je ________ aide quand il a un problème.
8. Tu prêtes tes compacts à Robert?	En général, oui, je ________ prête mes CDs.

Nom ______________________________

UNITÉ 9

E 7. Lettres de vacances

In the summer we like to write to people we know and let them know what we are doing. Complete the following sentences with the appropriate forms of **écrire** and **dire.**

▶ Francis ____écrit____ à sa copine.

Il lui ____dit____ qu'il veut lui rendre visite.

1. Nous ______________ à nos copains.

   Nous leur ______________ que nous passons des vacances extra!

2. Caroline ______________ à sa cousine.

   Elle lui ______________ qu'elle a rencontré un garçon très sympathique.

3. Tu ______________ à tes grands-parents.

   Tu leur ______________ qu'il fait beau et que tu apprends à faire de la voile.

4. Vous ______________ au professeur.

   Vous lui ______________ que vous êtes en France.

5. J' ______________ à ma mère.

   Je lui ______________ que j'ai besoin d'argent.

6. Cécile et Mélanie ______________ à leurs parents.

   Elles leur ______________ qu'elles sont très contentes de leurs vacances.

Nom ___________________________

WRITING ACTIVITIES Leçon 36 (cont.)

8. Communication: Êtes-vous serviable? *(Are you helpful?)*

Are you helpful? Of course you are! Write two things you would do for the following people in the circumstances mentioned below. Be sure to use the appropriate *direct* or *indirect* object pronouns. You may want to select some of the verbs in the box.

acheter	aider	donner	écrire	inviter
parler	prêter	rendre visite	téléphoner	

▶ Ma meilleure amie a un problème avec sa famille.

Je lui téléphone. Je l'aide. (Je lui parle. Je l'invite chez moi.)

1. Mes grands-parents sont malades.

____

2. Ma cousine est à l'hôpital.

____

3. Mes amis ont des problèmes avec la classe de français.

____

4. Mon meilleur copain a besoin d'argent.

____

5. Le professeur est malade.

____

6. Une amie organise une boum et a besoin d'aide.

____

Nom ______________________________

Classe ______________________ Date ______________

READING AND CULTURE ACTIVITIES Unité 9

A. Dîner en ville

1. Quel plat est-ce qu'on *ne* peut *pas* trouver dans ce restaurant?
- ☐ Salade de tomates.
- ☐ Omelette au jambon.
- ☐ Glace à la vanille.
- ☐ Yaourt.

GOVINDA
Repas Végétariens Économiques
Ouvert 7 jours
11 hrs à 22 hrs
300 Ontario Est
Près de St-Denis

2. Qu'est-ce qu'on peut faire dans ce restaurant?
- ☐ Manger des spaghetti.
- ☐ Manger de la nourriture chinoise.
- ☐ Parler japonais.
- ☐ Écouter de la musique.

EL MARIACHI
RESTAURANT MEXICAIN
2 ORCHESTRES
DINERS OU CONSOMMATIONS
62.rue P. Charron 8e (Champs-Elysées)
45.63.40.88 — Salle clim. Fermé Dim.

3. Quelles sont les spécialités de ce restaurant?
- ☐ La viande.
- ☐ Le poisson.
- ☐ Les fromages.
- ☐ Les desserts.

GARNIER
Le Restaurant de mer
Déjeuners,
Dîners, Soupers
Banc d'Huîtres
111, rue Saint-Lazare
75008 PARIS - 43.87.50.40
Commandes prises jusqu'à 2 h du mat.

4. Qu'est-ce qu'on peut manger dans ce restaurant?
- ☐ De la cuisine mexicaine.
- ☐ Des spécialités de la Martinique.
- ☐ Un bon steak.
- ☐ Des pizzas.

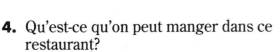

Spécialités des Iles
LA CREOLE
Le célèbre et renommé restaurant antillais
122, bd du Montparnasse 14e. Rés. 43.20.62.12 (Ouvert T.L.J

UNITÉ 9

READING AND CULTURE ACTIVITIES Unité 9 (cont.)

B. Vinaigrette

Vinaigrette
Mettez dans un petit bol :
– 1 cuillère à soupe de vinaigre,
– ½ cuillère à café de moutarde,
– 4 pincées de sel.
Ajoutez :
– 3 cuillères à soupe d'huile d'olive.
Mélangez bien avec une fourchette.
Versez la vinaigrette sur la salade.

1. Ce texte est . . .

☐ une recette *(recipe)*
☐ un menu
☐ une liste de courses
☐ la description d'un repas

2. Qu'est-ce que c'est «vinaigrette»?

☐ Un hors-d'oeuvre.
☐ Le nom d'un restaurant.
☐ Une sauce pour la salade.
☐ Le nom d'un magasin.

Nom ___

C. Petit déjeuner dans l'avion

Imaginez que vous allez passer une semaine de vacances en France avec votre famille. Maintenant vous êtes dans l'avion et c'est le moment du petit déjeuner.

Qu'est-ce que vous allez choisir?

Le Petit Déjeuner
sera servi avant l'atterrissage

Choix de Jus de Fruits Frais

Assiette de Fruits Frais de Saison

Choix de Yaourts
Sélection de Céréales

Assortiment de Pains
Danoise aux Graines de Pavot Gâteau aux Pommes
Croissants

- Est-ce que vous prenez un jus de fruits? ___
  Si oui, quel jus de fruits préférez-vous? ___
  ___
  Qu'est-ce que vous dites à l'hôtesse?
  ___
- Est-ce que vous voudriez *(would like)* des fruits? ___
  Si oui, quels fruits aimez-vous? ___
  Qu'est-ce que vous dites à l'hôtesse?
  ___
- Est-ce que vous allez prendre un yaourt? ___
  Si oui, quel parfum *(flavor)*? ___
  Qu'est-ce que vous dites à l'hôtesse?
  ___
- Est-ce que vous allez manger des céréales? ___
  Qu'est-ce que vous dites à l'hôtesse?
  ___
- Est-ce que vous allez choisir un pain? ___
  Si oui, quel pain? (Notez: «graines de pavot» = *poppy seeds*)
  ___
  Qu'est-ce que vous dites à l'hôtesse?
  ___

UNITÉ 9

READING AND CULTURE ACTIVITIES Unité 9 (cont.)

D. Les courses

Imaginez que vous êtes en France avec vos parents. Vous venez de faire les courses à La Grande Épicerie de Paris.
Maintenant votre mère, qui ne comprend pas le français, a des questions.

- How much did you spend for the following things?

bread? ______ + ______ = ______
butter? ______ = ______
cheese? ______ + ______ = ______
fruits and vegetables? ______ + ______ + ______ + ______ = ______
Total = ______

- Is the store open . . .

Monday at 9 A.M.?	yes	no
Tuesday at 9:30 P.M.?	yes	no
Wednesday noon?	yes	no
Thursday at 8 A.M.?	yes	no
Friday at 9:45 P.M.?	yes	no
Saturday morning?	yes	no
Sunday afternoon?	yes	no

* LA GRANDE EPICERIE DE PARIS *
OUVERT DU LUNDI AU SAMEDI

PAINS POILANE		10,45
PAINS POILANE		10,45
FROMAGE COUPE		93,65
FROMAGE COUPE		70,30
FRUITS ET LEGUMES		9,60
BEURRE CHARENTE/P.		10,60
FRAISE 1L		22,90
FRUITS ET LEGUMES		15,40
CONCOMBRE		6,90
****	TOT	250,25
ESPECES		250,25

26/06/91 11:03 4680 07 0124 138
DE 8H30 A 21H - LUNDI ET VENDREDI 22H
MERCI DE VOTRE VISITE A BIENTOT

READING AND CULTURE ACTIVITIES Unité 9 (cont.)

E. Aux Deux Magots

Vous avez visité le musée d'Orsay ce matin. Maintenant il est midi et demi et vous avez faim. Vous allez déjeuner aux Deux Magots. Regardez bien le menu.

- Regardez le choix de jus de fruits.

  Quel jus de fruit est-ce que vous allez choisir? ___________________

  Combien coûte-t-il? ___________________

- Regardez le choix de sandwichs.

  Quel sandwich avez-vous choisi? ___________________

  Combien est-ce qu'il coûte? ___________________

- Choisissez un dessert: une glace ou un sorbet ou une pâtisserie.

  Qu'est-ce que vous avez choisi? ___________________

  Combien coûte ce dessert? ___________________

- Maintenant faites le total.

  Quel est le prix de votre déjeuner en francs? ___________________

  Combien coûte-t-il en dollars? (Notez: $1 = approximativement 6 francs.) __________

DEPUIS 1885
LES DEUX MAGOTS
Café Littéraire
6, PLACE SAINT-GERMAIN-DES-PRES 75006 PARIS TEL. 45 48 5

BOISSONS FROIDES

Cola-cola	21,00
Schweppes indian tonic	21,00
Canada dry	21,00
Orangina	21,00
Limonade	21,00
Jus de fruit : Ananas, Abricot, Pamplemousse, Orange, Raisin et Jus de tomate	21,00
Eaux minérales (le 1/4) : Evian, Perrier, Vichy, Vittel, Badoit	21,00
Oranges ou citrons pressés	25,00
Lait aromatisé	20,00

LES SANDWICHS

Jambon de Paris	23,00
Jambon de Bayonne	30,00
Saucisson beurre	23,00
Mixte : jambon, Comté	30,00
Fromage Comté ou camembert normand	23,00
Le Croque Monsieur	30,00
La quiche Lorraine	28,00
La salade Deux Magots (salade verte, jambon, poulet, gruyère, tomate, oeuf dur)	43,00
Salade verte	25,00

LES FROMAGES

Crottin de Chavignol chaud sur pain Poilâne	35,00
Crottin de Chavignol goat cheese	31,00
Assiette de Comté	31,00
Camembert normand	24,00

LES PATISSERIES

Gâteau au chocolat	30,00
Tarte Tatin chaude	32,00
Avec crème fraîche supplément	6,00
Pâtisserie au choix	25,00
Cake	9,00

GLACES ET SORBETS
deux parfums au choix

Café, Vanille, Noisette, Pistache, Rhum raisin, Chocolat	30,00
Cassis, Citron, Fraise, Framboise, Fruits de la passion, Spécial tropic	32,00
Coupe des Deux Magots (glace Vanille, Sorbet et Sirop cassis)	35,00

COMMUNICATIVE EXPRESSIONS AND THEMATIC VOCABULARY

Unité 9 Les repas

CULTURAL CONTEXT: Foods and meals

COMMUNICATIVE EXPRESSIONS

Talking about what you like and don't like to eat or drink

J'aime le [gâteau].
Je préfère [la glace].
Je déteste [le poisson].

Offering a friend some food

Est-ce que tu veux | du pain? / de la glace?

Donne-moi | du fromage. / de la tarte.

Talking about food shopping

Je vais au marché.
Je vais faire les courses.

Asking for specific quantities

Vous désirez?
Donnez-moi / Je voudrais | un kilo de . . . / une livre de . . . / une douzaine de . . .

Interrelating with others: asking for and offering services

Tu me prêtes ton vélo?
D'accord, je te prête mon vélo.

Prête-moi ton vélo.

Tu nous invites à ta boum?
D'accord, je vous invite.

Invite-nous à ta boum.

Talking about people you know

Tu connais | Jérôme? / Christine? / ces filles?

Oui, je | le / la / les | connais.

Non, je ne | le / la / les | connais pas.

Talking about what we do for others

Tu téléphones à | François? / Pauline? / tes copains?

Oui, je | lui / lui / leur | téléphone.

Non, je ne | lui / lui / leur | téléphone pas.

UNITÉ 9

COMMUNICATIVE EXPRESSIONS AND THEMATIC VOCABULARY

VOCABULARY

Meals and food

un repas
le petit déjeuner — **prendre le petit déjeuner**
le déjeuner — **déjeuner**
le dîner — **dîner**

la nourriture — **aimer**
la cantine — **détester**
la cuisine *(cooking, cuisine)* — **préférer**

Setting the table

le couvert	**une assiette**	**mettre la table**
un couteau	**une cuillère**	
un verre	**une fourchette**	
	une serviette	
	une tasse	

UNITÉ 9

Foods and beverages

un plat — **une boisson**

le petit déjeuner

le beurre	**la confiture**
le pain	**les céréales**
un oeuf	

le déjeuner et le dîner

un dessert	**le riz**	**les frites** (f.)
le fromage	**le rosbif**	**la glace**
le gâteau	**les spaghetti** (m.)	**la salade**
un hors-d'oeuvre	**le thon**	**la soupe**
le jambon	**le veau**	**la tarte**
le poisson	**le yaourt**	**la viande**
le poulet		

quelques ingrédients (m.)

le ketchup	**le sucre**	**la mayonnaise**
le sel		

quelques fruits (m.)

un pamplemousse	**une banane**	**une orange**
	une cerise	**une poire**
	une fraise	**une pomme**

quelques légumes (m.)

des haricots verts	**une carotte**	**une salade** *(lettuce)*
des petits pois	**une pomme de terre**	**une tomate**

les boissons (f.)

le jus de pomme	**le lait**	**l'eau** (f.)
le jus d'orange	**le thé glacé**	**l'eau minérale**

COMMUNICATIVE EXPRESSIONS AND THEMATIC VOCABULARY

VOCABULARY *(continued)*

Verbs and expressions used with foods and beverages

je veux	**acheter**
je voudrais	**avoir**
	boire
voici	**manger**
voilà	**mettre**
il y a	**prendre**

Some irregular verbs

devoir	**apprendre**	**connaître**	**dire**
pouvoir	**comprendre**		**décrire**
vouloir	**prendre**	**boire**	**écrire**

Verbs used to describe interpersonal relationships

aider, **amener**, **connaître**, **inviter** | **quelqu'un**

parler, **rendre visite**, **répondre**, **téléphoner** | **à quelqu'un**

apporter, **dire**, **demander**, **donner**, **écrire**, **montrer**, **prêter** | **quelque chose à quelqu'un**

UNITÉ 9